Urban Planning, Management and Governance in Emerging Economies

Urban Planning, Management and Governance in Emerging Economies
Paradigm Shifts

Edited by

Jan Fransen

Senior Researcher of Urban Economic Development and Resilience, Institute of Housing and Urban Development, Erasmus University Rotterdam, the Netherlands

Meine Pieter van Dijk

Professor of Urban Management, Erasmus University Rotterdam and Professor of Economics, Maastricht School of Management, the Netherlands

Jurian Edelenbos

Professor of Interactive Governance, Faculty of Social and Behavioral Sciences, Erasmus University Rotterdam, the Netherlands

Edward Elgar PUBLISHING

Cheltenham, UK • Northampton, MA, USA

Published by
Edward Elgar Publishing Limited
The Lypiatts
15 Lansdown Road
Cheltenham
Glos GL50 2JA
UK

Edward Elgar Publishing, Inc.
William Pratt House
9 Dewey Court
Northampton
Massachusetts 01060
USA

A catalogue record for this book
is available from the British Library

Library of Congress Control Number: 2021936691

This book is available electronically in the **Elgar**online
Geography, Planning and Tourism subject collection
http://dx.doi.org/10.4337/9781800883840

ISBN 978 1 80088 383 3 (cased)
ISBN 978 1 80088 384 0 (eBook)

Printed and bound by CPI Group (UK) Ltd, Croydon, CR0 4YY

Contents

Figures

Contributors

Daniel Adamu, PhD, Urban Management and Governance Specialist, Department of Urban and Regional Planning, Nasarawa State University Keffi, Nigeria.

Taslim Adebowale Alade, PhD, Strategic Space Applications Department, National Space Research and Development Agency, Abuja, Nigeria; and Erasmus Graduate School of Social Sciences and the Humanities, Erasmus University Rotterdam, the Netherlands.

Aloysius N. Bongwa, Senior Expert Urban Finance, Urban Sustainability and Resilience, Institute for Housing and Urban Development Studies (IHS), Erasmus University Rotterdam, the Netherlands.

Marija Ćaćić, Lecturer, Faculty of Architecture, University of Montenegro, Montenegro.

Jurian Edelenbos, Professor of Urban Interactive Governance, Department of Public Administration & Sociology, academic director Vital Cities and Citizens, Erasmus University Rotterdam, the Netherlands.

Jan Fransen, Senior Expert, Assistant Professor Urban Economic Development and Resilience, research coordinator Smart Cities of EUR Vital Cities and Citizens initiative, Institute for Housing and Urban Development Studies (IHS), Erasmus University Rotterdam, the Netherlands.

Alberto Gianoli, Associate Professor Urban Sustainability and Resilience Department, Institute for Housing and Urban Development Studies (IHS), Erasmus University Rotterdam, the Netherlands.

Zvezdina Ivanova, Independent Researcher, Architect, Bulgaria.

Els Keunen, Institute for Housing and Urban Development Studies (IHS), Erasmus University Rotterdam, the Netherlands.

Yirang Lim, PhD candidate, Erasmus Graduate School of Social Sciences and the Humanities, Erasmus University Rotterdam, the Netherlands.

Indriany Lionggo, Urban Economic Development and Resilience, Institute for Housing and Urban Development Studies (IHS), Erasmus University Rotterdam, the Netherlands.

Darren McCauley, Professor in the Management of International Social Challenges, Department of Public Administration and Sociology, Erasmus University Rotterdam, the Netherlands.

Paula Nagler, Assistant Professor Urban Economic Development and Resilience, Institute for Housing and Urban Development Studies (IHS), Erasmus University Rotterdam, the Netherlands.

Peter Nientied, Independent Researcher, Netherlands and Research Fellow, POLIS University, Albania.

Saskia Ruijsink, Institute for Housing and Urban Development Studies (IHS), Erasmus University Rotterdam, the Netherlands.

Katarzyna Stachowiak-Bongwa, Independent Researcher, Netherlands/ Poland.

Rudina Toto, Professor of Environmental Planning, Co-PLAN Institute for Habitat Development, POLIS University, Albania.

Meine Pieter van Dijk, Professor of Entrepreneurship MSM of University of Maastricht; Emeritus Professor Urban Management Institute for Housing and Urban Development Studies (IHS), and International Institute of Social Studies (ISS), Erasmus University Rotterdam, the Netherlands.

Frank van Oort, Professor of Urban & Regional Economics, Erasmus University Rotterdam, the Netherlands.

Acknowledgements

We would like to thank Laura Quadros Aniche of the Institute of Housing and Urban development Studies (IHS), Erasmus University Rotterdam for her wonderful support in managing the contributions, organising a workshop, liaising with the authors, arranging meetings and constantly reminding us and following up. Without her support this book would not have been possible. We would also like to thank IHS and all authors for availing the time and resources needed to prepare the contributions.

1. Urban paradigm shifts in emerging economies

Jan Fransen, Meine Pieter van Dijk and Jurian Edelenbos

INTRODUCTION

The main purpose of this book is to identify and understand urban paradigms in emerging economies. Kuhn (2012: viii) defines paradigms as "universally recognized scientific achievements that for a time provide model problems and solutions to a community of practitioners". In this chapter we focus on models that indicate how to intervene in cities and identify paradigm shifts for which subsequent chapters of the book offer theoretical depth and/or case studies from different countries and domains. The ultimate objective of this book is to learn about the identified paradigms (how) as applied by different approaches (what) in different cities in emerging economies (where).

The reason to focus on emerging economies is that they face high rates of urbanization. Urban models predict that by 2025 nine of the twelve biggest cities will be in emerging economies. Asia alone is likely to have seven of the twelve biggest cities. In Africa, both Lagos and Kinshasa are each likely to have grown to more than 15 million residents (Roberts, 2011). Rapid urbanization has a major effect on the environment, poverty and the availability of resources worldwide. It demands an immense urban management effort, which far outstrips the current urban management capacity in emerging economies. Equally important, it demands a reflection on how we manage cities.

Urban paradigms have shifted over the past century. In broad brush terms, the way to intervene in cities altered from urban planning by central governments for most of the twentieth century, to decentralized urban management with privatized service delivery in the 1980s and 1990s, to urban governance in the new millennium (Table 1.1). The shifts exemplify a realization that effective and efficient service delivery on its own does not address wicked problems in increasingly complex urban systems. However, while new problems have attracted the attention of policy makers and researchers, old problems have not disappeared.

Table 1.1   *Urban paradigm shifts*

Time period	Problem addressed	Urban paradigm	Public administration paradigm
1900–1980	Shortage in services and infrastructure	Central planning as a reaction to market failure	Traditional Public Administration
1980–2000	Inefficient service delivery	Urban management as a reaction to government failure	New Public Management
2000–now	Wicked problems	Urban governance as a reaction to both market and government failure	New Public Governance

Source: Authors.

After describing these paradigm shifts, the chapter argues that any urban problem demands an eclectic mix of urban planning, management and governance. The reframing of problems results in new concepts such as smart, resilient, creative, sustainable cities. While these concepts partially pour the same wine in new bottles, they also offer inspiring entry points for urban development.

We end the chapter by anticipating the next paradigm shift, whereby the role of (local) government increases once again. Market-led development has been criticized due to its inability to deal with wicked problems. At the same time, governments have played a major role during the COVID-19 pandemic. With climate change and urban resilience high on the political agenda, the role of (local) governments is likely to increase. But urban managers work in highly differentiated political settings, local contexts and local capacities. As a novel approach, we introduce a 'governance possibility frontier' (adapted from Djankov et al., 2003), which describes minimum levels of planning, management and governance required under different political settings. We propose boundary spanning as an eclectic way to bring actors and processes together. The urban examples presented in the book subsequently offer rich examples of a reflexive stance on urban planning, management and governance.

REFRAMING URBAN PROBLEMS

Industrializing cities in the late nineteenth century resembled Charles Dickens' Coke Town, the fictional town he depicted in his 1854 novel *Hard Times*. In this industrial mill town every building looked the same and was covered in soot, the air quality was appalling, the society was unequal and segregated, infrastructure, housing and services were inadequate, and working hours were long and the work boring. Urban markets failed to deliver housing, drainage, education, health facilities and other basic services. This led to negative externalities such as pollution, segregation and depression. For most of the twentieth century, the problem of cities was framed in terms of poor infrastructure and service delivery caused by urbanization and industrialization (Bettencourt, 2013). To frame it more broadly: the identified problem was market failure. To the extent that resources allowed, a welfare state or socialist regime delivered centralized public services and infrastructure, funded from taxation and official development aid, in order to overcome market failure (Hemerijck, 2013). Governments worldwide set minimum wages and, when viable, offered unemployment benefits. In socialist countries, salaries were standardized. Keynes (1936) argued that these measures not only reduced poverty, but also stabilized demand thereby dampening recessions and smoothing economic progress. At the same time, developing countries supported industries and adopted import substitution industrialization (ISI) strategies in order to protect their investments. Labour-based industries relocated to developing countries, developing economies grew relatively quickly and despite neo-Marxist criticism there was an overall belief that developing countries would catch up over time (Jaret, 1983; Rostov, 1960).

To fund the welfare state, however, developing countries borrowed huge sums of money from international creditors. This proved to be a risky public investment, leading to a massive debt crisis in Latin American countries. It was quickly realized that not only Latin American governments had overspent. With countries being unable to fund basic services and infrastructure and repay loans, the development problem was reframed as government failure: nepotism, red tape, centralized decision making and a poor understanding of economic risks resulted in inefficient service delivery and failed industrialization investments (de Soto, 1989; Stiglitz, 1998). Privatization became the new saviour to enable developing countries to reduce costs, repay loans and deliver urban services more efficiently. Structural adjustment programmes brought down government expenditures, by privatizing services such as education almost overnight (Sahn et al., 1999; Stiglitz, 1991).

Over time, urban issues became more complex, facing wicked problems such as climate change, economic crises, traffic congestion and growing inequality (Head and Alford, 2015). A wicked problem is a problem that is difficult or impossible to solve because of incomplete, contradictory, and changing requirements (Rittel and Webber, 1973). 'Wicked' denotes resistance to resolution and implies that it has no determinable stopping point, because the interdependency between issues means that the effort to solve one aspect of a wicked problem may reveal or create other problems (Tonkinwise, 2015).

These kinds of wicked problems are highly visible in cities in emerging economies. For instance, the 30 most polluted cities are in emerging economies (WHO, 2018). For a wicked problem such as climate change, there is no clearly defined cause or solution. Different actors have different perspectives of the problems, priorities and solutions (Kickert et al., 1997). Wicked urban problems arise in complex systems such as cities (Bettencourt, 2013). Complex systems are self-organised, in the sense that markets and social networks create "order without design", as Bertaud's (2018) latest book is aptly called. Successful behaviour is reinforced by feedback mechanisms. Cities create positive feedback mechanisms in processes of matching, sharing and learning (Duranton and Puga, 2004). Firms in related industries are rewarded by productivity gains, as they benefit from matching in labour markets, sharing of infrastructure and learning in knowledge networks. This attracts more related industries (Neffke et al., 2018). However, the high density in cities also leads to negative externalities (the wicked problems), such as pollution, heat waves, traffic congestion, crime, stress, social exclusion and inequality.

EVOLVING PARADIGMS

The development of new urban paradigms reflects the reframing of urban problems and a related debate on the role of governments (and other stakeholders) in the urban realm. Public administration and public policy scholars have reacted to the reframing of problems by suggesting a shift from Traditional Public Administration to New Public Management, and a further shift to a, yet incoherently described, third paradigm, often called New Public Governance (Osborne, 2006).

Traditional Public Administration

Traditional Public Administration arose in the early twentieth century as a response to the challenges of, amongst others, industrialization, urbanization, and major market failure (Stoker, 2006). In an idealized form, politics and administration were separated, and neutrality as well as equality in government operations were highly valued, based on the rule of law. Public servants pursued politically provided objectives. There are basically two dominant logics within this paradigm: standardization and internal orientation (Nederhand et al., 2019). The primary logic is that of standardization (Weber, 1978). From this logic, the function of policy officials should be standardized and executed along the lines of predictable processes and rules. The explicit standardization of functions makes interaction with the bureaucratic organization perfectly predictable. This predictability is also safeguarded by the presence of impersonal and stable rules (Wilson, 1989). The second major characteristic is the internal orientation of policy officials. The emphasis on both administrative procedures and serving the political officeholders makes policy officials internally oriented. Hence, political decisions guide the actions of policy officials. This internal orientation on policy programmes and rules also enables policy officials to treat each citizen alike.

Urban development was perceived as a process of centralized planning. Planners produced master plans, delivered infrastructure and services and subsequently checked building permits and minimum building standards. Local authorities comprised departments that were devolved from national ministries. Highly detailed urban planning models, such as the garden city or Le Corbusier's Ville Radieuse, were implemented on a massive scale irrespective of the local context (Bertaud, 2018; Bettencourt, 2013). Centralized planning was inspired by engineering practices and control theories. While these control tendencies are criticized these days, centralized urban planning was instrumental in changing Dickensian 'Coke Towns' into serviced urban centres, whereby costs were reduced by mass production and ever-reducing transport costs (Bettencourt, 2013). The World Bank (2000) argues that even now successful urban development also requires strategic urban or regional planning in order to attract investments and physically locate employment, houses, amenities and transport infrastructure.

Urban Management

New Public Management (NPM) arose in the 1980s out of concern for government failure, and a belief in the efficiency and effectiveness of market mechanisms and economic rationality (Hood, 1991). It implied a break from centralized government towards decentralization, privatization and public–private partnerships (PPPs). Politically provided goals were now implemented by public managers using markets, managing inputs and outputs such that they ensured economic welfare and responsiveness to 'customers' (i.e. citizens) (Bryson et al., 2014). The managerial logic is grounded in a neoliberal approach. While it is difficult to provide a definitive image of NPM (Pollitt et al., 2007), most scholars agree on the main features. These include the focus on improving the efficiency and effectiveness of public service delivery through management of processes and systems. The use of business instruments (strategic and performance management techniques, performance indicators) is crucial to the conceptualization of NPM (Hood, 1991). After politicians have defined and set the main policy goals for the bureaucratic organization, public managers are expected to manage the delivery of these policy goals within budget (Du Gay, 2008). Consequently, problems are translated into managerial targets. Financial resources are subsequently disaggregated into specific organizational units that should realize these targets and results. Results measured in terms of outputs and outcomes are important for purposes of accountability and efficiency (Haque, 2007). There are basically two logics in this paradigm

(Nederhand et al., 2019): functional specialization and result-orientation. Policy ambitions are broken down into a large set of measurable smaller tasks that are allocated among functionally specialized departments and responsible policy officials. Achieving managerial results within budget is key for policy officials as that is what they are held accountable for. This potentially leaves little room and time for policy officials to deal with extra tasks that come up during interactions with citizens, and therefore fall outside their performance indicators (Bartels, 2016).

In time, the criticism of NPM led to the broader perspective of urban management. Van Dijk (2006: 7) defines urban management as 'the effort to co-ordinate and integrate public as well as private actions to tackle the major problems the inhabitants of cities are facing and to make a more competitive, equitable and sustainable city'. Urban management is multi-sector and multi-actor (Cheema, 1993) and should be concerned with the economic basis of the city, the environment, and participation of and equality among its citizens (Devas and Radkodi, 1993). The role of urban managers is to coordinate horizontally and vertically across government layers, outsource service delivery to private firms and public–private partnerships, improve urban competitiveness and foreign direct investments, enable community participation to ensure targeted service delivery, and manage municipal finance. At the same time, urban planning remains a core responsibility. Consensus building with inhabitants, entrepreneurs, organizations of inhabitants or entrepreneurs, environmental activists and project developers (or organizations of these actors) enables the development and execution of urban policies and strategies (Van Dijk, 2006).

Urban Governance

Since the 2000s, it is claimed that, although the challenges underlying the rise of the first two paradigms have not disappeared, new challenges have emerged. Our society is more complex than ever, facing wicked problems such as climate change, economic failure, urbanization, and growing inequality (Head and Alford, 2015). The public sector responses to these challenges within society do not constitute a coherent (third) paradigm yet, but scholarly work has been published on, for example, New Public Service (Denhardt and Denhardt, 2000), New Public Governance (Osborne, 2006), Public Value Management (Stoker, 2006) and Public Value Governance (Bryson et al., 2015). At the heart of the emerging paradigm lies the idea that policy goals and policy implementation are discussed and pursued not in a hierarchical way (Traditional Public Administration) or through markets (New Public Management), but by collaborative networks of public and private actors and citizens. Healey (1995: 18) states that urban governance departs from the control perspective, because it is realized that urban managers and planners cannot know all the information held by the immense number of heterogeneous agents in cities and cannot predict the dynamics of complex systems. In urban governance, many developmental choices are therefore left open and/ or are discussed in networks (Bettencourt, 2013). Moreover, the legitimacy of politically provided objectives is increasingly questioned.

In this third paradigm, which closely resembles the concepts and ideas of network governance (Koppenjan and Klijn, 2004), the primary logics are those of interdependency, external/context orientation and collaboration (Edelenbos and Teisman, 2011; Torfing et al., 2012). Every government agency depends on several stakeholders with specific resources that cannot be easily substituted (knowledge, legitimacy, formal consent, money, etc.). Network theories perceive the public domain as a complex governance network with layers and departments that are interconnected (Kooiman, 2003; Rhodes, 1996).

Network governance approaches result from the shift of emphasis away from structural devolution, disaggregation and single-purpose organizations and towards a so-called 'whole-of-government' or 'joined-up government' approach (Pollitt, 2003; Christensen and Lægreid, 2007). These initiatives are focused on coordinating and integrating government policy-making and service delivery across organizational boundaries (Mulgan, 2005). A whole-of-government approach needs a cooperative effort and cannot be imposed from the top down (Pollitt, 2003; Edelenbos and Teisman, 2011). Joined-up government is described as the opposite of departmentalism, tunnel vision and vertical silos, and denotes the aspiration to achieve horizontal and vertical coordination, leading to agencies working across portfolio boundaries to achieve a shared goal and an integrated government approach (Christensen and Lægreid, 2007). Whole-of-government activities span any or all levels of government and involve groups outside government (Pollitt, 2003). The emergence of joined-up government and whole-of-government shows similarities with trends in the United States that stress management of boundaries and networks and cross-sector collaboration (Bryson et al., 2014, 2015).

In the literature on governance networks, the idea of how to integrate a fragmented reality shifts from classic instruments like law, reorganization and force to more subtle and less static means, conceptualized as network management and interactive policy-making (Agranoff and McGuire, 2003; Edelenbos, 2005). Network management focuses on strategic attempts to manage interactions between actors and ongoing processes in networks.

In urban governance the notion of central coordination should be abandoned (Edelenbos and Teisman, 2011). The argument is that the interactions in complex systems are too numerous and diverse. Complex processes are dynamic due to the existing degree of self-organization. A more deliberate network management strategy is applied in these networks (Klijn and

Edelenbos, 2007). Deadlocks and disputes cannot be solved by force or authority. Integration in networks requires going beyond boundaries of layers and
departments. Within this holistic network approach, the capacity to connect
to other domains, levels, scales, organizations and actors becomes important,
addressing interrelationships and linkages among multiple, cross-cutting,
and often conflicting resource uses (Edelenbos et al., 2011; Edelenbos and
Teisman, 2013).

Urban governance is perceived to have an "evolutionary advantage", as
networking enables innovation and learning in a constantly changing environment, which is characterized by situations of complex reciprocal interdependence among relatively autonomously operating stakeholders with private and
shared interests, values and viewpoints (Jessop, 1998: 32–33). The capacity
to get things done "no longer lies (if it ever did) with government power and
authority in one place" (Kearns and Paddison, 2000: 847).

Eclectic Approaches

All paradigms have merits and weaknesses (Table 1.2). Public administration enables the top-down delivery of low-cost infrastructure and services
but may lead to government failure and does not differentiate between local
specificities. Urban management can tailor services to local needs, but may
lead to market failure and cannot address wicked problems. Urban governance, finally, can address wicked problems, but may lead to network failure
especially in cities with limited capacity to manage networks. Finding the
best approach, which navigates between market, state and network failure, is
space- and path-dependent.

In their constant search for solutions to problems, cities can explore
a number of new approaches, such as smart city, resilient city, green city,
competitive city and/or innovative city. Each addresses urban development
from a different content angle. They recommend the *what*, while paradigms
recommend the *how*. In practice, they may represent a fancy city brand, as all
cities want to be smart, resilient and inclusive. We discuss how these concepts
eclectically and implicitly integrate theory on governance, management and
public administration.

Resilient cities
A resilient city can recover from an external shock and disturbance, which
may be drought, flooding, an earthquake, a financial crisis, or a pandemic.
Resilience involves three distinct stages: the ability to resist, to recover and to
thrive (Elmqvist et al., 2019; Martin and Sunley, 2015). Resilience indicates
the ability, time and cost needed for urban systems to bounce back to their
previous equilibrium or to bounce forward (Martin and Sunley, 2015). The

Table 1.2   An overview of urban paradigms

Urban paradigm and main concepts	Public administration paradigm	Main mode of governance	Main strength	Main weaknesses
Urban planning – *Centralization* – *Standardization* – *Internal orientation* – *Top-down planning*	Traditional Public Administration	Public hierarchy	Standardized low-cost service and infrastructure delivery	Government failure Crowding out Power abuse Inefficiencies Patronage
Urban management – *Decentralization* – *Privatization/PPP* – *participation*	New Public Management	Market	Tailored low-cost service and infrastructure delivery	Market failure Information asymmetries Opportunism Bounded rationality
Complex urban systems – *Networks* – *Multilevel*	New Public Governance	Networks	Can address wicked problems	Network failure High transaction costs Limited control Vested interests Different scales

concept covers the resilience of urban social, environmental and economic systems (Ernstson et al., 2010; Martin and Sunley, 2015), urban communities (Fransen et al., 2021), urban organizations (Lebel et al., 2006) and/or the people living and working in a city (Peek, 2008).

The COVID-19 pandemic has placed urban resilience high on the political agenda. We witness that the phases of urban resilience roughly coincide with a paradigm shift. The immediate response to the COVID-19 pandemic has been one of centralized planning. Centralized and standardized rules (keep distance, wash hands, stay indoors, shops closed) have played a major role in the first (resist) and second (recover) phase of coping with the pandemic. Urban management enables a targeted and localized response, such as local policing, closing off public spaces and supporting community initiatives. At the same time, the multiple initiatives of communities and firms in providing much-needed medical equipment such as masks, offering solace to the lonely and shopping for the elderly, illustrate the need for urban governance and especially play a role in the second (recovery) and third phase (thriving). Learning and thriving from a crisis demands localized and adaptive governance (Olsson et al., 2004). It defines the city after the pandemic which learns to thrive through more resilient organizations, communities, economies and people. These phases and levels of resilience are interlinked and non-linear: the lessons learned, initiatives and solidarities at multiple layers during phases 1 and 2 lay the basis for phase 3. Phase 3 subsequently informs the ability to cope with the next crisis, be it a second wave of COVID-19 or some other crisis. This requires an eclectic mix of public administration, urban management and urban governance. This is easier said than done, as each phase has its own actors, objectives and speed.

Creative and competitive cities

Scholars widely discuss the role of actors and perspectives in urban economics. Hall and Soskice (2001) for instance identify two opposing paradigms, which they call varieties of capitalism: liberal market economies, which resemble New Public Management, and coordinated market economies, which resemble Network Governance. Markets steer development in a liberal market economy, while non-market forms of interaction are the primary drivers in coordinated market economies.

Porter (1996), as a proponent of liberal market economies, argues that firms locate industries and services close to markets, firms, research labs and universities. The role of urban managers is to create an enabling environment. At its core is the efficient urban management of inner-city revitalization, preferably in public–private partnerships (Porter, 1997). However, others argue in favour of network governance because urban competitiveness is not only dependent on local firms but also on creative people. Network governance can identify how to make cities attractive for the creative class (Florida, 2004) and how to operate in global value chains (Fransen and Helmsing, 2017). Katz and Wagner (2014) propose a specific role of government to develop geographically bounded innovation districts, which house leading-edge anchor institutions and clustered companies, business incubators and accelerators. They offer a breeding ground for start-ups. These innovation districts are physically compact, transit-accessible, technically wired and offer mixed use housing, office and retail. These urban economic approaches are discussed in forums such as economic development boards, comprising public, private and/or civil partners. This often links to a broader definition of competitiveness, arguing that not only productivity, but also sustainability and equality matter (Scott and Storper, 2015). A sole focus on creativity and competitiveness, alongside technological trends which take away jobs from the middle class, leads to inequality and a 'new urban crisis' (Florida, 2017; Fransen and Helmsing, 2016).

Green/sustainable cities

Green or sustainable cities reduce, recycle, and reuse waste, close their water cycle and address pollution. This demands a transition to integrated, circular and adaptive approaches in order to cope with increasing uncertainties generated, for example, by climate change (Van Dijk, 2012). In an ecological city, waste, energy and water management are integrated into a broader urban environment approach (Suzuki et al., 2010). Alongside environmental services, climate change adaption and mitigation, liveability and the quality of the urban environment are valued. As this is unknown territory, urban actors navigate the transition and discuss strategies in open governance processes. Urban governance thereby aims to promote the welfare of citizens in such a way that it does not have negative consequences for future generations.

Urban managers reassess risks, manage networks and co-create strategic, spatial and action plans to mitigate these risks. Urban management can therefore be defined as an integrated and comprehensive approach to deal with urban risks in cities (Van Dijk, 2009a). Climate change adds urgency and complexity. In forms of network governance, strategic and action plans create a shared vision and concrete activities for government, communities and firms. A more ecological approach to sustainable urbanization implies moving from traditional environmental technologies to more ecosan options (sanitary solutions with ecological characteristics) in the ecological city of the future (Van Dijk, 2009b).

Smart cities
While the concept 'smart city' has become powerful in influencing urban development worldwide, it lacks a uniform definition or practice. Instead, there are many different perspectives, narratives and practices leading to different urban development trajectories (Kummitha and Crutzen, 2017). The first definitions of a smart city focused on the role of information and communication technologies (ICTs), such as information and technology infrastructure, smart technologies, mobile technologies, virtual technologies and digital networks (Huovila et al., 2019: 145). In practice, this approach is closely interwoven with New Public Management, whereby city councils and ICT firms take the lead in introducing ICT into urban management. While the use of ICT has many advantages, scholars argue that it often leads to inequality, a digital divide and exclusion and it may reduce democratic processes (Datta, 2015; Kummitha and Crutzen, 2017; Nam and Pardo, 2011).

Later definitions place people and governance at the core of the smart city debate (Nam and Pardo, 2011: 286). This relates to the concept of soft smartness (Huovila et al., 2019). Knowledge, education, social learning and creativity constitute important criteria to enhance the performance of a smart city (Nam and Pardo, 2011; Castelnovo et al., 2016). Authors also emphasize the link between smart and sustainable (Höjer and Wangel, 2015). Others emphasize inclusive, democratic and polycentric approaches, whereby new solutions are co-created in living labs. This approach is used in Amsterdam for instance, but the practice also shows that many local experiments do not necessarily scale up to a smart city with smart citizens (Van Winden and van den Buuse, 2017).

WHAT IS NEXT?

After decades of market-led development, governments and networks appear to be taking up a larger role once again. Governments have played a central role in infrastructure-led development in emerging economies. This has materialized in constructing new cities which are smart, often implemented in public–private partnerships. The role of government has also (temporarily) been enlarged in coping with the COVID-19 pandemic. At the same time, the climate change transition has resulted in a critical outlook on the ability of the private sector to organize sustainable development.

We expect (local) governments and networks to carve out a larger role for themselves in the foreseeable future in order to manage transitions and navigate crises. The era of market-led development may have come to an end. This trend may lead to new (combinations of) paradigms. We introduce the Governance Possibility Frontier in order to assess the space for local actors to operate within different local contexts. We subsequently discuss boundary spanning as a tool to make the Governance Possibility Frontier work.

Governance Possibility Frontier

Social urban life is coordinated by hierarchies, markets and networks; neither one surpasses the others. For example, neither the market nor hierarchy will lead to proper coordination, as both neglect the informal mechanisms that typify a network (Thompson, 1991). Coordination of urban life will always require certain blends of the three where one can dominate over the other. Urban societies operate in different political settings within which either a government, market or network mode of governance dominates. They represent structurally different solutions to urban problems. While most urban societies combine approaches, their extremes are seen in socialist dictatorships, market-driven societies and network societies. We propose a Governance Possibility Frontier (adapted from Djankov et al., 2003), which indicates the minimum level of planning, management and governance required to address wicked urban problems and to protect people from misuse and opportunism of public, civil and private parties. Its defining characteristic is that different political settings offer different competences and comparative advantages in planning, management and/or governance. We argue that to function at a minimum level, a benevolent dictator would require a competent government in combination with a minimum level of resilient, competent and self-organized communities, functioning markets and social networks. If well-functioning, it is relatively likely to excel in top-down urban planning and perform worse in addressing varied needs, local initiatives, constant market fluctuations and wicked problems. By the same token, a competent network society may excel in framing wicked problems, but face challenges in effective and efficient service delivery. Besides networks, it therefore requires a minimum competence in government hierarchies and markets. Finally, a market-driven society may excel in responsiveness to fluctuations, but it requires a minimum competence of government hierarchy and networks to overcome market failure.

Boundary Spanning

The interdependency of government, market and networks implies that boundaries are permeable and not set in stone (Stoker, 1995). Coordinating and integrating urban planning, management and governance requires crossing boundaries, because solving problems in one domain might imply new issues and problems in others. Urban professionals have to become boundary spanners, defined as "people who proactively scan the organizational environment, employ activities to cross organizational or institutional boundaries, generate and mediate the information flow and coordinate between their 'home' organization or organizational unit and its environment, and connect processes and actors across these boundaries" (Van Meerkerk and Edelenbos, 2018: 3). Four types of boundary spanners are distinguished: fixer, bridger, broker and innovator, each with their specific focus and core competences as displayed in Table 1.3.

Boundaries can be spanned through boundary objects. Boundary objects provide a shared language that allows for representing the domain-specific knowledge in a structure and format that are known on the other side of the knowledge boundary (Carlile, 2002). Examples are work manuals, intranet and forms, which usually try to cross boundaries between management and workforce. Urban professionals – scientists, policy makers and representatives of stakeholder organizations – can generate, integrate and apply boundary objects and thereby relate to, understand and interact between planners, managers and governors across sectors and organizations (Edelenbos and Teisman, 2011; Van Meerkerk and Edelenbos, 2018).

CONCLUSION

Since the 1980s, paradigms to understand and intervene in cities have shifted from hierarchy (Traditional Public Administration), to markets (Urban Management) and finally to networks (Urban Governance). This reflects a radical change in the way we manage cities. The radical change reflects a pendulum, whereby market, government or network failure swing the pendulum back and forth. Rapid urbanization and shocks such as climate change and the COVID-19 pandemic make the pendulum swing faster and faster. We

Table 1.3   Four boundary spanning profiles

	Fixer	Bridger	Broker	Innovator
Is a person who …	is oriented at solving problems in cross-boundary endeavours and aligning organizational policies with external processes.	focuses on creating connections between people from different organizations and promoting cross-boundary endeavours.	is active in facilitating and mediating concrete interactions and dialogues among actors with different interests and organizational backgrounds.	explores new ideas, products and processes crossing public, private and societal boundaries, looking for opportunities to develop support and mobilize resources for proposed initiatives.
Main competences and activities	Represents external views in the organization and vice versa; reading the situation; pragmatic and implementation oriented; result driven; information scanning and exchange activities; relationship building	Strong network; trustworthy person with good reputation; ambassador activities for cross-boundary endeavours; highly developed interpretation, communication and translation skills	Highly developed facilitation and negotiation skills; finding and expressing common ground; empathetic; good listener; good interpreter and translator	Highly developed sense for seeing and seizing opportunities; entrepreneurial drive; motivating and inspiring; mobilizing capacity; daring to take risks

Source: Adapted from Van Meerkerk and Edelenbos (2018: 111).

expect that urban resilience will be placed higher on the urban agenda due to the current pandemic and climate change. As markets have failed to provide urban resilience, we expect government hierarchy and/or governance to play a larger role in the near future.

Cities in emerging economies ultimately require an eclectic mix of the three perspectives. This is easier said than done, as each perspective has its own actors, political priorities, decision-making model and speed. It requires constant reflection, learning, creativity and organizational innovation across different actors and levels. Urban governance is perceived to have an 'evolutionary advantage', as networking enables innovation and learning in a constantly changing environment (Jessop, 1998). Authoritarian or market-driven development are thus likely to face greater difficulty in adjusting their pendulum.

New approaches emerge on an almost daily basis and propose that urban managers should make their city smart, resilient, creative, inclusive and/

or sustainable. They all address urban development from different content angles, but the concepts often remain blurry with major conflicts of opinion between scholars within each approach. Cities in emerging economies adopt one or more of these approaches and do so in hierarchical, market-driven or network mode depending on their own context and history. In our experience, the choice of *how* to develop cities (the paradigms) is as important as *what* to develop (the approaches). We use a Governance Frontier Model to compare the perspectives internationally, whereby the frontier may differ per approach.

This book aims to explore the different paradigms (how) for different approaches (what) applied by different cities in emerging economies (where). That is ambitious. The endless variety of how cities deal with wicked problems in complex environments constitutes a worldwide evolutionary experiment. A lot is at stake, as urban managers in emerging economies often lack political, financial and human resources to deal with rapid urbanization, climate change and crises. This book offers inspiration and an update on recent theories and practices.

REFERENCES

Agranoff, R. and McGuire, M. (2003). *Collaborative Public Management: New Strategies for Local Governments*. Washington, DC: Georgetown University Press.
Bartels, K. P. R. (2016). Doing what's necessary: How encounters in practice shape and improve interactive governance work. In *Critical Reflections on Interactive Governance*, ed. J. Edelenbos and I. Van Meerkerk. Cheltenham, UK and Northampton, MA, USA: Edward Elgar Publishing, 352–375.
Bertaud, A. (2018). *Order Without Design: How Markets Shape Cities*. Cambridge, MA: MIT Press.
Bettencourt, L. M. (2013). The origins of scaling in cities. *Science*, 340(6139), 1438–1441.
Bryson, J. M., Crosby, B. C. and Bloomberg, L. (2014). Public value governance: Moving beyond traditional public administration and the new public management. *Public Administration Review*, 74(4), 445–456.
Bryson, J. M., Crosby, B. C. and Bloomberg, L. (eds.) (2015). *Public Value and Public Administration*. Washington, DC: Georgetown University Press.
Carlile, P. R. (2002). A pragmatic view of knowledge and boundaries: Boundary objects in new product development. *Organization Science*, 13(4), 442–455.
Castelnovo, W., Savoldelli, A. and Misuraca, G. (2016). Smart cities governance: The need for a holistic approach to assessing urban participatory policy making. *Social Science Computer Review*, 34(6), 724–739.
Cheema, G. S. (ed.) (1993). *Urban Management: Policies and Innovations in Developing Countries*. New York: Praeger.
Christensen, T. and Lægreid, P. (2007). The whole of government approach to public sector reforms. *Public Administration Review*, 67(6), 1059–1066.
Datta, A. (2015). New urban utopias of postcolonial India: 'Entrepreneurial urbanization' in Dholera Smart City, Gujarat. *Dialogues in Human Geography*, 5(1), 3–22.

De Soto, H. (1989). *The Other Path: The Invisible Revolution in the Third World.* New York: Harper & Row.

Denhardt, R. B. and Denhardt, J. V. (2000). The new public service: Serving rather than steering. *Public Administration Review*, 60(6), 549–559.

Devas, N. and Radkodi, C. (eds.) (1993). *Managing Fast Growing Cities: New Approaches to Urban Planning and Management in the Developing World.* Harlow: Longman.

Djankov, S., Glaeser, E., La Porta, R., Lopez-de-Silanes, F. and Shleifer, A. (2003). The new comparative economics. *Journal of Comparative Economics*, 31(4), 595–619.

Du Gay, P. (2008). Without affection or enthusiasm: Problems of involvement and attachment in responsive public management. *Organization*, 15(3), 335–353.

Duranton, G. and Puga, D. (2004). Micro-foundations of urban agglomeration economies. In *Handbook of Regional and Urban Economics*, vol. 4, ed. J. V. Henderson and J.-F. Thisse. Amsterdam: North-Holland, 2063–2117.

Edelenbos, J. (2005). Institutional implications of interactive governance: Insights from Dutch practice. *Governance*, 18(1), 111–134.

Edelenbos, J. and Teisman, G. R. (2011). Numéro spécial sur la gouvernance de l'eau. *Revue Internationale des Sciences Administratives*, 77(1), 5–30.

Edelenbos, J. and Teisman, G. (2013). Water governance capacity: The art of dealing with a multiplicity of levels, sectors and domains. *International Journal of Water Governance*, 1(1–2), 89–108.

Edelenbos, J., Van Buuren, A. and van Schie, N. (2011). Co-producing knowledge: Joint knowledge production between experts, bureaucrats and stakeholders in Dutch water management projects. *Environmental Science & Policy*, 14(6), 675–684.

Elmqvist, T., Andersson, E., Frantzeskaki, N., McPhearson, T., Olsson, P., Gaffney, O. and Folke, C. (2019). Sustainability and resilience for transformation in the urban century. *Nature Sustainability*, 2(4): 267–273.

Ernstson, H., van der Leeuw, S. E., Redman, C. L., Meffert, D. J., Davis, G., Alfsen, C. and Elmqvist, T. (2010). Urban transitions: On urban resilience and human-dominated ecosystems. *Ambio*, 39(8): 531–545.

Florida, R. (2004). *The Rise of the Creative Class.* New York: HarperCollins.

Florida, R. (2017). *The New Urban Crisis: How Our Cities Are Increasing Inequality, Deepening Segregation, and Failing the Middle Class – and What We Can Do About It.* New York: Basic Books.

Fransen, J. and Helmsing, A. H. J. (2016). Breaching the barriers: The segmented business and innovation system of handicraft exports in Cape Town. *Development Southern Africa*, 33(4), 486–501.

Fransen, J. and Helmsing, A. H. J. (2017). Absorptive capacity as a mediator: Innovation of handicraft exporters in Yogyakarta, Indonesia. *Tijdschrift voor economische en sociale geografie*, 108(6), 737–752.

Fransen, J., Peralta, D. O., Vanelli, F., Edelenbos, J. and Olvera, B. C. (2021). The emergence of urban community resilience initiatives during the COVID-19 pandemic: An international exploratory study. *The European Journal of Development Research*, Special Issue (January), 1–23.

Hall, P. A. and Soskice, D. (eds.) (2001). *Varieties of Capitalism: The Institutional Foundations of Comparative Advantage.* Oxford: Oxford University Press.

Haque, M. S. (2007). Revisiting the New Public Management. *Public Administration Review*, 67(1): 179–182.

Head, B. W. and Alford, J. (2015). Wicked problems: Implications for public policy and management. *Administration & Society*, 47(6), 711–739.

Healey, P. (1995). *Managing Cities: The New Urban Context*. New York: John Wiley & Sons.

Hemerijck, A. (2013). *Changing Welfare States*. Oxford: Oxford University Press.

Höjer, M. and Wangel, J. (2015). Smart sustainable cities: Definition and challenges. In *ICT Innovations for Sustainability*, ed. L. Hilty and B. Aebischer. Cham: Springer, 333–349.

Hood, C. (1991). A public management for all seasons. *Public Administration*, 69(1): 3–19.

Huovila, A., Airaksinen, M. and Bosch, P. (2019). Comparative analysis of standardized indicators for smart sustainable cities: What indicators and standards to use and when? *Cities* 89, 141–153.

Jaret, J. (1983). Recent neo-Marxist urban analysis. *Annual Review of Sociology*, 9, 499–525.

Jessop, B. (1998). The rise of governance and the risks of failure: The case of economic development. *International Social Science Journal*, 50(155), 29–45.

Katz, B. and Wagner, J. (2014). *The Rise of Innovation Districts: A New Geography of Innovation in America*. Washington, DC: Brookings Institution.

Kearns, A. and Paddison, R. (2000). New challenges for urban governance. *Urban Studies*, 37(5–6), 845–850.

Keynes, J. M. (1936). *Allgemeine Theorie der Beschäftigung, des Zinses und des Geldes* (Vol. 6). Berlin: Duncker & Humblot.

Kickert, W. J., Klijn, E. H. and Koppenjan, J. F. (eds.) (1997). *Managing Complex Networks: Strategies for the Public Sector*. London: Sage.

Klijn, E. H. and Edelenbos, J. (2007) Meta-governance as network management. In *Theories of Democratic Network Governance*, ed. E. Sørensen and J. Torfing. Basingstoke: Palgrave Macmillan, 199–214.

Kooiman, J. (2003). *Governing as Governance*. London: Sage.

Koppenjan, J. F. M. and Klijn, E. H. (2004). *Managing Uncertainties in Networks: A Network Approach to Problem Solving and Decision Making*. London: Routledge.

Kuhn, T. S. (2012). *The Structure of Scientific Revolutions*, 50th anniversary edition. Chicago: University of Chicago Press.

Kummitha, R. K. R. and Crutzen, N. (2017). How do we understand smart cities? An evolutionary perspective. *Cities*, 67, 43–52.

Lebel, L., Anderies, J. M., Campbell, B., Folke, C., Hatfield-Dodds, S., Hughes, T. P. and Wilson, J. (2006). Governance and the capacity to manage resilience in regional social-ecological systems. *Ecology and Society*, 11(1). http://www.ecologyandsociety.org/vol11/iss1/art19/.

Martin, R. and Sunley, P. (2015). On the notion of regional economic resilience: Conceptualization and explanation. *Journal of Economic Geography*, 15(1), 1–42.

Mulgan, G. (2005). Joined-up government: Past, present and future. In *Joined-Up Government*, ed. V. Bogdanor. New York: Oxford University Press, 175–187.

Nam, T. and Pardo, T. A. (2011). Conceptualizing smart city with dimensions of technology, people, and institutions. In *Proceedings of the 12th Annual International Digital Government Research Conference: Digital Government Innovation in Challenging Times*, ed. J. Bartot et al. New York: ACM Press, 282–291.

Nederhand, J., Van Der Steen, M. and Van Twist, M. (2019). Boundary-spanning strategies for aligning institutional logics: A typology. *Local Government Studies*, 45(2), 219–240.

Neffke, F., Hartog, M., Boschma, R. and Henning, M. (2018). Agents of structural change: The role of firms and entrepreneurs in regional diversification. *Economic Geography*, 94(1), 23–48.

Olsson, P., Folke, C. and Berkes, F. (2004). Adaptive co-management for building resilience in social-ecological systems. *Environmental Management*, 34(1), 75–90.

Osborne, S. P. (2006). The New Public Governance. *Public Management Review*, 8(3), 377–387.

Peek, L. (2008). Children and disasters: Understanding vulnerability, developing capacities, and promoting resilience—an introduction. *Children, Youth and Environments*, 18(1), 1–29.

Pollitt, C. (2003). Joined-up government: Survey. *Political Studies Review*, 1, 34–49.

Pollitt, C., van Thiel, S., and Homburg, V. (eds.) (2007). *New Public Management in Europe: Adaptations and Alternatives*. Basingstoke: Palgrave Macmillan.

Porter, M. E. (1996). Competitive advantage, agglomeration economies, and regional policy. *International Regional Science Review*, 19(1–2), 85–90.

Porter, M. E. (1997). New strategies for inner-city economic development. *Economic Development Quarterly*, 11(1), 11–27.

Rhodes, R. (1996). The new governance: Governing without governance. *Political Studies*, 44, 652–667.

Rittel, H. W. J. and Webber, M. M. (1973). Dilemmas in a general theory of planning. *Policy Sciences*, 4(2), 155–169.

Roberts, L. (2011). 9 Billion? *Science*, 333(6042), 540–543.

Rostov, W. (1960). *The Stages of Economic Growth*. Cambridge: Cambridge University Press.

Sahn, D. E., Dorosh, P. A. and Younger, S. D. (1999). *Structural Adjustment Reconsidered: Economic Policy and Poverty in Africa*. Cambridge: Cambridge University Press.

Scott, A. J. and Storper, M. (2015). The nature of cities: The scope and limits of urban theory. *International Journal of Urban and Regional Research*, 39(1), 1–15.

Stiglitz, J. E. (1991). *The Invisible Hand and Modern Welfare Economics* (NBER Working Paper 3641). Cambridge, MA: National Bureau of Economic Research.

Stiglitz, J. E. (1998). The private uses of public interests: Incentives and institutions. *Journal of Economic Perspectives*, 12(2), 3–22.

Stoker, G. (1995). Regime theory and urban politics. In *Theories of Urban Politics*, ed. D. Judge, G. Stoker and H. Wolman. London: Sage, 54–71.

Stoker, G. (2006). Public value management: A new narrative for networked governance? *The American Review of Public Administration*, 36(1), 41–57.

Suzuki, H., Dastur, A., Moffatt, S., Yabuki, N. and Maruyama, H. (2010). *Eco² Cities: Ecological Cities as Economic Cities*. Washington, DC: World Bank.

Thompson, G. (ed.) (1991). *Markets, Hierarchies and Networks: The Coordination of Social Life*. London: Sage.

Tonkinwise, C. (2015). Design for transitions: From and to what? *Design Philosophy Papers*, 13(1), 85–92.

Torfing, J., Peters, B. G., Pierre, J., and Sørensen, E. (2012). *Interactive Governance: Advancing the Paradigm*. Oxford: Oxford University Press.

Van Dijk, M. P. (2006). *Managing Cities in Developing Countries*. Cheltenham, UK and Northampton, MA, USA: Edward Elgar Publishing.

Van Dijk, M. P. (2009a). Urban water governance as part of a strategy for risk mitigation: What is different in third world cities? In *Building Safer Communities*, ed. F. Urbano. Amsterdam: IOS Press, 182–200.

Van Dijk, M. P. (2009b). Ecological cities, illustrated by Chinese examples. In *Climate Change and Sustainable Development: New Challenges for Poverty Reduction*, ed. M. A. M. Salih. Cheltenham, UK and Northampton, MA, USA: Edward Elgar Publishing, 214–233.

Van Dijk, M. P. (ed.) (2012). *Water Governance*. Special issue of the *International Journal of Water*.

Van Meerkerk, I. and Edelenbos, J. (2018). *Boundary Spanners in Public Management and Governance: An Interdisciplinary Assessment*. Cheltenham, UK and Northampton, MA, USA: Edward Elgar Publishing.

Van Winden, W. and van den Buuse, D. (2017). Smart city pilot projects: Exploring the dimensions and conditions of scaling up. *Journal of Urban Technology*, 24(4), 51–72.

Weber, M. (1978). *Economy and Society: An Outline of Interpretive Sociology*. Berkeley: University of California Press.

WHO (2018). Ambient air pollution. https://www.who.int/airpollution/data/cities/en/.

Wilson, J. Q. (1989). *Bureaucracy: What Government Agencies Do and Why They Do It*. New York: Basic Books.

World Bank (2000). *Attacking Poverty*. World Bank Development Report. New York: Oxford University Press.

2.   Urban management in practice, issues at stake and overview of the book

Meine Pieter van Dijk

This chapter looks at the practice of urban management and the issues urban managers have to deal with. It enumerates different approaches to urban management and governance. It links the main urban paradigms distinguished in Chapter 1 to the different issues discussed in the chapters of this book. A short history of urban management as a field of study will be given and some definitions of urban planning, management and governance will be reviewed, showing the changing emphasis over time.

URBAN MANAGEMENT AND GOVERNANCE: A NEW FIELD OF STUDIES

Urban management in the Global South used to just involve administering urban developments and indicating where the roads or houses should be located. A more dynamic version would entail checking building permits and insisting on respect for minimum building standards (Van Dijk, 2006). New approaches have emerged and old ones are disappearing. This is part and parcel of the dynamics of urban development reflected in the different terms used for the dynamics of cities which are discussed later in this chapter. It will be seen that there is now more attention given to the social fabric of the city, social networks, the cultural city and making cities competitive and inclusive. Cities are reflecting on their development and reinventing themselves continuously as reflected by terms such as smart, green or resilient cities.

The issues to be solved by local officials have changed and the urban management function has shifted from just managing to anticipating urban developments. The importance of the coordinating role for urban managers dealing with these issues and working at lower levels of local governments should not be underestimated. The essence of urban management is creating participatory decision structures and being inclusive: striving with all actors concerned in a decision structure for more equality, a better environment and a vibrant economy (Van Dijk, 2006).

Several trends can be observed in urban management. Table 2.1 lists some of the old and new issues for urban managers, dealing with societal changes, such as climate change and youth unemployment in cities. However, no distinction is made between knowledge, skills, attitudes and ways of working. Besides more knowledge, urban managers increasingly also need research skills, participatory skills and skills to manage networks. The change from the old to the new issues is not just a change from management to governance but also adaptation in knowledge, attitudes, mentality and skills.

Attention has moved from topics such as creating employment in cities, providing housing and looking after the environment to creating innovative, networked cities and making them more green or ecological. The literature is now about using information technology smartly and introducing forms of e-governance. Also the importance of an entrepreneurial attitude is recognized and many universities have become more entrepreneurial institutions (Mudde, 2020).

More attention is now given to participation and the situation of specific groups, such as young people, working parents and elderly or disabled people. There is also more research on the processes going on in cities (such as radicalization, gentrification and growing inequality) and there is more attention for the factors influencing inequality, life chances for different societal groups, genders or nationalities (Jacobs, 1965). We need to address whether urban management can be fair and equitable in education, healthcare, housing and the job market. We need people who can provide a strategic view on the future of the city, but also the visionary leadership to move in that direction. More attention is now paid to the role of urban finance and new ways of financing urban projects. New tools and methods are being used in urban management, such as strategic planning, stakeholder analysis, geographic information systems and policy impact studies.

The distinction between old and recent issues is not an absolute one. Some old issues are not solved; for example urban poverty, employment and housing remain issues to deal with. In terms of Chapter 1, we could say that the complexity of these issues has grown over time, and previous generations of urban managers have not been able to solve them. Solving one issue (urban transport) may make another issue worse (urban pollution). It is the complexity of some of the issues which calls for a system approach (Healy, 1997), but as will be shown in different chapters a comprehensive or integrated approach may be difficult to manage. In Chapter 1 and also in Edelenbos and Van Dijk (2017) it is noted that the response to increasing complexity in managing cities calls for governance approaches and abandoning the pure urban management approach as this latter approach bets on complexity reduction and project management approaches trying to reduce complexity in content, organization and time required. The complexity of some of the issues mentioned in Table 2.1 will be

Table 2.1   Old and new issues for urban managers

Old issues	Some recent issues
– Unemployment, insufficient housing and the degradation of the environment	– Dealing with climate change and other urban risks, making the city inclusive
– The importance of information technology (IT) and digital data	– Creating innovative, networked cities
– Using IT to inform and involve stakeholders	– Becoming green or ecological cities
– Attention for the social fabric of the city, the role of social networks	– Urban governance becomes more important
– Deal with sectoral issues like transport, water, sanitation, waste collection and environmental issues in isolation	– New forms of e-governance existing in major world cities
– A focus on improving tax collection	– The importance of visionary leadership using strategic planning
– Using existing tools in urban management: cost–benefit analysis, stakeholder analysis, geographic information systems and gender analysis	– Use ICT to make a smarter city
– Attention for participation of specific groups, such as migrants, women and poor people	– Attention for specific groups, such as young people, working parents and elderly or disabled people
– Deal with rural–urban migration and the problems of absorbing migrants in slums	– A focus on processes going on in cities: radicalization, gentrification and growing inequality
– Slum upgrading programmes and relocation	– More attention for urban finance and new ways of financing urban projects
– Public–private partnerships (PPPs) to finance urban renewal, infrastructure and other urban services	– Original ways of involving the private sector in inner city revival, infrastructure provision and service delivery

discussed below after providing definitions of urban management and governance and summing up some changes in society affecting them.

URBAN MANAGEMENT IN PRACTICE

What does the urban manager do in real life? There is a proliferation of ideas as to what urban management is and what makes it an interesting topic. In the 1990s there were two different approaches. One approach stemmed from a spatial urban planning tradition (based on geography or on physical planning theories) and the other took a more economic and management approach to urban management. The first group of urban managers believed that urban development also requires some, if only strategic planning. This view proposes that urban development requires strategic city-wide or regional planning to guide trunk investments and identify the most appropriate locations for jobs, residences and transportation (World Bank, 2000). The World Bank considered at that time that the key issues that urban managers have to deal with included: governance and municipal finance; competitiveness of cities and enhanced capacity to attract private sector investment and promote employment; capacity to deliver public services in an efficient manner, including environmental managerial capacity.

Traditionally local authorities were supposed to plan and coordinate activities in the city in conjunction with other levels of government. They provided services such as water and transportation, dealt with municipal finance and regulated the behaviour of the major actors and important urban markets. However, something essential is missing in this approach to urban management, namely that the local authorities should focus on the major issues identified by the population together with other stakeholders. That was the definition of urban management suggested by Van Dijk (2006). The emphasis is then more on the implementation of policies and managing the outcomes of the urban development process with the stakeholders. In short, urban management involves putting urban plans into practice with less emphasis on the planning process itself, while urban governance is defined as creating opportunities to involve more stakeholders in the visioning and implementation process.

The emphasis shifted again from looking at urban management as management of a stock of houses and a bundle of infrastructure to managing the flows of information in a smart way. At the beginning of this century the main tenets of urban management were as follows (Van Dijk, 2006):

- Cities compete and should be made more competitive.
- Decentralization is a precondition for urban management. It makes urban management possible since it allows urban managers to take action and decide for themselves.
- New Public Management theory suggests the way to go: involve the private sector, make organizations responsible, transparent and accountable, go for customer and market orientation.
- Good governance offers guidelines on how to involve more stakeholders in decision making, planning and implementation and eliminate corruption.
- The idea is that cities can be governed differently if more stakeholders are involved. Urban governance has become more important and this has implications for urban management (Edelenbos and Van Dijk, 2017; Van Dijk et al., 2017).
- The challenge for urban managers is to use information technology smartly, ranging from electronic voting to registering births online, and from managing urban flows to using surveillance equipment in a smart way. Managing information flows is a bigger challenge than managing bricks and asphalt (Van Dijk, 2018).

Whereas most scholars and practitioners would agree that decentralization and a smart use of technologies have remained important, New Public Management is criticized widely these days (Kintu, 2019). We have become aware that excessive authority is given to the private sector, which has not always led to appropriate solutions. At the core of the criticism of NPM and other urban management paradigms is the awareness that none of the old paradigms fully captured the increasing complexity of cities and the growing importance of wicked problems such as climate change. Neither did they (or could they) fully appreciate the possibilities of using new technologies.

Concerning urban governance, we note that since 2006 a generally hierarchical, top-down type of urban management has been replaced by a more bottom-up adaptive kind of management. New forms of governance are developing, dealing with complexity, and promoting collaboration between elected politicians and activist stakeholders fighting for their own interests. Transparent urban governance systems are required, where stakeholders can also be held accountable for what they are contributing to the decision process.

The emphasis in urban management has shifted from looking at the stock of houses and infrastructure to managing the flows of knowledge, information, capital, people, food, water and waste. This perspective leads to a different way of managing cities, focusing on managing flows in cities and using information and communication technologies (ICT) and geographic information systems (GIS) to do that in an integrated way. Technology allows the urban manager to tackle issues differently. Flows, which will be discussed in later chapters, include the water cycle (Chapter 6), the knowledge of how to organize the flow of people (e.g. light-rail systems to move people around, discussed in Chapter 8) and flows of capital (Chapter 9). There are also flows of goods and the resulting waste flows which require waste minimization and integrated waste management. Mobility is a flow of people and goods and requires the development of integrated infrastructure and transport policies. Sensors can be put at critical points (on bridges, traffic lights and parks) and digitally inform the authorities about traffic congestion, air pollution, noise pollution, or concentrations of toxic substances in surface water. The short definition of urban management used in this approach is that urban managers have to get the food into and the waste out of the city. Using new technologies wisely is a challenge and it often comes together in the smart cities concept discussed below and in Chapter 5.

SOCIETAL CHANGES INFLUENCING URBAN MANAGEMENT

The new issues listed earlier require another approach in urban management. A number of societal changes have also affected urban management and will be discussed first, because they also have consequences for the definition of urban management and governance:

1. Climate change and pollution can be considered as risks for cities, requiring strategies for risk mitigation and adaptation to the new situation (Rotterdam, 2016).
2. This leads to the issue of resilience, the capacity of a city to deal with shocks, and how to become more resilient as a city or region (Liang, 2018).
3. Pollution has become widespread and people want ecological, green or sustainable cities (Kenworthy, 2006).
4. Competition requires innovative cities, which constantly reinvent themselves (Suzuki et al., 2010).

These are challenges which are not always compatible with the old slogan: cities need integrated urban planning and management to deal with them. Each challenge will now be described in slightly more detail.

Regarding the first point, climate change and its consequences for cities have become more important. The consequences of climate change can be seen as risks.

With regard to the second issue, strategic planning and urban governance can be considered as strategies for mitigating these risks. In that case urban management can be defined as an integrated way of dealing with the risks that cities are now facing. Urban management will usually opt for a comprehensive approach to manage urban risks. In the context of climate change such an approach is complicated because of the acuteness of the problems raised. Action and strategic planning approaches are highly relevant tools that can be used for the purpose of identifying the major risks for cities and the strategies to deal with them.

In relation to the third issue, urban management and governance want to achieve sustainable urban development. This means urban management is defined in terms of promoting the welfare of citizens in such a way that it does not have negative consequences for the environment and could continue without financial support from outside the urban system. This theme is discussed in several chapters in the book.

Finally, the last societal change stems from the desire to make cities, in the process of globalization, more competitive. Van Oort et al. discuss this in Chapter 4 where they look at the economic dynamics of a region and its cities. For example, the eco^2 approach of the World Bank tries to combine sound economic policies with environmental policies (Suzuki et al., 2010).

Table 2.2   *Examples of changing emphasis in urban interventions*

Issues and the relevant chapter	Urban planning	Urban management	Urban governance
Urban planning	Physical planning	Focus is on implementing plans	Strategic planning with stakeholders
Housing (Chapter 10)	Where to build new houses, roads and access to energy	How to get people to build these houses	How to involve project developers and construction firms in sustainable construction
Finance (Chapter 9)	How to collect the necessary taxes	How to tap private sources of finance	How to use new sources of finance, from crowd funding to targeted subsidies
Employment (Chapter 4)	Can space for formal enterprises be reserved?	How to stimulate the formal and informal sector	How to develop innovative networks
Transport (Chapter 8)	How to provide the necessary infrastructure	How to stimulate alternative forms of transportation	What are appropriate solutions for connecting people and work?
Public–private partnerships (PPPs) to execute urban projects (Chapter 9)	Originally only for urban renewal projects: how to use PPPs for the plans	How to promote PPPs for housing, services and urban infrastructure (Chapter 10)	How to generate collaborative efforts for creative solutions for specific issues
Environmental issues (Chapter 7)	Administer pollution, how to plan spaces for polluting activities	How to deal with pollution and waste as flows and how to reduce them	How to make the transition to reuse and recycle at household and city level
Climate change (Chapter 6)	Not an issue yet	How to achieve climate mitigation	How to achieve climate adaptation

CHANGING ISSUES AND SOCIETAL DEVELOPMENTS HAVE CONSEQUENCES FOR SECTORAL INTERVENTIONS

The changing issues and societal developments have consequences for framing the issues urban managers have to deal with. In Table 2.2 the three main paradigms used in the book are linked to a number of sectors and it is shown that other questions are being asked over time, depending on whether one looks at the sector from an urban planning perspective, or with an urban management or an urban governance paradigm in mind. Examples of these changes can be found in the different chapters of this book as indicated in the table.

DIFFERENT CONCEPTS USED

The practice of urban management is very much linked to what the politicians see as the major issues, and to the concepts used to express what urban management should achieve. In this section we list ten concepts which express an ambition. After giving a reference, we define the concept and provide some more information. The concepts are put in the order of the date of the reference. We have included green, sustainable and smart cities, which will be discussed in more detail in subsequent chapters, as will be indicated.

Global cities (Sassen, 1991): Sassen argues that New York, London and Tokyo are global cities because of the networks in which they function and points out how crucial such networks are to be a successful, global city. The role of networks is also emphasized in Van Oort et al. in Chapter 4. In Chapter 6 it is shown that cities learn from international experiences through networks and use this experience to deal with their own issues.

Competitive cities (Porter, 1998): This idea has been around since the 1990s. Cities have to be competitive and should use the ideas of New Public Management to do so. This approach figures in several contributions to this book, notably in Van Oort et al. (Chapter 4).

Cultural city (Florida, 2004): Florida emphasized that cultural activities are the key to modern cities. He showed the importance of cultural activities in modern cities and developed the idea that they are part of the city of the future. Cities are no longer places of manufacturing but of 'cultural' activities and will become more and more important in the future.

Climate proof cities (Rotterdam, 2008): The negative effects of climate change call for climate proof cities. Recent disasters have shown the serious consequences for cities of excessive or lack of rain, more heat or pollution (Zhang et al., 2019). Hence more attention is being given to climate proof, resilient cities, and carbon neutral, green, eco and sustainable cities, as discussed in Chapter 3. The focus is often on reduction of greenhouse gas emissions and on introducing climate resilience.

Green cities (Lindfield and Steinberg, 2012): In a green city the land and waterscape is also important. Different urban projects focus on achieving zero carbon emissions. They are discussed in Chapter 9. The approach intends to make cities greener, more environmentally friendly and liveable.

Eco-cities (Van Dijk, 2015): Eco cities pay attention to the eco-system approach: the quality of urban life, the physical environment or ways cities deal with pollution, waste and wastewater, etc. In the eco city literature the emphasis is on the quality of the environment and a similar concern can be found in the green and sustainable cities concept. Van Dijk (2018) argues in favour of smart eco cities. The smart eco city concept intends to integrate the smart and eco approaches, as discussed in Chapter 6.

Sustainable cities (UN Habitat, 2016): Sustainable cities promote good environmental governance at all levels to support local and national partners to adopt environmental planning management processes and integrate good practice into national policy and legal frameworks, as discussed in Chapter 6. A sustainable city should reduce waste in an efficient way, recycle it, and reuse it as much as possible. Such a city should close its water and energy cycles and deal with pollution.

Resilient cities (Rockefeller Foundation, 2017): De Jong (2016) defines urban resilience as "The ability to learn, plan, and recover from the hazards to which they are exposed". The Rockefeller Foundation developed tools to assess the ability to learn, plan, and recover from the hazards to which cities are exposed.

Sponge city concept (Liang, 2018): The Chinese have developed the sponge city concept to deal with flooding. The sponge city technology should slow, spread, sink, and store runoff. Related terms are resilient cities, a more defensive concept, while the eco city concept addresses the question of what a city should be, as discussed in Chapter 6 on urban water management.

Smart cities (Lim in Chapter 5): Smart cities aim to better connect human capital, social capital and ICT, i.e. to use ICT in an intelligent way. The challenge is to achieve integration of sectoral interests in the framework of urban management, using modern information technology (Hajer and Dassen, 2014). Cities are no longer regarded simply as a collection of houses and roads, but rather the sum of a number of flows that need to be managed. Important flows are the water cycle and the energy cycle (including the reduction of CO_2 and other greenhouse gas emissions) and creating relevant governance structures for this. In this definition smart eco cities focus on managing flows, including flows of people and money. This is discussed in more detail in Chapter 5.

The concepts reviewed here tend to differ substantially in their scope (from the narrow focus of the sponge city concept to the broad goals of the green and sustainable city concepts). Green and sustainable cities think mainly in terms of using government structures, while in eco cities citizens want to be involved. In resilient cities the potential victims of negative events may even be involved in urban management, while in the sponge city the idea is to involve the private sector. We now present an issue based discussion of urban management and its central themes.

FROM URBAN MANAGEMENT TO URBAN GOVERNANCE: NEW ISSUES DETERMINE THE DEFINITION

Urban issues have become more complicated because of new challenges and the growing complexity of the challenges. Urban development has become more and more a multi-actor event, with many stakeholders wanting and deserving a role. Urban management is more than physical or urban planning because the aim is to get things done with the stakeholders. They need to be involved in order to indicate what would be good solutions for the issues identified and to mobilize the necessary know-how and resources. In the consultation process consensus building is necessary to take the decisions and execute the results of the strategic planning exercise successfully. Inhabitants, entrepreneurs, organizations of inhabitants or entrepreneurs, environmental activists and project developers (or organizations of these actors) all want to be involved in the urban development process. The urban governance approach is more appropriate to deal with wicked and complex problems.

In the following we summarize each chapter and provide a critical perspective placing the chapters in the context of changing paradigms and popular concepts.

Chapter 1: Paradigms for Urban Management and Governance of the City of the Future

Three paradigms are introduced in Chapter 1 concerning urban development. The paradigm of urban planning corresponds with the public administration paradigm of hierarchical control. When urban management becomes important, the public administration paradigm embraced is the New Public Management. Finally public administration suggests using new public urban governance as a paradigm to deal with wicked urban problems.

The editors argue that responding to urban issues requires a mix of elements from the urban planning, management and governance paradigms. The wide range of issues has resulted in new conceptualizations of smart, resilient, creative, green and environmental cities. While these concepts partially pour the same wine in new bottles, they offer inspiring entry points for managing urban development as will be shown in subsequent chapters.

The editors point to a paradigm shift, whereby the role of government may increase once again. Indications are the critique on market-led development and the increasing role of government during the COVID-19 pandemic in 2020. With climate change and urban resilience high on the political agenda, the role of local government is also likely to increase.

In Chapter 1 the editors introduce a 'Governance Possibility Frontier', which describes minimum levels of planning, management and governance required in different political settings. They also propose to use boundary spanning as an eclectic way to bring actors and processes together, but it is not yet clear how that would work in practice.

Chapter 3: Just Transitions to Deal with the Challenge of Climate Change

Darren McCauley writes about urban transition, and how to make the step from the current situation to a desired situation in a just way. He points to the need to make a *just* transition. This raises an important moral issue that should also play out in the other chapters: how to ensure inclusive urban development with equal access to urban services for everybody.

The chapter describes environmental challenges in Berlin and Paris and provides details on a research agenda to respond to these challenges, with climate proof cities in mind. McCauley argues in favour of networked governance as an indicator of successful transition management in cities. He uses Paris and Berlin as case studies. After identifying the key actors the author looks at how the transition away from fossil fuel was made. He considers the use of procedural justice in the energy transition from fossil fuel in Berlin and away from the dependence on nuclear energy in Paris. Procedural justice is the idea of fairness in the processes that resolve disputes and allocate resources.

One may ask whether the findings for Berlin and Paris are also valid for cities in emerging and developing countries. In these countries priorities may be unemployment or pollution, the lack of services or infrastructure. However, transition management is always important if one wants to go from one situation to another. In the same way, ethical discussions (very important in this chapter) need to be held each time, even if the decisions may be different given the local circumstances. Can we agree on the values and norms to be used in urban development?

Chapter 4: Structural Change, Labour Markets and Regional Economic Policy

Van Oort et al. situate urban development in a regional context. This links to a discussion about the competitive cities concept. How do we make cities and regions more innovative? How do we get a dynamic urban economy? Such an economy would allow all kinds of urban development initiatives to be undertaken.

The authors focus on the importance of the regional economy, of innovative networks, labour markets and metropolitan development. Cities are part of bigger regions and their development fits into metropolitan development strategies. The labour market is the key institution for regional development. In an innovative environment it will work better to create jobs and achieve urban dynamics.

The urban labour market in emerging economies may not function in the same way as in a dynamic Western city. Van Oort et al. look at it from a market economics perspective, while in a developing context an institutional approach (developing new and redirecting existing institutions) is more important. This points to the role of the state in a capitalist urban economy. The varieties of capitalism debate has shown that there are big variations between the role of the state in the economy: in Europe, for example, between France and Germany, and similarly in China between the role of provincial and local governments in Yunnan and Zhejiang provinces.

In a developing countries context the urban informal sector is also very important. The authors pay attention to it since the sector can make up more than half of the urban economy in some African countries. The point is that this sector has its own dynamic, which is not always captured by Western economic theories. Finally it is important to distinguish policies to create competitive cities and regions formulated and implemented at different levels of government: the national, regional and local levels.

Chapter 5: What Use Can Be Made of Modern Information Technology in Smart Cities?

Yirang Lim asks the question: what use is made of modern information technology in smart cities? What are the strong and the weak points of different technological solutions? The predecessor of this book (Van Dijk, 2006) also dealt with using ICT in urban management. In 2006 information technology mainly had a supportive function, facilitating urban administration and development. ICT allowed the population to participate in voting over municipal budgets or was used to inform citizens about recent developments. The technology was a step forward, but around 2010 the perspective changed.

Lim shows that technology will not just help the authorities in managing the cities, but the city would function differently if conceived as a technological challenge. The focus will change to incentivizing people to behave differently by using technology, or what is called 'nudging' (Thaler and Sunstein, 2008). Information technology will change the relation between living and working areas, including urban mobility (cities go from building roads to managing mobility), building houses and developing the internet of things, and will also involve a change from simply avoiding pollution to exploiting flows of waste and sewerage by using ICT.

The author looks at the advantages and disadvantages of a smart city concept. The main idea of the chapter is that smart cities better connect human capital, social capital and ICT infrastructure in order to generate greater and more sustainable economic development and an improved quality of life for urban citizens. The EU has also emphasized the human dimension in a policy study on smart cities (European Parliament, 2014). The EU launched the smart cities and communities initiative in 2011 and supported actors in the development and implementation of smart cities through the European Innovation Partnership on Smart Cities and Communities (EIP-SCC).

Lim rightly also looks at the disadvantages of using the smart cities approach. This leads to a discussion about the techno-surveillance state. Does the use of all this information still guarantee the privacy of its citizens? China is often called a surveillance state given the high number of cameras in cities and the use of face recognition software.

Chapter 6: Different Approaches to Urban Water Management

This chapter analyses three different approaches to urban water management. The sustainable, green and smart eco cities concepts and the corresponding interventions to deal with urban water issues at different levels of government (national, regional, urban, local and neighbourhood) and at the household level are discussed. Van Dijk suggests using technological options, which are available and make sense in economic terms, within a governance structure.

Cities are facing increasing water problems because of urbanization, additional economic development and climate change. Climate change asks for climate proof cities and the literature emphasizes climate change mitigation and adaptation policies. What should cities do in case of climate change? This may imply higher temperatures (heat waves), and usually more volatility in rainfall. This situation may make it necessary to store water, to prohibit building on low lying areas, to experiment with new technologies (for example heat exchange systems using the water under the ground), to start rainwater harvesting, to address water penetration in the soil and to separate grey and brown water. It is important to take action at different levels of government, and to involve households as well.

Three conceptual frameworks to deal with the resulting issues are analysed, in particular how sustainable cities, green cities and smart eco-cities deal with urban water issues. Often similar interventions are suggested in the framework of these concepts. Examples of the interventions to deal with water issues are analysed drawing from evidence from Europe and Asia. The technical options range from water infiltration systems and rainwater harvesting systems to introducing the separation of grey and brown water. The use of concepts like the green, sustainable or sponge city may help to get the necessary focus, attention, support and finance. However, to what extent are these concepts just fashions and do they really suggest a coherent approach to the issues mentioned?

Another important theme is the nexus of water and energy and experiences with water and energy saving technologies. Existing technologies discussed are rainwater harvesting, which can be at the level of a house, a public building or a neighbourhood; solar water heaters, which are placed by households; and water turbines, which are placed by a community, a neighbourhood, a city or a higher level (involving the regional or the national government). A cost–benefit analysis of the technologies chosen shows that the societal benefits are often high, but much depends on the governance structures, which are left out of the analysis. The chapter recommends policies and incentives to promote the introduction and use of these water management technologies, distinguishing different target groups. It is realized that smaller cities may not be able to follow an integrated approach.

Chapter 7: Governing Urban Public Places, or Urban Commons

This chapter deals with the governance of urban public open spaces. Toto et al. study urban commons in cities in Eastern Europe and explore forms of collaboration between stakeholders (commoners). The leading question in this chapter is whether urban commoning can be complementary to or is part of urban governance, defined as a framework for making the city liveable. Urban commoning is defined as community-led network governance.

The examples explored concern public open spaces (squares), as objects that encompass ecosystem functions, infrastructure, property rights, and social interaction and values. The underlying issue is how to make the most of open spaces. In the cities studied public open space is usually owned by local governments, but the pool of users – commoners who benefit in various ways from the bundle of property rights – is large and complex. The public open space is a space of human and social representation, where citizens anchor or claim values, in a typical act of city appropriation. Consequently, the governance approach to deal with its optimal use should include more than local governments.

The problem of the commons is that their management requires some kind of regulation, or a governance structure. Coase (1936) received the Nobel Prize in economics because he proved commons need to be managed. They need a governance structure to take decisions and finance to achieve the plans. The authors ask the question of what drives the care taken over these common spaces. Elinor Ostrom received the Nobel Prize in economics in 2009 for demonstrating how local property can be successfully governed in common, without state intervention or privatization. The management of urban commons requires a governance approach (regulations and design principles) that, in addition to common pool resources, should carefully consider the values system attached to public open space, which goes well beyond utilitarian considerations (Ostrom, 1990).

The authors develop a framework for what potentially defines public open space as urban commons, which should be considered in urban governance processes. These are called dimensions and encompass: drivers (of space formation and functioning), boundaries (property rights and users' pool), governance (rules), and values (attributed to space). They explore also the challenges that are present in each case. They opt for a case comparison to find patterns that allow them to draw conclusions. Then follows the presentation of the cases as per this framework, and a discussion section on the three types of selected spaces. In the central spaces local government has to do the management, while in intermediate space there may be conflicting interests and there is a possibility for community-based development. In the neighbourhood open spaces there is higher potential for commoning.

They conclude that in most of the cases the local governments are in charge, but inconsiderate of the interests of users of these public squares. However, the users – commoners – attach values to the spaces and the larger the pool of commoners (central squares) the larger the variety of values, but the lower the interest of commoners to participate in management, limiting their rights to access and withdrawal. In the neighbourhood squares, commoners are engaged more in management and sometimes have also exclusion rights, but values depend on the historical ties among commoners and between them and the space.

The authors suggest that the governance of urban commons is and should be part of urban governance. In practice, the responsibility lies with the local government in the cities studied, but bottom-up stakeholder involvement brings added value and effectiveness to the urban governance of public open space. In addition, values attributed to public open space should be carefully accounted for, when choosing the most appropriate/optimal governance rules and mechanisms to administer it.

The examples represent the situation in Eastern European cities, but the repository of cases should be expanded further for the findings and conclusions to lead to universally corroborated approaches. The authors do not explore the conditions for robust commons governance in detail, and do not deal extensively with the importance of collective action and the role of values pertaining to urban commons. However, they conclude that a bottom-up, community-led approach to commoning of public spaces is the most effective.

Chapter 8: Co-creating Knowledge in a Light-Rail Transport Project in Addis Ababa

This chapter is about improving infrastructure and urban transport to become a global city. However, the emphasis is on collaboration between countries when infrastructure is transferred. The light-rail system built in the capital of Ethiopia came from China. The underlying hypothesis is that without knowledge transfer, countries remain dependent on external knowledge resulting in financial outflows.

The themes covered in this chapter are knowledge sharing in constructing and operating mass transportation systems using Chinese equipment, construction companies and capacity building. The story is that a light-rail system has been successfully built in Addis Ababa, but a similar project in Nigeria has faced delays for years. What are the reasons for such a different performance?

The chapter is written from the Ethiopian perspective. Alade and Gianoli conclude that the structured absorptive capacity by the Ethiopian railroad company to acquire knowledge and skills from the Chinese consortium was the main determinant for responsibilities, knowledge and skill transfer. The actors involved in the Ethiopian case made various efforts to acquire these skills and knowledge and the initial knowledge base, which facilitated the acquisition of the explicit knowledge provided by the Chinese, using a knowledge transfer structure, knowledge transfer ratio plans and streams, and other unique approaches to knowledge transfer.

What would be the motivation of the Chinese counterparts to transfer knowledge if they can also sell it? Is it because of contractual obligations (else they would not be paid), or because of close ties of trust with their Ethiopian counterparts? The chapter portrays the case study as a best practice. This may be true as far as knowledge transfer is concerned, but it is important to mention the limitations of the case study approach, of not looking at the actual functioning of the system and the implied financial obligations to China.

Chapter 9: Alternative Ways of Financing Urban Infrastructure, African Examples

This chapter by Bongwa and Van Dijk deals with urban finance issues: how is urban development financed? Infrastructure is the foundation of modern economies and societies. A robust, efficient, and well-maintained infrastructure system is critical to support and sustain the nation's economy, improve quality of life, and strengthen global competitiveness. This chapter looks not only at the rationale for public provision and regulation of urban infrastructure but also at how currently African cities need to cope with financing and providing basic infrastructure services in the face of rapid urban growth globally and especially in Africa. How can they become global cities?

The focus of this chapter is on urban infrastructure financing. The underlying concepts are clarified, so that the myriad urban infrastructure financing vehicles available to local governments today are understood in their proper context. This chapter looks at what strategies are used in financing urban infrastructure in Africa and how effective they are. The chapter emphasizes that it is necessary to follow a coordinated approach including public–private partnerships and asset leveraging, developing domestic financial institutions, using multilateral and bilateral financial institutions, pension funds, insurance companies and endowments. However, capital markets and new innovative mechanisms for infrastructure finance could go a long way in resolving the financial bottlenecks facing the urban infrastructure. This approach enables cities to realize their full functional responsibilities as regards infrastructure and service financing and their developmental potential.

The question is whether this approach of accessing capital markets is also possible for smaller cities. In the Netherlands there is a bank for the Dutch municipalities (BNG), which issues bonds on behalf of these smaller cities. It saves them the trouble of getting a credit rating themselves.

Chapter 10: Collaborative Capacity of PPP Projects: The Influence of Partnership Models

Adamu and Gianoli analyse the influence of different partnership models in the urban housing sector in Nigeria, and pay attention to financing housing and the role of different stakeholders. Themes include the role of PPPs as governance mechanisms, alliances, and housing effectiveness and efficiency.

The results from two PPP-led housing projects from Nigeria show that the concession PPP model possesses limited internal relational capacities as the public partners are often limited to the pre-implementation phases of the project's life cycle and the private partners have dominance in the implementation phases. Hence, the emphasis is placed on the independent organizational capacities of partners. By contrast, projects that adopt an alliance model have positive internal relational capacities which, invariably, boost project capacity.

The authors conclude that the choice of a partnership model influences the result of the project. But little attention is given to the specific influence of the local context, compared to other such projects in African cities.

Chapter 11: Selecting Multi-Stakeholder Tools in Urban Planning

Keunen and Ruijsink studied strategic planning experiences to define guiding principles for selecting multi-stakeholder tools for urban planning. Such plans posed the question what is your city going to look like in 20 years' time? Strategic planning in the context of territorial and spatial based planning uses different tools. The objectives of Keunen and Ruijsink are to assess to what extent the tools lead to engagement of different stakeholders and what we can learn from them.

Strategic planning became an important tool for urban management in the 1980s. The organization City Alliance helped cities all over the world to prepare strategic plans. City Alliance introduced the strategic planning approach for cities in the Global South in a big way. Such a plan was often a condition for the World Bank to start lending to cities to develop their cities. Reviews of the work of City Alliance in the field of strategic planning are available. The authors also reviewed efforts to make strategic plans for some specific cities and found that they pay little attention to the spatial dimension and suggest an alternative approach.

The strategic planning tool can be put in the broader context of tools for urban management and governance. A number of tools are available to deal with urban issues. Policies are formulated at different geographical levels (the national, provincial or state, metropolitan, city or district level), but the objectives must be in agreement with the strategic plan. Then there should be tools to implement the agreed policies and programmes. The tools may be different in different cities, as is apparent in the more empirical chapters in this book.

The authors rightly emphasize the importance of phases in strategic planning and show how participation and spatiality can operate in these different phases. However, the proposed participatory mapping approach is still quite general, while preparing for climate change is a very specific issue, which requires concrete activities.

CONCLUSION

The work of an urban manager in local government has changed over time as shown in the different chapters. The body of knowledge and experience on how to deal with various urban issues is growing rapidly. What is new in urban management and governance? The emphasis is currently on the use of innovation to achieve the full potential of cities. It is all about smart and creative cities, about experimenting, about managing flows and paying attention to resources, such as the capacities of the local governance structures and local entrepreneurs.

REFERENCES

Coase, R. (1936). The nature of the firm. *Economica*, 4(16), 386–405.

De Jong, M. (2016). Sustainable urban and infrastructural development in China: Why intergovernmental relations are the key. Inaugural Address, Delft University of Technology.

Edelenbos, J. and Van Dijk, M. P. (2017). Introduction: Urban governance in the realm of complexity. In *Urban Governance in the Realm of Complexity*, ed. M. P. Van Dijk, J. Edelenbos and K. van Rooijen. Rugby: Practical Action Publishing, 1–24.

European Parliament (2014). *Mapping Smart Cities in the EU*. Brussels: European Parliament.

Florida, R. (2004). *The Rise of the Creative Class*. New York: HarperCollins.

Hajer, M. and Dassen, T. (2014). *Smart about Cities: Visualizing the Challenge for 21st Century Urbanism*. The Hauge: PBL Netherlands Environmental Assessment Agency.

Healy, P. (1997). *Collaborative Planning: Shaping Places in Fragmented Societies*. Basingstoke: Macmillan.

Jacobs, J. (1965). *The Death and Life of Great American Cities*. London: Cox & Wyman.

Kenworthy, J. R. (2006). Dimensions for sustainable city development in the Third World. *Environment & Urbanization*, 18, 67–86.

Kintu, P. (2019). Juridical performance of the court system in Uganda: A case of the High Court. DBA Maastricht: Maastricht School of Management.

Liang, X. (2018). Integrated economic and financial analysis of China's sponge city program for water-resilient urban development. *Sustainability*, 10(3), 669. https://doi.org/10.3390/su10030669.

Lindfield, M. and Steinberg, F. (2012). *Green Cities*. Manila: Asian Development Bank.

Mudde, H. L. M. (2020). Universities in the midst of society: Entrepreneurship and youth employment in Ethiopia, Indonesia and the Palestinian Territories. Maastricht: Universiteit van Maastricht.

Ostrom, E. (1990). *Governing the Commons: The Evolution of Institutions for Collective Action*. Cambridge: Cambridge University Press.

Porter, M. E. (1998). *On Competition*. Boston: Harvard Business School Press.

Rockefeller Foundation (2017). *City Resilience Framework*. New York City: The Rockefeller Foundation and ARUP.

Rotterdam (2008). *Rotterdam, Climate Proof*. Rotterdam: Municipality.

Rotterdam (2016). *Rotterdam Resilience Strategy: Ready for the 21st Century*. Consultation document. 100 Resilient Cities. http://lghttp.60358.nexcesscdn.net/8046264/images/page/-/100rc/pdfs/strategy-resilient-rotterdam.pdf.

Sassen, S. (1991). *The Global City: New York, London, Tokyo*. Princeton: Princeton University Press.

Suzuki, H., Dastur, A., Moffatt, S., Yabuki, N. and Maruyama, H. (2010). *Eco² Cities: Ecological Cities as Economic Cities*. Washington, DC: World Bank.

Thaler, R. H. and Sunstein, C. R. (2008). *Nudge: Improving Decisions About Health, Wealth, and Happiness*. London: Penguin.

UN Habitat (2016). *Sustainable City Programme*. Nairobi: United Nations Habitat.

Van Dijk, M. P. (2006). *Managing Cities in Developing Countries*. Cheltenham, UK and Northampton, MA, USA: Edward Elgar Publishing.

Van Dijk, M. P. (2015). Measuring eco cities, comparing European and Asian experiences: Rotterdam versus Beijing. *Asia Europe Journal*, 13, 75–94.

Van Dijk, M. P. (2018). Smart eco cities are managing information flows in an integrated way: The example of water, electricity and solid waste. In *Smart Futures:*

Challenges of Urbanization and Social Sustainability, ed. M. Dastbaz, W. Naude and J. Manoochehri. Berlin: Springer, 149–169.

Van Dijk, M. P., Edelenbos, J. and van Rooijen, K. (eds.) (2017). *Urban Governance in the Realm of Complexity*. Rugby: Practical Action Publishing.

World Bank (2000). *Attacking Poverty*. World Bank Development Report. New York: Oxford University Press.

Zhang, M., Huan, W., Wei, J. and van Dijk, M. P. (2019). Assessing heat wave vulnerability in Beijing and its districts, using a three dimensional model. *International Journal of Global Warming*, 17(3), 297–314.

3. Managing a just transition in urban contexts

Darren McCauley

MANAGING TRANSITIONS

There has been a plethora of literature designed to demonstrate that transitions are to be managed (Mullally and Byrne, 2016; Sareen and Haarstad, 2018; Schot et al., 2016; Scrase and Smith, 2009; van Welie and Romijn, 2018). This literature emphasizes the importance of proactive administering of positive societal forces that drive desired outcomes and processes. Scholars in this field have built conceptual frameworks that are applicable on all governance levels, from the global to the city. Transition management literature focuses on three conceptual levels, at the macro, meso and micro levels (Jenkins et al., 2018). This is not to be confused with local, national and international. The three levels of transition management are designed around the meso level of thinking. This is a group of institutions, processes and ideas that underpin the current system. They all seek to maintain the status quo. Transition management is about empowering the micro and macro levels of institutions, processes and actors. The objective is to destabilize current thinking through the active management of change.

Sustainability is a core principle in transition management. The idea is to encourage a series of stages that will lead to more sustainable outcomes, from pre-development, take-off, and acceleration to the new form of civilization. While destruction is an important part of the process, the objective is to attain a new form of stability which is more sustainable. Transition management has been applied to both Global South (Castán Broto et al., 2018; Goddard and Farrely, 2018; Verbitsky, 2014) and Global North (Delina and Sovacool, 2018; Healy and Barry, 2017; Miller et al., 2015) contexts. The centrality of the city in these studies is evident. Literature on urban contexts has emphasized the critical nature of participatory, reflexive and adaptable forms of networked governance as crucial indicators of transition management in cities (Mullen and Marsden, 2016; van Welie and Romijn, 2018). This has led to literature focusing on transition experiments at a city level which is then designed to be upscaled to other governance levels (Bulkeley et al., 2014). We see the same combination of ideas around how best to destabilize the meso level to achieve a new more sustainable system for the city.

I seek therefore to understand the transition management approach and then apply it to the case study of Paris and Berlin. I take each core component of the transition management approach in turn. The micro level of transition management, referred to as the niche level in some literature, is frequently connected with technology. This reflects a growing acceptance that technology is a disrupter of current established regimes. Electric vehicles are a classic example of a major disrupter at an urban level. The growing uptake of electric vehicles has shifted the established norms of urban transportation, even in urban contexts in China (Yang et al., 2018; Zhang, 2014). Some argued that the growth of electric vehicles in cities threatened sustainability as they move the argument back towards individual, rather than shared, mobility (Mullen and Marsden, 2016). Others argue that electric vehicles promote sustainability through replacing existing petrol-based transportation with more renewable vehicles (Han et al., 2014). Transition management in this case focuses on shifts in transportation and modes of transport and seeks to identify key actors that drive forward this change in a positive way. Innovation at the micro level is an inherent component of shifting the status quo. The emerging concern in this context is not simply sustainability as an endpoint. We must also question to what extent this technology is going to lead to more just outcomes, and crucially what actors can do to proactively ensure that it does. I return to this point in the case study later.

From another perspective, the macro level of transition management is equally important to the ultimate change of dominating institutions, ideologies and actors. It can be referred to as the landscape level. It is the least researched level of transition management. Many argued that its application is not possible considering its abstract nature (Calvert et al., 2019). This level of transition management involves broad cultural shifts or changes in norms and values in the society that puts pressure in a complementary way on the positive change desired at the micro level. To continue the electric vehicle example, transition management scholars would argue that growing environmental awareness is a complementary cultural shift that is enabling the disruption of the automobile industry (Wu et al., 2016). I argue that its application at the city level may prove more fruitful than what we find in existing research. Each city has a different culture and way of doing things. Too much literature on micro level thinking has restricted itself to broad abstract global level changes. We need more investigations into technologically driven change and its relative success in Copenhagen, say, as opposed to London. The answer may lie more in the culture, norms and values of the city rather than the technology or the actors seeking to promote this shift.

The meso level, or regime as it is often referred to, is a crucial component of transition management. It is the level at which existing elite actors and institutions attempt to resist change. There are many examples of this in the existing literature. The avoidance, limited rollout or blocked retrofitting schemes in cities have attracted much attention from scholars. The need to insulate and provide more sustainable buildings in cities disrupts the existing regime which has sought to use tactics for avoiding this change (Howden-Chapman et al., 2005). This research has equally emphasized the importance of inequalities (Vilches et al., 2017). It is in socio-economically deprived areas where we find the least activity in retrofitting living quarters or homes (Gillard et al., 2017). Changing the meso level is the commonly understood objective of transition management.

Fairness, equity and justice are understudied concepts in transition management. This is surprising considering that sustainability is a key objective. Intergenerational justice should play a central role in transition management. It remains side-lined. I therefore seek to integrate core ideas of justice through delving into debates first on the just transition concept, and then applying such concepts to the examples of Berlin and Paris.

UNDERSTANDING JUST TRANSITION

The term 'just transition' was originally proposed by global trade unions in the 1980s. It became a mobilizing term for promoting green jobs as a necessary component of the transition away from fossil fuels (Abraham, 2017). From this perspective, the move away from fossil fuels entailed the wholesale shutdown of multiple associated industries. The development of new energy industries offered the potential for green jobs. I argue, instead, that it could have the potential for uniting environmental, climate and energy justice in order to provide a more comprehensive framework for analysing and ultimately promoting fairness and equity throughout the transition away from fossil fuels.

The just transition is defined here as "a fair and equitable process of moving towards a post-carbon society". By its very nature, this transition must take place at a global scale, whilst connecting effectively with multi-scalar realities. It involves the development of principles, tools and agreements that ensure both a fair and equitable transition for all individuals and communities. Just transition has more to offer than what is currently realized in its usage by environmental, climate and energy justice scholars. I argue that its analytical reach must move beyond the simplicity of its origins, which focus on promoting a jobs-based solution to climate change. It can offer a space to bring together the three major justice scholarships.

Environmental justice has provided a wide range of studies in this area based upon exploring proximity as a central concept (Clough and Bell, 2016;

Hricko et al., 2014; Childs, 2014). McKenzie et al. (2016) demonstrate that 78,000 people in Colorado live within one mile of oil and gas wells as a classic study of the burdens associated with environmental bads such as polluted rivers (Loo, 2007), water tables (Cotton et al., 2014) and more broadly the environmental implications of living close to major infrastructures (Laurian, 2008). From a distributional perspective, research scholars in this area have revealed where community resistance takes place. Carruthers (2007) demonstrates where protest movements against the actions of companies take place along the US–Mexico border. With the increased need to build new energy infrastructure, proximity will remain an important component to be assessed when considering a just transition. The central argument of contemporary environmental justice scholarship is, however, set out by Walker (2009), Walker and Day (2012) and Schlosberg (2013) who argue that there is an urgent need to explore injustices that take place outside the analytical framework of proximity.

This analytical turn emerged from frustration with the dominance of quantitative studies in exploring the proximity issue by largely US scholars. It has, partly, resulted in a focus upon the qualitative (though not exclusively of course) dimensions of injustice often reflected in procedural studies (as explored below) as well as in new distributional frameworks in the form of (a) capabilities and well-being, (b) risk and responsibility, (c) vulnerability and (d) recognition. The concept of capability centred justice was developed by Sen (2011). He argues that a person's freedom to pursue functions (which constitutes a person's being, including both well-being and agency) is as important as individual rights. As our societies transition towards a post-carbon world, individuals' capabilities, not just their rights, may be infringed. Alternatively, Damgaard et al. (2017) show that adopting renewables can lead to greater functions for communities and individuals. Whilst we observe such distributional research in environmental justice beyond proximity (Acey, 2016; Reese and Jacob, 2015), climate and energy justice scholarships have adopted more readily these new frameworks of distributional analysis.

The linking of climate and energy justice has allowed researchers to explicitly reflect upon the distribution of risks and responsibilities (Barrett, 2013; Olawuyi, 2016; Shaw, 2016; Thorp, 2014). Climate change involves "a double inequality" (Barrett, 2013: 1819), where the distribution of risk and responsibility is inversed. The Global North is responsible for the large part of the negative consequences associated with climate change but remains the least affected. Conversely, the Global South is less responsible for such consequences, but is set to experience the major consequences through impacts upon livelihoods, assets and security. Distributional injustices are therefore conceptually untied from proximity as a central concept. This allows us to explore more broadly the ways in which inequalities are distributed throughout the world, no longer bound to geographical proximity. The identification of where risks and responsibilities lie lends itself directly to exploring where the most vulnerable communities are and how they adapt.

The transition away from fossil fuels will generate new senses of injustice surrounding processes of engagement and involvement in urban areas. Procedural justice has concentrated around the siting of new infrastructure within the environmental justice literature (Higginbotham et al., 2010; Kohli and Menon, 2016). Hess (2016) and Acuna (2015) argue that procedural justice is often the platform for justice demands – albeit often inadequate by itself to ensure a resolution. Procedural justice can instigate long-term engagement processes with the affected community. Marques et al. (2015) show us that procedural approaches in environmental justice are indeed often site-specific but also based upon an awareness of local identity, as in their study of the construction of two dams in Portugal.

A second debate in the procedural component of justice is evident in the climate justice literature. A key component of the transition to a post-carbon society is energy efficiency. The site of study, in this sense, has moved away from large-scale industry and communities towards households in cities where traditional practices are reimagined within a post-carbon society (Stern et al., 2016). This has been driven by Shove (2010) in demonstrating the challenges involved in understanding the behaviours and practices of householders. Externally driven engagement practices are replaced by self-initiated practices. A third extension of the procedural concept emerges from the energy justice literature. The focus on energy systems brings an inherent multiplication of study sites in a city. Procedural justice is reconceptualized as taking place in multiple locations (Heffron and McCauley, 2014; McCauley et al., 2013).

In summary, a just transition must be distributional and procedurally fair. As the transition is centred on usurping the existing regime of elites found at the meso level, proponents of this transition must be aware of where and how injustices may emerge. To explore this awareness, I move on to the real-world examples of Berlin and Paris. In attempting to overthrow the meso level, I assess the ways in which advocacy organizations frame a just transition. I focus on the ways they frame distributional and procedural justice.

WHY WE NEED AN URBAN JUST TRANSITION

Cities are at the forefront of the climate transition (Bulkeley et al., 2013; McKendry, 2016). We are now living in a world with 400 ppm (parts per million) of CO_2, with levels unlikely to drop below this symbolic milestone in our lifetime (World Bank, 2017). The world is witnessing an acceleration of associated events in different locations of the world that demonstrate that too many damaging events are occurring (van Asselt, 2018). In researching transitions within urban contexts, there needs to be a full appreciation of the multiple urban realities. A just transition is needed to capture the 'just' process when urban societies move towards an economy free of CO_2 emissions. Justice is an important element to the transition. Often the rhetoric of governments, companies, institutions and researchers mentions "a transition to low carbon economy" and then there is no mention of 'just'.

An urban just transition is defined here as "a fair and equitable process of a city moving towards a post-carbon society" (Goddard and Farrely, 2018; Healy and Debski, 2017; Heffron and McCauley, 2018; McCauley and Heffron, 2018). By its very nature, this transition must take place at a global scale, whilst connecting effectively with multi-scalar realities such as at urban scales. It involves the development of principles, tools and agreements that ensure both a fair and equitable transition for all individuals and communities within cities. We currently live in a world which is dominated by fossil fuels, amounting to 82 per cent of the world's energy supply (IEA, 2016). It has only experienced a small drop from 90 per cent in 1973. The Paris Climate Change Agreement marked a drastic step away from a carbon-based world. This change will not happen overnight. Most projections suggest that fossil fuels will continue to dominate, in the most optimistic view, until 2035 (World Energy Council, 2016). Added to this, rates of consumption – driven by global urbanization processes – are expected to increase by around 25–34 per cent globally in the next twenty years, with the world's population reaching 8.8 billion (BP, 2017). Throughout the foreseeable future, the world's cities must move away from fossil fuels, both production and consumption.

Cities must drive our efforts to shift these patterns (Gossling, 2016). But it must be fair and equitable. The 'just transition' is a concept receiving more attention in the literature. So far there is some confusion as many disciplines and different research areas all define it differently. Further, for energy, environmental and climate scholar communities, the transition means different things. This is due to these three research areas all having different meanings of what 'justice' is. Therefore in terms of ensuring a 'just transition' how can society support such a process when there are mixed visions of what it means? For too long, the research communities on justice have failed to connect their work and this leads to much distortion of what 'justice' and the 'transition' mean.

Inequalities in cities are as important as the inequality of countries (Jordan, 2016). They are often intense mirrors of larger scale trajectories but encased within smaller geographical areas (Souche et al., 2012). This intensity brings historically more social and political uprisings, driving change in society (Ziervogel et al., 2017). And yet inequality is more frequently studied within the context of countries rather than cities (Kelly-Reif and Wing, 2016). Justice research needs to engage with cities beyond the US context. The development of North America has led it to be the central geographical point for the exploration of inequalities (Kyne, 2016). European and indeed non-European cities should receive the same level of attention. This chapter details a research agenda for responding to this challenge. The need for global societies to transition away from fossil fuels is resulting in distributional and procedural inequalities that take place in urban areas. This chapter explores how the climate emergency drive can be combined with inequalities research in such areas. It then demonstrates how this can be managed, and who is critical for its management.

Timing is crucial in transitions research. The concept of transition is time sensitive. The idea is to move from point A to point B over a given period. The key idea within this is at which point do we make the change (Normann, 2015). Considering the climate realities, a growing global social movement is gathering to claim that the time for substantial change must be now (Meyer and Sanklecha, 2017). Climate records are regularly broken. In 2016, scientific reports recorded that seven climate records were broken in that year including the melting of Arctic ice, consecutive hottest months, the hottest day that India has ever experienced, the highest temperature in Alaska, consecutive and largest annual increases in carbon dioxide, the hottest autumn in Australia, and the highest amount of destruction of the Great Barrier Reef. By 2020, we witnessed the exacerbation of such problems with climate record-breaking negative observations including yet again the hottest year on record.

At the time of writing, the climate emergency driving the need to transition away from fossil fuels is challenged additionally by a global pandemic. The need for societies to move into lockdown and cease most economic activity has sparked a new consciousness of the fragility of today, and the potential of tomorrow. The global health crisis is temporarily halting the production of fossil fuels whilst driving down economic growth. Global societies are at what is referred to in the literature as a critical juncture. The two stark choices of renouncing or embracing the climate emergency face all of us. This chapter helps us to reflect on who will manage this transition. It also poses the question, will this transition, however conceived, lead to further inequalities? The city will be both the context and actor (not so much the focus of this chapter) that will in large part determine this.

I consider this within the context of managing a just transition within an urban context. I first outline the key debates in 'managing transitions' before exploring 'just transition'. I then apply this to efforts from advocacy organizations to manage the transition in Berlin and Paris through assessing their framing processes. I then conclude with priorities for future research in this area.

FRAMING AN URBAN JUST TRANSITION: LESSONS FROM BERLIN AND PARIS

This case study was designed as an early research phase as part of a larger project on the USA and Europe. As such, the focus is limited to exploring the emergence of just transition frames in advocacy organizations in two specific cities: Berlin and Paris. These cities were selected for two key reasons. First, an existing knowledge of the political landscape in each city was essential to gain access to relevant organizations. Second, an initial scoping exercise in each city revealed the existence of just transition campaigns around consumption and production. For each city, a desktop mapping exercise was carried out to identify relevant organizations and campaigns. This mapping allowed an initial insight into activities within a city, as well as generating contextual information to allow for field-based interviews with 24 advocacy organizations.

Berlin and Paris are net importers of energy (particularly oil and gas) – i.e. they rely upon oil and gas nationally or more so internationally. They have, in comparison to the energy consumed, negligible production industries in the city – with a clear reliance on oil and gas plants. Solar/PV is the most evident renewable energy source in the cities. This picture does change somewhat when we look at the surrounding region. Both cities and surrounding areas have experienced different trajectories with regards to production. In Berlin-Brandenburg, renewable energy sources have gradually increased their share (now around 25 per cent) over the traditional coal power stations. In the 1960s, coal production reached as high as 73 per cent – with the 2013 percentage at 44 per cent. There is, moreover, a substantial (and increasing) mining industry in Berlin-Brandenburg. Berlin is set within a national context defined most recently by the nuclear phase out. The Paris-Ile de France context is devoid of any coal-derived energy generation. In its place, oil and gas and surrounding hydro schemes dominate. There is, controversially, significant potential in untapped geothermal energy in Paris-Ile de France. The national electricity generation context is largely dependent upon nuclear energy.

The two cities are proportionally net consumers of energy. Efforts in this area are centred on reducing the carbon footprint of the cities. Heating and electricity sources of consumption are difficult to quantify on a city level as they draw from a national grid. Oil and gas remain the two biggest sources in consumption estimates. More notably, the highest consuming sectors in the three cities are residential and transport, followed by industry and agriculture when the city region is considered. This variable (i.e. sector rather than energy source) has largely defined each city's approach to reducing consumption. In each of the cities, their respective energy strategies prioritize energy efficiency and retrofitting schemes in the residential sector, as well as 'greening' transport in a wide variety of ways.

It is also important to consider the landscape of environmental inequalities, which suggests that justice is an issue for political action. For example, one study that considers patterns of inequality in France highlights that "towns with higher proportions of immigrants are more likely to have a variety of hazardous sites and to host greater numbers of sites" (Laurian, 2008: 55). The Ile de France region has officially the highest immigrant population in both total numbers (1.5 million in 2011) and percentage (12.7 per cent in 2011) than any other French region. Berlin-Brandenburg (with Berlin as a city joint top with Hamburg) also has the largest immigrant population in Germany. Groups with lower socio-economic status and foreign citizenship are disproportionately exposed to environmental risk.

I assess which production and consumption issues are raised by advocacy organizations in each city. I find evidence of frames around promoting 'good' energy technology, which relates to policy constraints and enablers around renewable energy such as solar PV or micro-generation. The central focus for energy activism in each city is, however, around the suppression of 'bad' energy. In Berlin and Paris, there is a link made between the suppression of renewables and the promotion of 'bad' technologies. As one NGO proclaimed, "energy issues in France are defined by the nuclear issue" (activist organization, Paris), decrying the lack of progress on renewable energy. For Berlin, the move away from nuclear was leading to the "greening of coal" (advocacy organization, Berlin) rather than any new uptake in renewables.

The consumption frame includes the promotion of energy cost savings for households and the energy efficiency of buildings. On energy savings, Parisian organizations focus on promoting education rather than further market deregulation – "we need to be more proactive in telling people of the deals out there" (advocacy organization, Paris). Infrastructural efficiency activism is evident in all three cases, but most prominently in Berlin. Their efforts concentrate on innovative projects in reaching above baseline efficiency targets through "think(ing) creatively about what the city offers ... [such as our] fantastic district heating system" (advocacy organization, Paris).

I now turn our attention to the differences in problem framing in each city, in order to reveal which issues are *outside* the problem frame of just transition in some cases. The empirical research reveals, firstly, variation in the breadth of justice concerns in the problem frames in each city. The problem frame is significantly larger in the Berlin case. In terms of production, a wide range of concerns on 'good' and 'bad' energy technologies falls within their energy justice action, including coal, nuclear, oil, gas, biomass and district heating systems. Parisian activities focus almost uniquely on nuclear. From a consumption perspective, it appears there is less variation in the breadth of justice concerns. All organizations frame the problem around the duality of achieving energy cost savings for households – including for example new household micro-production schemes in Berlin and the energy efficiency of buildings such as the promotion of a wide range of retrofit schemes in Paris.

However, the interviews reveal further notable differences in prioritization across the production and consumption spectrum. The balance between production and consumption is, indeed, different for each city. While the nuclear issue dominates the energy frame in Paris, all organizations interviewed linked together the production, waste and electricity consumption processes. One interviewee underlined that the abundance of cheap 'nuclear' electricity in Paris hindered low carbon behavioural changes among households. In Berlin, the main problem was seen to comprise achieving community awareness of production to change consumption patterns:

> The consumer must become [more] aware of where their energy comes from ... we believe greater municipal ownership would bring energy into the community mind-set ... just look at the success of Bethel Hospital ... they actually make money from energy production! (advocacy organization, Berlin)

There are, therefore, notable differences in what is *inside* and *outside* the problem frames in each city, with regards to both the breadth of justice concerns and the level of concentration on production or consumption issues. The decision on what to include in a problem frame significantly influences the solutions put forward (Van Dijk et al., 2011).

The key distributional theme emerging in relation to just transition is the articulation of vulnerability. This is significant because, as noted above, the existence of a perceived injustice and any resulting intervention – either activism or advocacy – is largely based either on the identification of a group as vulnerable or the set of characteristics which are seen to contribute to the existence of vulnerability. In this study, we found that the focus was on relatively 'visible' groups, identified from characteristics such as income, race or class. In Paris vulnerable populations were framed as "poor North African immigrants". Vulnerability was defined largely in terms of income, in common with many academic and policy debates about fuel poverty. For example, in Berlin there was clear targeting of low-income areas of city, areas of sub-standard housing and areas of high immigrant population. As such, claims for distributional justice were made based on targeting specific groups that were perceived to display characteristics of vulnerability.

Claims and interventions for procedural justice were based on identifying groups for the purposes of engagement. For example, in Paris, one organization noted the importance of engaging with young people: "Of course, our main activity will always remain education focused. It is important as a new organization to really engage with people, especially young people". As such, vulnerability was presented as an issue that could be at least partially addressed by collaborative working in order to enact policy change.

We could assume that the management of just transitions must take place through powerful elite structures and processes. This would be a misunderstanding. Sustainability transitions remind us that bottom-up driven changes are required for a transition to occur (Castán Broto et al., 2018). Both the Paris and Berlin examples underline the need to engage with the framing processes of non-elite actors. Advocacy organizations in both cities are seeking to disrupt the status quo. In assessing transitions, our focus is on the niche level disruptors (Kuchler and Bridge, 2018; Sareen and Haarstad, 2018). Unlike in sustainability transitions, this does not need to be technology-only focused. The Berlin and Paris case studies show that ideas are as powerful as technologies. They demonstrate that, in this case, feelings of justice are integral components to driving positive transitions.

The energy component of the city case studies shows the dominance of production related actors in maintaining the status quo. The meso level is where we find the dominant elites struggling to maintain production and their related consumption patterns. Both cities are devoid of their own production sources. They rely on national, and more importantly international sources. This is the starting point for understanding how new transitions can be imagined or framed. Urban transitions within the energy field must critically connect with national and international levels. The dominant framing process in Paris revealed that nuclear energy was viewed as a critical instigator of inequalities. Oil and gas, and even coal, especially in the Berlin case, were at the forefront of framing the barriers to the transition. The meso level elite in energy transitions are therefore less the city councils, or regional committees, but rather national and international companies that drive the potential or not for transition.

The macro level of both case studies offered interesting conclusions around the influence of cultural shifts. The framing of advocacy organizations in both cities targeted the growing desire from urban dwellers for more sustainable communities. In contrast to the sustainability transitions literature (Jenkins et al., 2018), the macro level appears as more influential in these cases than what would normally be recognized. A growing awareness among consumers of the need to move away from fossil fuels is the most critical influential component of the transition. This is too often viewed as a niche level phenomenon. But the advocacy organizations do not frame on individuals that drive this change. They ignite mass consciousness through mobilizing cultural connections. This has of course to do with cultural shifts in environmental or climate awareness. It is a cultural shift that also moved beyond the environment, to also include complementary ideas of inequalities such as immigration and social and economic deprivation.

PRIORITIES FOR FUTURE RESEARCH

The first priority area for future research is understanding the management of cities as self-dependent entities. This chapter has focused on energy transitions. A brief detour to consider future food transitions shows the potential of assessing the management of cities as separate self-sufficient geographical areas (Majima, 2014). Research in this field must continue to engage with niche level disruptors, both technological and non-technological. This chapter encourages rather a detailed assessment of the macro level of transitions. It opens new lines of thinking with regards to how non-elite actors encourage, enable and enact cultural shifts among urban communities. A first stop for a researcher in this area must be critically reflecting on energy production and consumption. Too little research has focused on how urban centres can drive a self-sufficient future that disconnects from fossil fuels. The managers of such a future lie outside mainstream political actors. Their strategies must connect distributional and procedural inequalities with successful attempts to shift cultural dynamics associated with production and consumption.

The second priority for future research lies in the management of urban 'prosumption', i.e. where an urban dweller produces and consumes at the same time and rate. This is a new term that has emerged, originating in technological futures and science fiction (Xie et al., 2007). It has recently been adopted in European regulations for energy consumers. The promotion of the dual activity of producing and consuming electricity and heating is a key driver for sustainability transitions in urban environments. The focus in the literature has been the rollout of retrofitting and energy savings in buildings (Gonzalez, 2010; Heyman et al., 2005; Howden-Chapman, 2015). Future research must critically reflect not only on the consumption but also the production activities of urban dwellers. The beginning of such a move has focused on electricity generation through solar panels for example (Parag and Sovacool, 2016). New thinking is needed on how to encourage this prosuming behavioural rollout, with an explicit mindset of achieving fairness and equity. Prosumption in this regard is likely to become a wider phenomenon for future research in urban contexts.

The third priority for future research is managing critical junctures. The studies of Paris and Berlin demonstrate that timing is crucial in transitions. At the time of writing, we are in the midst of the COVID-19 pandemic outbreak. Reflection is emerging on what this means for the climate transition. This is coupled with anxiety about rising inequalities, especially in the transition out of COVID-19 lockdown. The city is positioned as a landscape on which both transitions will take place. The management of sustainability transitions relies on the action of niche level actors at the right time (McCauley, 2013). Public and private organizations must seize the opportunity of reshaping urban communities at such a time. In contrast to traditional public management, moments of disruption are to be embraced. Bottom-up actors need to mobilize. Future research must be time sensitive and seek to engage with such moments.

The fourth priority for future research is the assessment of how agents of change and continuity seek to manage a just transition. Sustainability transitions literature concentrates on agents of change. These are normally NGOs or small community groups that activate during such critical junctures as explored above or more gradually to ensure cultural shifts achieve positive outcomes. Such actors will remain the focus of how just transitions are managed. The Paris and Berlin city examples remind us that agents of continuity are equally valid for our assessments. If a just transition is to be achieved, we need to understand why agents of continuity, such as energy producers who continue to produce fossil fuels or city councils that refuse to engage in energy efficiency activities, act in this way and how they can be tackled (McCauley et al., 2018). This chapter focused on the agents of change in relation to advocacy organizations. Future research should also consider how agents of continuity frame their strategies for refusing transitions.

REFERENCES

Abraham, J. 2017. Just transitions for the miners: Labor environmentalism in the Ruhr and Appalachian coalfields. *New Political Science* 39(2): 218–231.

Acey, C. 2016. Managing wickedness in the Niger Delta: Can a new approach to multi-stakeholder governance increase voice and sustainability? *Landscape and Urban Planning* 154: 102–114.

Acuna, R. 2015. The politics of extractive governance: Indigenous peoples and socio-environmental conflicts. *Extractive Industries and Society* 2(1): 85-92.

Barrett, S. 2013. Local level climate justice? Adaptation finance and vulnerability reduction. *Global Environmental Change* 23: 1819–1829.

BP. 2017. *Energy Outlook: 2017 Edition*. London: BP.

Bulkeley, H., J. Carmin, V. Castán Broto, G. A. S. Edwards and S. Fuller. 2013. Climate justice and global cities: Mapping the emerging discourses. *Global Environmental Change* 23(5): 914–925.

Bulkeley, H., G. A. S. Edwards and S. Fuller. 2014. Contesting climate justice in the city: Examining politics and practice in urban climate change experiments. *Global Environmental Change* 25: 31–40.

Calvert, K., K. Greer and M. Maddison-MacFadyen. 2019. Theorizing energy landscapes for energy transition management: Insights from a socioecological history of energy transitions in Bermuda. *Geoforum* 102: 191–201.

Carruthers, D. V. 2007. Environmental justice and the politics of energy on the US–Mexico border. *Environmental Politics* 16(3): 394–413.

Castán Broto, V., I. Baptista, J. Kirshner, S. Smith and S. Neves Alves. 2018. Energy justice and sustainability transitions in Mozambique. *Applied Energy* 228: 645–655.

Childs, J. 2014. From 'criminals of the earth' to 'stewards of the environment': The social and environmental justice of Fair Trade gold. *Geoforum* 57: 129–137.

Clough, E. and D. Bell. 2016. Just fracking: A distributive environmental justice analysis of unconventional gas development in Pennsylvania, USA. *Environmental Research Letters* 11(2). doi:10.1088/1748-9326/11/2/025001.

Cotton, M., I. Rattle and J. Van Alstine. 2014. Shale gas policy in the United Kingdom: An argumentative discourse analysis. *Energy Policy* 73: 427–438.

Damgaard, C., D. McCauley and J. Long. 2017. Assessing the energy justice implications of bioenergy development in Nepal. *Energy, Sustainability and Society* 7(8): 1–16.

Delina, L. and B. Sovacool. 2018. Of temporality and plurality: An epistemic and governance agenda for accelerating just transitions for energy access and sustainable development. *Current Opinion in Environmental Sustainability* 34: 1–6.

Gillard, R., C. Snell and M. Bevan. 2017. Advancing an energy justice perspective of fuel poverty: Household vulnerability and domestic retrofit policy in the United Kingdom. *Energy Research & Social Science* 29: 53–61.

Goddard, G. and M. Farrely. 2018. Just transition management: Balancing just outcomes with just processes in Australian renewable energy transitions. *Applied Energy* 225: 110–123.

Gonzalez, G. 2010. Energy efficiency and sustainable consumption: The rebound effect. *Environmental Politics* 19(2): 312–315.

Gossling, S. 2016. Urban transport justice. *Journal of Transport Geography* 54: 1-9.

Han, H., O. Xunmin, D. Jiuyu, W. Hewu and O. Minggao. 2014. China's electric vehicle subsidy scheme: Rationale and impacts. *Energy Policy* 73: 722–732.

Healy, N. and J. Barry. 2017. Politicizing energy justice and energy system transitions: Fossil fuel divestment and a 'just transition'. *Energy Policy* 108: 451–459.

Healy, N. and J. Debski. 2017. Fossil fuel divestment: Implications for the future of sustainability discourse and action within higher education. *Local Environment* 22(6): 699–724.

Heffron, R. J. and D. McCauley. 2014. Achieving sustainable supply chains through energy justice. *Applied Energy* 123: 435–437.

Heffron, R. J. and D. McCauley. 2018. What is the 'just transition'? *Geoforum* 88: 74–77.

Hess, D. J. 2016. The politics of niche-regime conflicts: Distributed solar energy in the United States. *Environmental Innovation and Societal Transitions* 19: 42–50.

Heyman, B., B. E. Harrington, N. Merleau-Ponty, H. Stockton, N. Ritchie and T. F. Allan. 2005. Keeping warm and staying well: Does home energy efficiency mediate the relationship between socio-economic status and the risk of poorer health? *Housing Studies* 20(4): 649–664.

Higginbotham, N., S. Freeman, L. Connor and G. Albrecht. 2010. Environmental injustice and air pollution in coal affected communities, Hunter Valley, Australia. *Health & Place* 16(2): 259–266.

Howden-Chapman, P. 2015. How real are the health effects of residential energy efficiency programmes? *Social Science & Medicine* 133: 189–190.

Howden-Chapman, P., J. Crane, A. Matheson, H. Viggers, M. Cunningham, T. Blakely, D. O'Dea, C. Cunningham, A. Woodward, K. Saville-Smith, M. Baker and N. Waipara. 2005. Retrofitting houses with insulation to reduce health inequalities: Aims and methods of a clustered, randomised community-based trial. *Social Science & Medicine* 61(12): 2600–2610.

Hricko, A., G. Rowland, S. Eckel, A. Logan, M. Taher and J. Wilson. 2014. Global trade, local impacts: Lessons from California on health impacts and environmental justice concerns for residents living near freight rail yards. *International Journal of Environmental Research and Public Health* 11(2): 1914–1941.

IEA. 2016. *CO2 Emissions from Fuel Combustion.* Paris: IEA.

Jenkins, K., B. K. Sovacool and D. McCauley. 2018. Humanizing sociotechnical transitions through energy justice: An ethical framework for global transformative change. *Energy Policy* 117: 66–74.

Jordan, A. 2016. The problem-solving capacity of the modern state: Governance challenges and administrative capacities. *West European Politics* 39(4): 908–909.

Kelly-Reif, K. and S. Wing. 2016. Urban–rural exploitation: An underappreciated dimension of environmental injustice. *Journal of Rural Studies* 47: 350–358.

Kohli, K. and M. Menon. 2016. The tactics of persuasion: Environmental negotiations over a corporate coal project in coastal India. *Energy Policy* 99: 270–276.

Kuchler, M. and G. Bridge. 2018. Down the black hole: Sustaining national socio-technical imaginaries of coal in Poland. *Energy Research & Social Science* 41: 136–147.

Kyne, D. 2016. Living with the invisible risks in the U.S. urban areas: Potential nuclear power-induced disasters, urban emergency management challenges, and environmental justice issues. *Risk Hazards & Crisis in Public Policy* 7(4): 176–208.

Laurian, L. 2008. Environmental injustice in France. *Journal of Environmental Planning and Management* 51(1): 55–79.

Loo, T. 2007. Disturbing the peace: Environmental change and the scales of justice on a northern river. *Environmental History* 12(4): 895–919.

Majima, S. 2014. A brief thought on the future of global ethics: Military robots and new food technologies. *Journal of Global Ethics* 10(1): 53–55.

Marques, S., M. L. Lima, S. Moreira and J. Reis. 2015. Local identity as an amplifier: Procedural justice, local identity and attitudes towards new dam projects. *Journal of Environmental Psychology* 44: 63–73.

McCauley, D. 2013. Sustainability, governance and time: Exploring 'critical junctures' in the governance of genetically modified organisms in France. *Environmental Policy and Governance* 23(5): 283–296.

McCauley, D., A. Brown, R. Rehner, R. Heffron and S. Van de Graaff. 2018. Energy justice and policy change: An historical political analysis of the German nuclear phase-out. *Applied Energy* 228: 317–323.

McCauley, D. and R. Heffron. 2018. Just transition: Integrating climate, energy and environmental justice. *Energy Policy* 119: 1–7.

McCauley, D., R. Heffron, H. Stephan and K. Jenkins. 2013. Advancing energy justice: The triumvirate of tenets. *International Energy Law Review* 3: 107–111.

McKendry, C. 2016. Cities and the challenge of multiscalar climate justice: Climate governance and social equity in Chicago, Birmingham, and Vancouver. *Local Environment* 21(11): 1354–1371.

McKenzie, L. M., W. B. Allshouse, T. Burke, B. D. Blair and J. L. Adgate. 2016. Population size, growth, and environmental justice near oil and gas wells in Colorado. *Environmental Science & Technology* 50(21): 11471–11480.

Meyer, L. H. and P. Sanklecha. 2017. *Climate Justice and Historical Emissions.* Cambridge: Cambridge University Press.

Miller, C. A., J. O'Leary, E. Graffy, E. B. Stechel and G. Dirks. 2015. Narrative futures and the governance of energy transitions. *Futures* 70: 65–74.

Mullally, G. and E. Byrne. 2016. A tale of three transitions: A year in the life of electricity system transformation narratives in the Irish media. *Energy, Sustainability and Society* 6. doi:10.1186/s13705-015-0068-2.

Mullen, C. and G. Marsden. 2016. Mobility justice in low carbon energy transitions. *Energy Research & Social Science* 18: 109–119.

Normann, H. E. 2015. The role of politics in sustainable transitions: The rise and decline of offshore wind in Norway. *Environmental Innovation and Societal Transitions* 15: 180–193.

Olawuyi, D. S. 2016. Climate justice and corporate responsibility: Taking human rights seriously in climate actions and projects. *Journal of Energy & Natural Resources Law* 34(1): 27–44.

Parag, Y. and B. Sovacool. 2016. Electricity market design for the prosumer era. *Nature Energy* 1: 1–12.

Reese, G. and L. Jacob. 2015. Principles of environmental justice and pro-environmental action: A two-step process model of moral anger and responsibility to act. *Environmental Science and Policy* 51: 88–94.

Sareen, S. and H. Haarstad. 2018. Bridging socio-technical and justice aspects of sustainable energy transitions. *Applied Energy* 228: 624–632.

Schlosberg, D. 2013. Theorising environmental justice: The expanding sphere of a discourse. *Environmental Politics* 22(1): 37–55.

Schot, J., L. Kanger and G. Verbong. 2016. The roles of users in shaping transitions to new energy systems. *Nature Energy* 1(5): 16054. doi:10.1038/nenergy.2016.54.

Scrase, I. and A. Smith. 2009. The (non-)politics of managing low carbon socio-technical transitions. *Environmental Politics* 18(5): 707–726.

Sen, A. 2011. *The Idea of Justice*. Cambridge, MA: Harvard University Press.

Shaw, C. 2016. The role of rights, risks and responsibilities in the climate justice debate. *International Journal of Climate Change Strategies & Management* 8(4): 505–517.

Shove, E. 2010. Beyond the ABC: Climate change policy and theories of social change. *Environment and Planning A* 42(6): 1273–1285.

Souche, S., C. Raux and Y. Croissant. 2012. On the perceived justice of urban road pricing: An empirical study in Lyon. *Transportation Research* 46(7): 1124–1136.

Stern, P. C., K. B. Janda, M. A. Brown, L. Steg, E. L. Vine and L. Lutzenhiser. 2016. Opportunities and insights for reducing fossil fuel consumption by households and organizations. *Nature Energy* 1(5): 16043. doi:10.1038/nenergy.2016.43.

Thorp, T. M. 2014. *Climate Justice: A Voice for the Future*. Basingstoke: Palgrave Macmillan.

van Asselt, H. 2018. International climate change law. *Carbon & Climate Law Review: CCLR* 12(1): 70–73.

Van Dijk, T., N. Aarts and A. De Wit. 2011. Frames to the planning game. *International Journal of Urban and Regional Research* 35(5): 969–987.

van Welie, M. J. and H. A. Romijn. 2018. NGOs fostering transitions towards sustainable urban sanitation in low-income countries: Insights from transition management and development studies. *Environmental Science and Policy* 84: 250–260.

Verbitsky, J. 2014. Just transitions and a contested space: Antarctica and the Global South. *Polar Journal* 4(2): 319–334.

Vilches, A., Á. Barrios Padura and M. Molina Huelva. 2017. Retrofitting of homes for people in fuel poverty: Approach based on household thermal comfort. *Energy Policy* 100: 283–291.

Walker, G. 2009. Globalizing environmental justice: The geography and politics of frame contextualization and evolution. *Global Social Policy* 9(3): 355–382.

Walker, G. and R. Day. 2012. Fuel poverty as injustice: Integrating distribution, recognition and procedure in the struggle for affordable warmth. *Energy Policy* 49: 69–75.

World Bank. 2017. CO2 emissions (metric tons per capita) | Data. Washington, DC: The World Bank.

World Energy Council. 2016. *World Energy Trilemma: Defining Measures to Accelerate the Energy Transition.* London: WEC.

Wu, T., Z. Shang, X. Tian and S. Wang. 2016. How hyperbolic discounting preference affects Chinese consumers' consumption choice between conventional and electric vehicles. *Energy Policy* 97: 400–413.

Xie, C., R. P. Bagozzi and S. V. Troye. 2007. Trying to prosume: Toward a theory of consumers as co-creators of value. *Journal of the Academy of Marketing Science* 36(1): 109–122.

Yang, S., D. Zhang, J. Fu, S. Fan and Y. Ji. 2018. Market cultivation of electric vehicles in China: A survey based on consumer behavior. *Sustainability* 10(11): 4056. https://doi.org/10.3390/su10114056.

Zhang, X. 2014. Reference-dependent electric vehicle production strategy considering subsidies and consumer trade-offs. *Energy Policy* 67: 422–430.

Ziervogel, G., L. Pasquini, M. Pelling, A. Cartwright, E. Chu, T. Deshpande, K. Michael, L. Harris, L. Rodina, K. Hyams, J. Kaunda, B. Klaus, R. Pharoah, P. Zweig and D. Scott. 2017. Inserting rights and justice into urban resilience: A focus on everyday risk. *Environment and Urbanization* 29(1): 123–138.

4. Structural change, labour markets and urban economic policy in emerging economies

Frank van Oort, Paula Nagler and Indriany Lionggo

INTRODUCTION

Economic and spatial policies in cities and regions around the world are on the eve of a major joint task: that of renewed economic growth, vitality and resilience – aspects that after the Great Recession of 2008/2009 have not been everywhere addressed. Rising prosperity is generally accompanied by challenges such as the energy transition, growing inequality, changing content of occupations through digitization, and an increasing level of knowledge in every step in the value chain of goods and services. It has been suggested for some time that the policy areas of economics and space are joining forces to cope with this complexity (Raspe and van Oort, 2007). It is undeniably the case that in recent decades the policy field of space has served the objectives of economic growth and dynamism – economic policy has largely shifted to the region and cities. Even complex themes such as energy transition, sustainable housing stock and internet of things (e.g. to create smart cities) are expected to be shaped at the sub-national level. Regardless of whether city and regional authorities have the expertise to manage this complexity, it fits with two universal trends: these are the trends of (1) network scaling up of the economy to a select group of ever larger urban regions, best expressed by Glaeser's (2011) *Triumph of the City* and Florida et al.'s (2008) "Rise of the megaregion", and simultaneously (2) the ever-increasing desire to reduce the administrative scale at which economic and social policy is formulated, most strongly expressed by Barber's (2013) *If Mayors Ruled the World* and even descending to the level of self-organization of the individual citizen in the sub-economy of Botsman and Rogers (2010), in which sharing becomes the central element ("what's mine is (y)ours").

The simultaneous scaling up of the economic playing field and the scaling down of the administrative level, aimed at the economy, are prompted by the network society and network economy in which we currently find ourselves (Batty, 2013): people and companies are becoming increasingly complexly interwoven in networks of interaction at different spatial scale levels – from daily activities in the daily urban system to knowledge-intensive and strategic business relations, job hoppers and cultural exchange for highly educated people in an (inter)national system of cities. Inevitably linked to a scaling up of the network economy, is the creation or confirmation of inequalities and the sorting out of population groups and sectors in the successful or failing cities. In larger cities, companies benefit from agglomeration advantages: companies can learn more easily from each other and from knowledge institutions, can match labour supply better with their vacancies, and have advantages of sharing expertise, market demand and suppliers. Theoretical and empirical research on agglomeration advantages, innovation and economic growth in cities is embedded in the processes of structural change towards a knowledge economy, and multilevel governance structures that are both triggered by this and facilitate this.

In a burgeoning literature, structural economic change towards diversified, export and innovation-oriented production structures is commonly witnessed in Western societies (Frenken et al., 2007; Content, 2019), being beneficial for economic growth. Although it is also suggested to be important in an emerging regions context (Hausmann et al., 2013; McMillan et al., 2014), arguing that there may be more to gain economically than anywhere else, fundamentally different institutional conditions compared to Western societies may hamper such processes (Rodrik et al., 2002). Interestingly, alongside the economic debate on structural change, public administration sciences simultaneously hypothesize a new form of urban management based on interactive, cooperative networks of governance, where public and private stakeholders jointly determine best practices fitting in divergent contexts (Teisman and Edelenbos, 2011; see also Chapter 1, this volume). Yet, implementing such participatory governance may not be so easy in emerging economies, due to the institutional barriers and lock-in, e.g. relying on either conservative hierarchical lines of government, or on market mechanisms in, for instance, foreign direct investments (Cheema, 1993). There may be opportunities for a successful implementation of the new governance paradigm on the urban and regional level though, as especially informal institutions and social capital tend to be attached to that level (Van Dijk, 2006; Cortinovis et al., 2017; Katz and Nowak, 2017). In recent years, regional economic policy and governance have been attributed more and more relevance throughout the world, while less structured effort and investment are allocated to economic bottlenecks and opportunities at a sub-regional level by governments (Glaeser, 2011; Barber,

2013). The societal challenges of innovation-driven competitiveness and technological complexity, and also of sustainability and increasing inequality, and the flexibility needed to deal with them at an ever-accelerating pace, are putting further pressure on regional economic development processes.

This chapter aims to investigate the question of which factors drive regional economic development, focusing particularly on the factors that are identified as key in this process. We argue that especially a well-functioning regional labour market and related institutions and policies are the most important ingredients for further favourable economic development of regions; not only in developed countries but also (and arguably most urgently) in emerging ones. The public value of labour market policies ranges from capitalizing on innovative talent, sectoral crossovers and ecosystems of entrepreneurship, to matching training, retraining and new vacancies for employees and jobseekers threatened by automation. We confirm that to economically benefit optimally from structural change, the involvement of many different actors is indeed required, both private and public, simultaneously at scale levels ranging from employers and municipalities to (labour market) regions, which may jointly facilitate regional economic success by means of spatial and administrative organizational investments, but are strongly dependent on the cooperating and self-organizing capacity of economic sub-markets (Mitlin and Satterthwaite, 2012; Bertaud, 2018). This complexity of structures, policies and institutions, broadly defined, requires strong urban management and governance. Urban governance refers to how government (local, regional and national) and stake-holders decide how to plan, finance and manage urban areas (Van Dijk, 2006; Van Dijk et al., 2017). As Devas et al. (2004: 1) note:

> It involves a continuous process of negotiation and contestation over the allocation of social and material resources and political power. It is, therefore, profoundly political, influenced by the creation and operation of political institutions, government capacity to make and implement decisions and the extent to which these decisions recognize and respond to the interests of the poor. It encompasses a host of economic and social forces, institutions and relationships. These include labour markets, goods and services; household, kin and social relationships; and basic infrastructure, land, services and public safety.

Large gaps often exist between poor and better-off urban residents in terms of access to social, economic and political opportunities (particularly decision-making) and the ability to participate in, and leverage, the benefits associated with urban living. While city government is the largest and most visible urban governance actor, much of what affects the life-chances of the urban poor lies outside the control of city administrations. Instead, it is the market and private businesses, agencies of the central state or the collective action of civil society that determine the daily experiences of urban dwellers (Venables, 2015). In emerging economies, the quality and functioning of formal and informal institutions enabling structural change in both the economy and its governance are therefore crucial, but less well understood. This imposes challenges for regional economic policies in addressing, facilitating and profiting from structural economic change (Henderson, 2002).

This chapter deals with these topics in the following manner. The next section introduces structural economic change as a regional phenomenon, and embeds this in recent literature on economic geography and regional economics. The fundamental role of labour market conditions and opportunities for localized structural change are discussed in the third section. The fourth section then links regional structural change to traditional and new governance paradigms. The fifth section discusses how fundamentally different levels of formal institutions in emerging economies compared to those in the Western world, pose a large challenge to the organizing capacity of both governance and markets. The bringing about of structural change in emerging economies may be more dependent on informal institutions (trust, social capital) rather than formal ones.

STRUCTURAL CHANGE AS A REGIONAL ECONOMIC PHENOMENON

Structural change of regional economies is dependent on the economic specialization opportunities of such regions, and their abilities to diversify into new and growing markets, building on their existing knowledge stock. How the existing knowledge stock is built up, in firms, people and ideas, gives clues on the localization aspect of the present and future knowledge economy and the evolution (structural change) towards such a new paradigm. Key concepts in both the structural change and governance paradigm shift (see Chapter 1) are networks, knowledge economy, diversification, variety, innovation and self-organization. Starting from the crucial role of knowledge in fostering innovation, productivity and development, many have investigated how localized network relations mediate and allow for the diffusion of ideas and technologies. Early contributions (e.g. Coe and Helpman, 1995) have focused on local spillover effects of patents and trade relations as channels for knowledge exchange. More recently, these contributions have been extended by looking at spatial, market, investment and technological relations as sources of productivity and innovation, both at country level (Keller, 2002; Lumenga-Neso et al., 2005) and firm and entrepreneur level (Keller and Yeaple, 2009). While studies at country and firm level focus on specific channels, economists have provided less detailed evidence at regional level, with most of the literature merely referring to spatial spillovers. With the increasing regional level focus of the organization of economic activities in clusters, industrial districts, creative hotspots, 'smart cities', and high quality of life in urban regions (see the third and fourth sections), there is a clear need for identifying the relationship of institutions and governance with structural change at the urban and regional level.

The economic geography literature has more to offer in explaining the effects of space and networks on structural change and economic growth. Putting as theoretical cornerstones the concepts of proximity and relatedness, this stream of research investigates and empirically tests what types of relatedness mould local knowledge interaction, learning and innovation (Boschma, 2005; Frenken et al., 2007). Whereas traditionally more interested in the role of local factors and conditions, the proximity-based literature has increasingly investigated the role of wider spatial relations and networks (Cortinovis and van Oort, forthcoming). Different contributions have considered the effects of spatial spillovers, co-patenting, industrial and technological similarity, labour mobility, and migration as channels for the diffusion of knowledge (Caragliu and Nijkamp, 2016; Maggioni et al., 2007; Miguelez and Moreno, 2017). Apart from co-inventorship relations, these contributions (except for Thissen et al., 2016) have paid less attention to the traditional factors – such as trade and investments – identified by the growth literature. Given the unequal distribution of knowledge, assets and innovating capabilities across cities and regions, not all linkages are equally important for each region (Hoekman et al., 2009) and conditions for profiting locally from knowledge relations may exist (Miguelez and Moreno, 2017). Based on these intuitions, it is generally found that knowledge linkages (moderated by FDI, cooperation, patent citation or trade) to most advanced regions provide a significant benefit for recipient regions (Cortinovis and van Oort, 2019). This line of research aims to determine whether the knowledge base – like the stock of learning or internalizing capabilities of regions' population and firms, captured on an educational level – acts as a precondition for regions to benefit from network relations with most advanced regions (Miguelez and Moreno, 2017). As endogeneity is involved, econometric identification strategies are needed, such as instrumental variable (IV) estimation, for determining the exact impact of knowledge endowments and knowledge networks on local development.

Much research underlines that knowledge and growth potentials are neither equally accessible nor equally relevant for economic actors. This has led research to focus on the importance of cognitive proximity, among other forms of proximity (Boschma, 2005), for the transmission of knowledge across an economy. In this sense, the more related the knowledge bases of different actors, the easier it is for ideas, capabilities and knowledge to be profitably exchanged and applied, resulting in local structural change where new industries enter, and mature and declining industries may exit. When the cognitive distance is significant and actors do not 'speak the same language', knowledge spillovers and economic renewal are less likely to take place (Breschi et al., 2003). This idea of relatedness between local actors has been tested in studies on agglomeration economies (Frenken et al., 2007; Cortinovis and van Oort, 2015) and on employment growth due to FDI attraction (Cortinovis et al., 2020). This emerging body of literature focuses predominantly on the implications of relatedness for the process of regional diversification and structural change. Incumbent firms are more likely to enter industries that are relatively close (technically, cognitive or institutionally) to the one they are already operating in. Similarly, new firms are more likely to start off and be successful in a sector that is closely related to other sectors in the region, as they can benefit from relevant local capabilities (such as related knowledge and skills), or what has been referred to as 'local related externalities' (Neffke et al., 2011). Interestingly, it has also been found that the presence and quality of formal *and* informal institutions at the regional level play a crucial role in accommodating diversification and growth opportunities (Rodriguez-Pose, 2013; Cortinovis et al., 2017).

This implies that regional diversification can be considered to a large degree a path-dependent process, in which the industrial history of regions provides opportunities but also sets limits to economic diversification. This process of relatedness-driven diversification has been referred to as regional branching, since new activities draw upon and combine capabilities from existing local activities. Empirical studies have confirmed the predominance of this process of related diversification both at the national and regional scales (Neffke et al., 2011), for productivity and employment gains. Unrelated diversification is rare, yet has large growth and innovation potential in breakthrough technologies in regions (Castaldi et al., 2015). This has not yet been much researched, and especially in the light of the present and upcoming societal transitions (that are path-creating in many senses) this is an important avenue for policy-relevant research (Schwab, 2018).

THE LABOUR MARKET AS KEY DRIVER OF URBAN AND REGIONAL STRUCTURAL CHANGE

Closely related to the local processes of structural change, diversification and specialization, are opportunities to attract (mobile, high-skilled) labour and capital investments. Labour mobility and its recombination capacities, or the absence of it and its lock-in consequences, have been studied extensively from a proximity approach over recent years (Eriksson, 2011; Csáfordi et al., 2020). Interestingly, because many medium-high and lower-skilled labour flows and dependencies in everyday life take place in (commuting defined) daily urban systems, the conceptualization and spatial footprint of this specific network typically defines proximity in terms of labour market regions. The labour market is one of the main drivers and transfer mechanisms of knowledge exchange, innovation and economic renewal, and we will focus on why this is the case in more detail in this section.

The innovative capacity of the economy, its sectors and urban regions is high on the policy agenda of practically all countries, regions and cities worldwide (Katz and Nowak, 2017). As simple as this local task of innovation and growth promotion seems to be,[1] its identification and implementation are complicated. Not everything can develop everywhere, despite wishful thinking. After all, how the innovative capacity of cities and regions can actually be measured, how innovation comes about, how it fits in with existing economic strengths and structural development paths of regions, and how innovation can actually be managed by urban authorities are still largely unknown. For understanding that, we must know the 'DNA' of cities and regions: What is the regional economy good at (specialized in) and what knowledge and skills (in human capital) does it have in-house to innovate and grow? The idea that economic dynamism is linked to a locally diversifying production structure has been gaining ground for some time now. A balance has to be found between specialization in sectors – industries located close to each other that benefit from the advantages of learning (from competitors and knowledge institutions), matching (in the labour market and housing market), and sharing (of production resources, suppliers and outsourcing possibilities) – and the innovation that results from diversification into related yet different industries, occupations and skills. A specialized economy is also vulnerable, and a region may become too dependent on one or more economic activities, and is therefore exposed to major risks if demand for products from those sectors falls. Regions and cities are therefore ideally both specialized, so that they benefit from economies of scale, and diversified, so that they benefit from crossover opportunities.

We argue that, to understand the potential of regional structural change, this 'DNA' must be analysed by looking at the extent to which employees' knowledge and skills can be exchanged between industries and made productive in new combinations (innovation). If activities in sectors require (partly) comparable knowledge and skills, this is referred to as 'skill-related' (Neffke et al., 2011). By exploring the extent to which there is skill-relatedness between the industries in a region, detailed sector opportunities and threats in that region can be identified. Regions differ in economic density and sectoral specializations, which means that processes of regional diversification and renewal have different focus and mass in each of them, but these processes are relevant everywhere. Often, existing knowledge in companies is combined with new knowledge, and new growth pathways can then emerge from these crossovers. The skills of employees present in a city or region determine what the local workforce can produce, what business processes it contributes to, and what type of occupations and sectors thrive through those skills.

One of the most informative and productive relationships between sectors is thus reflected in the overlap of the demand that sectors place on their human capital – the most important input material in today's knowledge economy (Glaeser et al., 2014). Wikipedia defines human capital as "the stock of competences, knowledge, social and personal skills, including creativity, which is embodied in the ability of the human being to work in an economy, so that economic value can be produced". In the labour market economy, a person's human capital is often related to his or her level of education. This results in classifications such as high- versus low-skilled or technical versus administrative employees (blue collar/white collar). However, such classifications do not do justice to the high degree of specificity of human capital in the twenty-first century. After all, although both groups are highly educated, media scientists and biologists have a completely different type of human capital. This does not only apply to employees with an academic degree: vocational education also trains a wide range of specialists, each with their own area of expertise. In addition, human capital develops further as an employee gains work experience. A modern labour market is therefore characterized by a rich range of specialisms. In fact, it is precisely this distribution of knowledge over an enormous variety of experts – from bricklayers to accountants and from bakers to surgeons – that makes the complex and distributed production chains in developed countries possible. Adam Smith already noticed in 1776 that the state or society has a sorting and structuring role in this: "Though in a rude society there is a good deal of variety in the occupations of every individual, there is not a great deal in those of the whole society [...]. In a civilized state, on the contrary, though there is little variety in the occupations of the greater part of individuals, there is an almost infinite variety in those of the whole society" (2008 [1776]: 430).

In this reading of the concept of 'human capital', labour market regions have a great diversity of experts (because people have an average commuting tolerance of about 35 minutes' travel time; highly educated people commute further than the low-skilled, and in emerging economies this may be hampered by sub-optimal infrastructure endowments). The human capital of a region is therefore specific to the economic activities that can make use of it. The measurement of (developments in) the crossover potential of human capital then poses new challenges for researchers. Often it is not the skills of employees that are studied, but their job changes (van Oort et al., 2016). The specificity of human capital is not only important for regional economic growth, but also limits employees' ability to find new jobs. Indeed, this specificity means that the hard-won skills needed for the current job will remain unused in most other jobs. As potential employers are generally unwilling to reward employees for irrelevant knowledge and skills, employees will not readily accept such a job. Most job transitions will therefore take place between activities that have more or less the same human capital requirements for their workers. The sectors requiring similar human capital are then called 'skill-related', and this appears to be a good predictor of regional economic growth and innovation. The presence of skill-related industries in a labour market region has many advantages: for both employers and workers who are more likely to match, for the creation of economies of scale in employee training at regional level, for resilience as economic hardship in one industry can be offset by growth in growing skill-related industries that can take over any redundant workers from related declining industries, and for the potential for knowledge exchange between related industries. This all facilitates, and is at the core of, regional economic structural change.

GOVERNANCE IMPLICATIONS

What is the organizing and creative capacity of governance in regional structural change processes? The message of Mazzucato (2013), optimally exemplifying the 'structural-change-by-governance-thinking', is clearly that it is not the entrepreneur, but the government that is creating major breakthroughs and economic growth. According to her, it is therefore governments that can provoke innovative ideas, and ultimately also scale up and thus achieve economic growth. In countries other than the USA, too, public administration and various forms of policy are ascribed a more dominant role in the creation of economic growth. Examples are given in SOB (2016), which suggests that the Netherlands misses out on economic opportunities because of the sub-optimal functioning of public administration. In the wake of this idea, a recent plea has also been made for a leading role for regional and urban governments in innovation, growth, up-scaling and valorization (Raspe et al., 2017). It is increasingly assumed that the urban region is the level of scale at which economic growth and innovation are achieved, and that spatial and economic policy can therefore also best be deployed at that level. The creative and structuring capabilities of governments, in line with Mazzucato's arguments, are hypothesized to be impacting on localized clustering, innovation and growth – even at the scale of science parks, neighbourhoods, or districts within cities (Katz and Bradley, 2013).

The idea of regional ecosystems of entrepreneurship and the role of public governance is the final aspect of the 'governance of the economy' approach that seems to combine all ingredients (Stam, 2015). As Oosterwaal et al. (2017: 7–8) introduce it: "You don't do business alone and success depends strongly on the context in which new initiatives are developed. An ecosystem in which the necessary actors and factors are present and well attuned to each other is necessary for productive entrepreneurship to flourish. Such an ecosystem for entrepreneurship encompasses all interdependent actors and factors that are coordinated in such a way that they enable productive entrepreneurship in a given region." Stam (2015) concluded earlier about this concept that it does not add new insight, but that its value lies in the integration of already existing insights. And the regional focus that is so central to the approach is not cast in concrete according to Oosterwaal et al. (2017: 9): "Regional governments take part in new collaborative arrangements, make agreements and conclude covenants with incidental or representative representatives of the business community and the knowledge world. These new partnerships each follow their own boundaries and do not adhere to the traditional boundaries of local authorities or to divisions such as labour market regions." This links to the idea of 'wicked problems of urban governance' which is identified as a paradigm shift since 2000 in Chapter 1 in this volume.

The problematic issue with place-based development strategies and their hypothesized impact on economic development – as they are presented on various spatial scales, from regions (Barca et al., 2012) to innovation districts, enterprise zones and neighbourhoods in cities (Katz and Bradley, 2013) – is that they do not identify convincingly that there is a place-based effect besides selective sectoral, market-driven self-organization (Neumark and Simpson, 2015; Bertaud, 2018). In such cases, the distributional effects of place-based policies are unclear (Koster et al., 2019). For example, beneficiaries of local selective investments or subsidies may be the richer people or firms in the impacted area, thereby increasing inequalities within the city or region. Moreover, the spatial extent of the effects of place-based investments may be unpredictable, so choosing a scale for a place-based policy can be problematic. There usually is a large heterogeneity in workers' and firms' effects regarding place-based local policies, that by interregional relations of commuting, sub-contracting, trade and cooperation leads to unpredictable welfare effects. The empirical results on the effectiveness and the welfare costs of place-based policies are therefore at least mixed (see for an overview Neumark and Simpson, 2015). Most studies find that positive effects are offset by substantial displacement effects within adjacent localities, but virtually all of the empirical studies on place-based policies examine programmes for deprived areas in developed countries. The welfare effects may be different when applied to place-based policies for leading areas in emerging economies. Policies stimulate relatively productive firms and people, and foster positive rather than negative spillovers. While almost unstudied, China, India, Brazil, South Africa, Russia, and many other transition economies extensively apply place-based policies and special economic zones to promote development. A scarcity of data on detailed added value and employment creation is argued to hamper strong conclusions on place-based policies in these countries (Frick et al., 2018).

One market that is very important in terms of self-organization of local economies is, in line with the arguments of the previous sections, the local labour market (and related to that the housing market). The human capital of a region is specific to the economic activities that can make use of it. The structural change and labour mobility arguments in the previous section mean that the knowledge, experience and skills of the local workforce largely determine which activities can be developed in a region (van Oort et al., 2016). A better understanding of the human capital that is present in a region – and the latent development opportunities it contains – enables one to map out the innovation potential of a region. But the absence of promising human capital also poses a regional challenge for policy makers. The labour market has a strong local effect. Jobseekers, non-participants, informal workers and benefit recipients are overrepresented in larger cities, and city governments worldwide are responsible for matching the supply and demand of labour. Connecting the skills specializations of the labour force and the business community seems obvious, but is not always a priority in policy: the creation of creative urban, engineering or scientifically driven hotspots (campuses), for example, is prominent on many municipal agendas, but cannot be thought of in isolation in one specific place – they will lead to greater sorting effects of higher educated people, with consequences that are also felt elsewhere and do not necessarily contribute to the integration of lower educated people (Ponds et al., 2015). The local 'pull in the chimney' or trickle-down hypothesis, in which growth in the number of higher educated people is accompanied by growth in the number of lower educated people in catering, security and supply, is much less valid than often assumed, at least outside the USA (Moretti, 2012). The opportunities but also threats to local economies are accumulating, resulting from economic structural changes, with an ever greater emphasis on services and smart, small-scale production with more complex value chains, automation that especially puts pressure on professional profiles of vocational education, technological and social transitions with great impact such as that of energy supply, increasing inequality in cities, and international competition that is becoming increasingly fierce. Effective place-based and people-based policies are needed from urban and regional governments to mitigate the threats and ensure that opportunities are not missed.

Skill-relatedness between industries in relation to the labour market is a recognized, but relatively unknown and difficult to quantify factor by urban policy (van Oort et al., 2016). It can be important for urban and regional economic policy in two ways: as a mediator for the unemployed, and as a stimulus for knowledge exchange and innovative cross-fertilization. For labour market policies that focus on shrinking clusters, it is wise to take skill-relatedness into account (Diodato and Weterings, 2015). Both in the training of employees and in the mediation of the unemployed, it can play a useful role. For example, future employees can be made more resilient against labour market turbulences by designing training courses that explicitly consider skill relationships.

To this end, training programmes can be set up, in cooperation with companies from skill-related industries, offering a set of skills that are both coherent (i.e. related) and transcend the narrowly formulated needs of the individual industry. It is also easier to mediate between the unemployed by considering their employability in skill-related industries.

Several actors are involved in such a policy. Training has been mentioned as an important structuring factor for skills now and in the future, and training institutions (such as high schools, universities, and universities of applied sciences) therefore have an important role to play. Sectoral (in-house) training organized by companies themselves is also important, as are internships and on-the-job training. Cities and municipalities are important, because they are locally responsible for (emptying) the card index with job seekers. Nevertheless, many labour market relations cross municipal boundaries, and regional coordination is therefore indispensable. However, because the responsibility for participation and matching on the labour market for jobseekers has been assigned to each municipality, competition between municipalities is more likely than cooperation between them (Broersma et al., 2016). This is a worldwide phenomenon. Lesser educated people do not automatically follow in the footsteps of higher educated people either. Insight into future structural changes means that soon more complex external effects of economic dynamics and challenges will have to be tackled, and bottlenecks in the labour market will have to be solved. The latter does, however, lead to value creation for both society and the individuals involved. An important (f)actor is therefore also the administrative organization of municipalities, cities and regions.

In addition, skill-relatedness between sectors is an important factor to consider in policies aimed at stimulating innovation. Here too, public value is created for companies, employees and society. There are several reasons, although not as far-reaching as Mazzucato (2013) suggests, why governments at different levels are engaged in innovation, productivity and job creation – while the primary mandate lies with companies and knowledge institutions. The basic idea is that information asymmetry and the lack of recognition of innovation opportunities leads to sub-optimal local growth. Broadly speaking, there are two visions for policy aimed at innovation: government intervention versus participation. In both cases, regional governments should consider facilitating regional economic and spatial policy instruments, using the factors mentioned above, such as the educational offer of knowledge institutions, the innovation and entrepreneurial ecosystem, labour market matching, and housing construction and accessibility. However, the structuring effect is assessed differently in the two visions. A feasible system approach is based on various forms of market failure (external effects or growth opportunities are missed), system failure (the insufficient presence of a system of cooperation and interactions between market parties, government, knowledge institutions and society) and government failure (larger social objectives and challenges are not achieved) that must and can be tackled. According to this vision, the government itself, as an enterprising stakeholder, can exert a great deal of influence on the actual development of the economy. However, this active government role is also increasingly being offset by the fact that market dynamics worldwide are so complex that at the level of countries and regions only policy can be moved along ('go with the flow'), especially in the labour market and the associated housing market. The question of which of the two visions is most effective or efficient is difficult to answer, but for both visions it is a condition that the 'regional DNA must be known': What is the region good at, what knowledge and skills does it have to innovate and grow in an increasingly global market? Empirical studies on skill-relatedness in the regional labour market provide an interpretation of this that can be used to shape policy in a more targeted way. What opportunities and threats play a role in the regional labour market and which can lead to innovation and value creation? These are appropriate questions for local policy.

Whether and how exactly the more productive use of this 'DNA' is given substance depends on the assessment of the degree of controllability of economic processes, policy priorities and sometimes also political preferences. The self-organizing capacity of industry, producers, consumers and markets in economies is generally large: innovation is created by market parties and knowledge institutions, their interactions, and how they develop from existing knowledge, craft and expertise. In a well-functioning system with many possibilities for interactions between entrepreneurs and employees, crossovers that lead to innovation therefore largely come about automatically; an oiled system is therefore a prerequisite for the process of economic innovation. Such an economic system benefits from a physical and institutional system that is in line with this – but it is mainly the case that an economy is hindered by a system that does not function properly. Policy that takes skill-relatedness into account requires the deployment of various policy fields, from the labour market to innovation and accompanying spatial policy, and therefore also of different levels of government. The central government creates the frameworks for education policy, the mediation of job seekers with and without a (formal) job, generic talent policy, industrial policy (e.g. the top sectors focus) and social policy. Regions and cities are responsible for economic portfolios, often in consultation with local firms. Finally, the sorting effect of self-organization of citizens is important, and the increasing extent to which informal institutions (norms, values, trust) are steering them instead of formal institutions – this creates both solidarity within the 'own' region, and it potentially builds bridges to (cultures in) other regions (Cortinovis et al., 2017). All levels of scale benefit from the insight into innovative capacity that emerges from the current analysis method.

INSTITUTIONAL CHALLENGES FOR EMERGING ECONOMIES

The labour market is a central and localizing theme for every city, and especially aimed at the bottom of that market. Municipalities often have the legal task to organize the matching of jobs to the job-seeking labour force. As the American economists Ford (2015) and Reich (2015) conclude in their latest books: jobs for the middle-educated will be put at risk because of structural change toward knowledge-intensive, but also automatable occupations. Much of the debate on regional labour market dynamics is concentrated on experience and market structures of developed, Western regions and cities, and the economic literature on emerging countries' labour markets is scarcer. Economic theories will apply in emerging economies equally as in developed ones (Zenou, 2009; Desmet and Henderson, 2015), yet the impact of divergent institutional settings on urban governance and market organization in emerging countries warrants a closer look at experiences in such countries.

The link between work and human development is synergistic. Work enhances human development by providing incomes and livelihoods, by reducing poverty and by ensuring more equitable growth. Human development – by enhancing health, knowledge, skills and awareness – increases human capital and broadens opportunities and choices (UNDP, 2015). Also in emerging economies, the technological (r)evolution leads to routine-biased technical change: the idea that the net effect of new technologies reduces demand for routine-skilled workers, typically medium-skilled, while increasing demand for non-routine skilled ones at the upper and lower ends of the skills distribution (Goos et al., 2014). Such change favours people with high and low human capital, but less so with medium human capital, polarizing work opportunities. The specific role of human capital accumulation (related especially to education) and the quality of institutions have been introduced by UNDP (2015) as a further explanation of development opportunities. Costatini and Monni (2008) argue that emerging economies positively affected by the globalization process are those that succeeded in modernizing their institutions in a democratic manner, investing in infrastructures, ensuring macroeconomic stability, and above all investing the relative benefits of education and skill development to enlarge people's choices. Like the discussion in developed countries, a combination of private-sector worker training and public-sector skills development and educational subsidies could drive the expansion of a diverse, skilled workforce. Specific for emerging economies is the emphasis that this would encourage multinational firms to hire locally, as well as promote home-grown business growth.

Campbell and Ahmed (2012) argue that there are some stark differences in the structure of labour markets in developed and emerging countries. The four most prominent are according to them: (1) the characteristics of non-market or informal work;[2] (2) the labour force participation of women;[3] (3) the status in and of employment;[4] and (4) the dispersion of occupational productivity.[5] State intervention can play a crucial role both in capability building and in fostering structural and technological change addressed to the most advanced development regimes. Therefore, according to Vivarelli (2014), policies should target advanced sectors and technologies in order to create new absolute advantages (related to but markedly different from existing ones), rather than specialize in the existing comparative advantages. This resembles the structural change and evolutionary development process discussed before.

David et al. (2019) specifically focus on informal work opportunities (in Latin American case studies), and notice that employment growth across regions was very strong in the 2000s but has moderated noticeably since. Informality is a major feature of Latin American labour markets and those countries with high informality relative to their level of development have the lowest and most stable levels of unemployment, suggesting that the informal/ formal margin can act as a substitute for the employment/unemployment margin. Naudé (2011) and Amorós (2011) report that the positive relationships between improved opportunity-driven entrepreneurship activities (utilized as a proxy for productive entrepreneurship) and 'control of corruption' and 'political stability' indicate that real opportunity ventures can be developed if government institutions in emerging economies are of adequate quality. It should be noted that appropriate policies for entrepreneurship, particularly in those countries where institutional checks and balances are often not robust, should consider that entrepreneurship may not always promote economic development (Naudé, 2011). Concerning structural change, De Vries et al. (2015) observe that in Africa and Latin America there has been a transformation to more productive distribution services[6] over the last 40 years, yet only in Asia is this also accompanied by the development of service industries that yield even larger productivity gains. Structural change in the long run has positive effects for the catching up of economies in emerging countries – not only in trade and production (and higher productivity), but also in less gender inequality, more social cohesion and more community trust (i.e. improved informal institutions) (Rendall, 2012). Brain-drain though may be caused by migration of mobile people, who want to capitalize on their acquired skills and education in places where labour demand is higher, and institutional settings (even) better.

From this review of publications on structural change in emerging economies' regions and cities, we learn that institutional settings (informal work, lack of basic infrastructures, educational programmes, legislation) may hamper development into a full knowledge economy as known in the Western literature and practice. Concerns for the labour market of the middle and lower educated in cities worldwide appear to be justified, and with human capital as the most important building block of today's knowledge economy, this is an important point of attention for urban and regional policy (see Sparreboom, 2017 for four countries in sub-Saharan Africa). While most of the empirical literature on the quantitative and qualitative employment impact of technological change is centred on the OECD countries (starting with older contributions like Griffin, 1999), in recent times some attention has also been devoted to the specificities of the middle-income and low-income countries (Vivarelli, 2012). Typically, technological change in emerging countries is mainly imported and innovation is inherently connected with trade, FDI, and consequent international technology transfer (Coe et al., 1997). "Even though these imported technologies are not always the most updated, they are far more advanced than those traditionally adopted by local firms in most developing countries. It is therefore reasonable to expect that transferred technologies are relatively more updated than those in use domestically, which are generally characterized by a lower capital intensity" (Vivarelli, 2012: 26–27). Yet, such foreign investments may create dependencies of emerging countries on developed ones, as they initiate from the more developed countries (which have their own interest in financing them), may focus on the lower end of value chain activities in the emerging countries, and may favour only a select group of firms in actual knowledge transfer (Aitken and Harrison, 1999; Narula and Dunning, 2000; Damijan et al., 2003; Arnold and Javorcik, 2009; Fu et al., 2011). At the same time, 'traditional' factors of regional-economic dynamics related to the labour market also remain important, such as accessibility, the housing and property market, the land market, entrepreneurship, area development, urban facilities and legislation, and regulations for citizens and entrepreneurs. In many emerging economies these necessary conditions lack maturity, despite signs of convergence and catching up (Diodato, 2017). Evidence based on micro data for these factors is becoming increasingly available (Cirera and Sabetti, 2019).

REFLECTION

"It has become impossible to think straight about the state. The only permissible discourse is to talk of shrinking, fragmenting and privatising it – opening it up to competition and market forces. It is accepted as axiomatic that a public institution will be bureaucratic, self-serving and [...] lazy", Will Hutton wrote in *The Observer* on 18 October 2015. After changes of power in the United States of America, the United Kingdom and Italy, nobody denies the quest for a scale that suits an engaged and individual society: more local involvement. How different is this sentiment to Mazzucato's view reported earlier in the chapter? However, local development policies seem less appropriate in emerging economies, where necessary basic facilities and institutions may not be fully developed. Before more attention can be directed at the local level, advances in educational attainment, appropriate entrepreneurship policies, and an improved institutional setting must be addressed.

Back to Adam Smith in 1775: "Little else is requisite to carry a state to the highest degree of opulence from the lowest barbarism, but peace, easy taxes, and a tolerable administration of justice; all the rest being brought about by the natural course of things" (quoted in Stewart, 1895: section IV, 25). Although Smith's *The Wealth of Nations* (2008 [1776]) is often seen as a plea for administrative laissez-faire, it also reads above all as an advocate of a smart state: tempering negative externalities caused by the market, promoting social opportunities and the division of labour, and proposing that the state is responsible for public works and education. And of course, public administration (not necessarily the state) must ensure that this is done in the smartest way possible. The pros and cons of government intervention meet regularly in the economic and administrative debate. The government is not a substitute for decentralized information in niche markets, and intervention provokes rent-seeking, according to Friedrich Hayek in 1974 when he received the Nobel Prize for economics. But: "the idea that the government can disengage from specific policies and just focus on general framework conditions in a sector neutral way is an illusion based on the disregard for the specificity and complexity of the requisite publicly provided inputs and capabilities [...]. We are doomed to choose", Hausmann and Rodrik (2006: 24) argue. The specific roles that local governments may play in the development of labour markets and regional economies once they have to choose can be manifold (Zenou, 2009).

In emerging countries, policies may be equally relevant as in developed ones, yet priorities may be set differently, and budgets may be more restricting. Local governments provide unemployment benefits, and strive for full employment and, ideally, also participation. Regional and urban social welfare programmes may be put into place, with also indirect investments impacting on labour market conditions, such as the quality of housing and the living environment, accessibility in (public) transport, amenities and retail provision. These latter investments are both private and public in character, but governmental efforts can be essential in the creation of economies of scale. Governments can further invest in (people-based) education and entrepreneurship programmes, and in place-based developments like enterprise zoning, science parks and knowledge locations, as discussed in this chapter. The welfare benefits of place-based policies are less clear to identify than those of people-based policies (Neumark and Simpson, 2015). Facilitating foreign investments may be high on the priority ladder in emerging countries, as these may come with knowledge and labour (although it may, as discussed, also create dependencies). All these aspects contribute to structural change actively – e.g. by the introduction and development of new technologies, the development of local industries and skills, transitions to more sustainable and inclusive production, and transitions towards service industries.

In emerging economies all these policies are more challenging than elsewhere, as market, institutional and governance failures are prevalent on a substantial scale. A prerequisite of smart public administration is the diagnostic monitoring of what is going on in the economy and society. What is then required of public administration varies per region and per theme. Not every level of government can, will or may interfere in economic development as prominently as Mazzucato (2013) outlines. However, the labour market is proving to be a future 'Achilles heel' of regional economic development in any local economy worldwide, which therefore deserves the full attention of all levels of public administration. The suggested links to structural change, skills and institutions presented in this chapter may help in identifying the opportunities for urban governance.

NOTES

1. Katz and Bradley (2013) suggest that all that is needed is a good planning of knowledge locations such as innovation districts, which can be done practically everywhere.
2. Non-market work in lower income countries frequently takes the form of livelihood contributions and subsistence farming. It is difficult to estimate the overall economic contribution of this type of work, although it is recognized that it presents an "important contribution to the maintenance of living standards and a buffer against extreme poverty" (Campbell and Ahmed, 2012: 10)
3. Female labour force participation differs by economic development: it is high in low-income contexts (due to necessity, and typically in non-market and informal work), decreases with increasing economic development (as necessity declines), and increases again in advanced economies (due to a desire to participate in the labour force, and fewer barriers in doing so) (Campbell and Ahmed, 2012).
4. The share of wage employment increases the higher the level of economic development (Campbell and Ahmed, 2012).
5. Productivity differences tend to be higher in lower development contexts, due to less integrated product markets, worse infrastructure and more information asymmetry. The same product is produced in widely diverse quality levels which typically coexist and do not compete due to highly segmented product markets (Campbell and Ahmed, 2012). See also McMillan et al. (2014).
6. Distribution services include transport services and distributive trade as well as hotels and restaurants (De Vries et al., 2015: 678).

REFERENCES

Aitken, B. J. and A. E. Harrison (1999). Do domestic firms benefit from direct foreign investment? Evidence from Venezuela. *American Economic Review* 89: 605–618.

Amorós, J. E. (2011). The impact of institutions on entrepreneurship in developing countries. In W. Naudé (ed.), *Entrepreneurship and Economic Development*. Basingstoke: Palgrave Macmillan, 166–186.

Arnold, J. M. and B. S. Javorcik (2009). Gifted kids or pushy parents? Foreign direct investment and plant productivity in Indonesia. *Journal of International Economics* 79: 42–53.

Barber, B. (2013). *If Mayors Ruled the World: Dysfunctional Nations, Rising Cities*. New Haven: Yale University Press.

Barca, F., P. McCann and A. Rodriguez-Pose (2012). The case for regional development intervention: Place-based versus place-neutral approaches. *Journal of Regional Science* 52: 134–152.

Batty, M. (2013). *The New Science of Cities*. Cambridge MA: MIT Press.

Bertaud, A. (2018). *Order without Design: How Markets Shape Cities*. Cambridge, MA: MIT Press.

Boschma, R. (2005). Proximity and innovation: A critical assessment. *Regional Studies* 39: 61–74.

Botsman, R. and R. Rogers (2010). *What's Mine Is Yours: How Collaborative Consumption Is Changing the Way We Live*. London: Collins.

Breschi, S., F. Lissoni and F. Malerba (2003). Knowledge relatedness in firm technological diversification. *Research Policy* 32: 69–87.

Broersma, L. A. Edzes and J. van Dijk (2016). Human capital externalities: Effects for low-educated workers and low-skilled jobs. *Regional Studies* 50: 1675–1687.

Campbell, D. and I. Ahmed (2012). *The Labour Market in Developing Countries*. Bonn: Institute for Labour Studies (IZA).

Caragliu, A. and P. Nijkamp (2016). Space and knowledge spillovers in European regions: The impact of different forms of proximity on spatial knowledge diffusion. *Journal of Economic Geography* 16: 749–774.

Castaldi, C., K. Frenken and B. Los (2015). Related variety, unrelated variety and technological breakthroughs: An analysis of US state-level patenting. *Regional Studies* 49: 767–781.

Cheema, G. S. (ed.) (1993). *Urban Management: Policies and Innovations in Developing Countries*. New York: Praeger.

Cirera, X. and L. Sabetti (2019). The effects of innovation on employment in developing countries: Evidence from enterprise surveys. *Industrial and Corporate Change* 28: 161–176.

Coe, D. and E. Helpman (1995). International R&D spillovers. *European Economic Review* 39: 859–887.

Coe, D. T., E. Helpman and A. Homaister (1997). North–South spillovers. *Economic Journal* 107: 134–149.

Content, J. (2019). The role of relatedness and entrepreneurship in regional economic development. PhD dissertation, Utrecht School of Economics, USE 048.

Cortinovis, N., R. Crescenzi and F. G. van Oort (2020). Multinational enterprises, industrial relatedness and employment in European regions. *Journal of Economic Geography* 20: 1165–1205.

Cortinovis, N. and F. G. van Oort (2015). Variety, economic growth and knowledge-intensity of European regions: A spatial panel analysis. *Annals of Regional Science* 55: 7–32.

Cortinovis, N. and F. G. van Oort (2019). Between spilling over and boiling down: Network-mediated spillovers, local knowledge base and productivity in European regions. *Journal of Economic Geography* 19: 1233–1260.

Cortinovis, N. and F. G. van Oort (Forthcoming). Economic networks, innovation and proximity. In A. Torre and D. Gallaud (eds.), *Handbook of Proximity Relations*. Cheltenham, UK and Northampton, MA, USA: Edward Elgar Publishing.

Cortinovis, N., J. Xiao, R. Boschma and F. G. van Oort (2017). Quality of government and social capital as drivers of regional diversification in Europe. *Journal of Economic Geography* 17: 1179–1208.

Costatini, V. and S. Monni (2008). Environment, human development and growth. *Ecological Economics* 64: 867–880.

Csáfordi, Z., L. Lőrincz, B. Lengyel and K. M. Kiss (2020). Productivity spillovers through labor flows: Productivity gap, multinational experience and industry relatedness. *Journal of Technological Transfer* 45: 86–121.

Damijan, J., M. Knell, B. Majcen and M. Rojec (2003). Technology transfer through FDI in top 10 transition countries: How important are direct effects, horizontal and vertical spillovers? William Davidson Working Paper No. 549.

David, A. C., F. Lambert and F. Toscani (2019). More work to do: Taking stock of Latin-American labour markets. IMF Working Paper 19/55.

De Vries, G., M. Timmer and K. de Vries (2015). Structural transformation in Africa: Static gains, dynamic losses. *Journal of Development Studies* 51: 674–688.

Desmet, K. and V. Henderson (2015). The geography of development within countries. In G. Duranton, J. V. Henderson and W. Strange (eds.), *Handbook of Regional and Urban Economics Volume 5A*. Amsterdam: Elsevier, 1457–1518.

Devas, N., P. Amis, J. Beall, U. Grant, D. Mitlin, F. Nunan and C. Rakodi (2004). *Urban Governance, Voice and Poverty in the Developing World*. London: Earthscan.

Diodato, D. (2017). Technological and structural change: Understanding economic growth in countries and regions in Europe and South-America. Dissertation, Utrecht University.

Diodato, D. and A. Weterings (2015). The resilience of regional labour markets to economic shocks: Exploring the role of interactions among firms and workers. *Journal of Economic Geography* 15: 723–742.

Eriksson, R. (2011). Localized spillovers and knowledge flows: How does proximity influence the performance of plants? *Economic Geography* 87: 127–154.

Florida, R., T. Gulden and C. Mellander (2008). The rise of the mega-region. *Cambridge Journal of Regions, Economy and Society* 1: 459–476.

Ford, M. (2015). *Rise of the Robots: Technology and the Threat of a Jobless Future*. New York: Basic Books.

Frenken, K., F. G. van Oort and T. Verburg (2007). Related variety, unrelated variety, and regional economic growth. *Regional Studies* 45: 685–697.

Frick, S. A., A. Rodriguez-Pose and M. D. Wong (2018). Towards economically dynamic special economic zones in emerging countries. *Economic Geography*. https://doi.org/10.1080/00130095.2018.1467732.

Fu, X., C. Pietrobelli and L. Soete (2011). The role of foreign technology and indigenous innovation in the emerging economies: Technological change and catching-up. *World Development* 39: 1204–1212.

Glaeser, E. (2011). *Triumph of the City*. London: Penguin.

Glaeser, E., G. Ponzetto and K. Tobio (2014). Cities, skills and regional change. *Regional Studies* 48: 7–43.

Goos, M., A. Manning and A. Salomons (2014). Explaining job polarization: Routine-biased technological change and offshoring. *American Economic Review* 104: 2509–2526.

Griffin, K. (1999). *Alternative Strategies for Economic Development*. Basingstoke: Palgrave Macmillan.

Hausmann, R., C. A. Hidalgo, S. Bustos, M. Coscia, A. Simoes and M. A. Yildrim (2013). *The Atlas of Economic Complexity: Mapping Paths to Prosperity*. Cambridge, MA: MIT Press.

Hausmann, R. and D. Rodrik (2006). Doomed to choose: Industrial policy as predicament. Conference paper, J. F. Kennedy School of Government, Harvard University.

Henderson, V. (2002). Urbanization in developing countries. *World Bank Research Observer* 17: 89–112.

Hoekman, J., K. Frenken and F. G. van Oort (2009). The geography of collaborative knowledge production in Europe. *The Annals of Regional Science* 43: 721–738.

Katz, B. and J. Bradley (2013). *The Metropolitan Revolution: How Cities and Metros Are Fixing Our Broken Politics and Fragile Economy*. Washington, DC: Brookings Institution.

Katz, B. and J. Nowak (2017). *The New Localism: How Cities Can Thrive in the Age of Populism*. Washington, DC: Brookings Institution.

Keller, W. (2002). Geographic localization of international technology diffusion. *American Economic Review* 92: 120–142.

Keller, W. and S. R. Yeaple (2009). Multinational enterprises, international trade, and productivity growth: Firm-level evidence from the United States. *The Review of Economics and Statistics* 91: 821–831.

Koster, H., F. Cheng, M. Gerritse and F. G. van Oort (2019). Place-based policies, firm productivity and displacement effects: Evidence from Shenzhen, China. *Journal of Regional Science* 59: 187–213.

Lumenga-Neso, O., M. Olarreaga and M. Schiff (2005). On 'indirect' trade-related R&D spillovers. *European Economic Review* 49: 1785–1798.

Maggioni, M., M. Nosvelli and E. Uberti (2007). Space versus networks in the geography of innovation: A European analysis. *Papers in Regional Science* 86: 471–493.

Mazzucato, M. (2013). *The Entrepreneurial State: Debunking Public vs. Private Sector Myths*. London: Anthem Press.

McMillan, M., D. Rodrik and I. Verduzco-Gallo (2014). Globalization, structural change and productivity growth, with an update on Africa. *World Development* 63: 11–32.

Miguelez, E. and R. Moreno (2017). Networks, diffusion of knowledge, and regional innovative performance. *International Regional Science Review* 40: 331–336.

Mitlin, D. and D. Satterthwaite (2012). *Urban Poverty in the Global South: Scale and Nature*. Abingdon: Routledge.

Moretti, E. (2012). *The New Geography of Jobs*. New York: Mariner Books.

Narula, R. and J. Dunning (2000). Industrial development, globalization and multinational enterprises: New realities for developing countries. *Oxford Development Studies* 28: 141–167.

Naudé, W. (2011). *Entrepreneurship and Economic Development*. Basingstoke: Palgrave Macmillan.

Neffke, F., M. Henning and R. Boschma (2011). How do regions diversify over time? Industry relatedness and the development of new growth paths in regions. *Economic Geography* 87: 237–265.

Neumark, D. and H. Simpson (2015). Place-based policies. In G. Duranton, J. V. Henderson and W. Strange (eds.), *Handbook of Regional and Urban Economics Volume 5A*. Amsterdam: Elsevier, 1197–1288.

Oosterwaal, L., E. Stam and J. P. van der Toren (2017). *Openbaar bestuur in region-ale ecosystemen van ondernemerschap*. The Hague: Ministerie van Binnenlandse Zaken.

Ponds, R., G. Marlet and C. van Woerkens (2015). Trickle down in the city: The influ-ence of higher educated people on the labour market of lower educated people. The Hague: Platform31.

Raspe, O., M. van den Berge and T. de Graaff (2017). *Urban Regions as Engines of Economic Growth: What Can Policy Do?* The Hague: Netherlands Environmental Assessment Agency.

Raspe, O. and F. G. van Oort (2007). *Spatial-economic policy in the knowledge economy*. The Hague: Ruimtelijk Planbureau.

Reich, R. B. (2015). *Saving Capitalism: For the Many, Not the Few*. New York: Alfred A. Knopf.

Rendall, M. (2012). Structural change in developing countries: Has it decreased gender inequality? *World Development* 45: 1–16.

Rodriguez-Pose, A. (2013). Do institutions matter for regional development? *Regional Studies* 47: 1034–1047.

Rodrik, D., A. Subramanian and F. Trebbi (2002). Institutions rule: The primacy of institutions over geography and integration in economic development. NBER Working Paper 3905.

Schwab, K. (2018). *Shaping the Future of the Fourth Industrial Revolution*. London: Portfolio/Penguin.

Smith, A. (2008 [1776]). *An Inquiry into the Nature and Causes of the Wealth of Nations*. Oxford: Oxford University Press.

SOB (2016). *Make a Difference: Responding Strongly to Regional Economic Challenges*. The Hague: Study Group Public Administration.

Sparreboom, T. (2017). Structural change, employment and education in four countries in sub-Saharan Africa. *African Journal of Economic and Management Studies* 8: 172–185.

Stam, E. (2015). Entrepreneurial ecosystems and regional policy: A sympathetic cri-tique. USE Discussion Paper 15-07.

Stewart, D. (1895). *Account of the Life and Writings of Adam Smith LLD*. London: Macmillan.

Teisman, G. and J. Edelenbos (2011). Towards a perspective of system synchronization in water governance: A synthesis of empirical lessons and complexity theories. *International Review of Administrative Sciences* 77: 101–118.

Thissen, M., T. de Graaff and F. G. van Oort (2016). Competitive network positions in trade and structural economic growth: A geographically weighted regression analy-sis for European regions. *Papers in Regional Science* 95: 159–180.

UNDP (2015). *Human Development Report 2015: Work for Human Development*. New York: United Nations Development Programme.

Van Dijk, M. P. (2006). *Managing Cities in Developing Countries*. Cheltenham, UK and Northampton, MA, USA: Edward Elgar Publishing.

Van Dijk, M. P., J. Edelenbos and K. van Rooijen (eds.) (2017). *Urban Governance in the Realm of Complexity*. Rugby: Practical Action Publishing.

Van Oort, F. G., A. Weterings, L. Nedelkoska and F. Neffke (2016). Labour mobility, skill-relatedness and urban innovation. *Tijdschrift voor Politieke Economie Digitaal* 10: 104–121 (in Dutch).

Venables, T. (2015). Making cities work for development. IGC Growth Brief 2. London: International Growth Centre.

Vivarelli, M. (2012). Innovation, employment and skills in advanced and developing countries: A survey of the literature. IZA Discussion Paper 6291.

Vivarelli, M. (2014). Structural change and innovation as exit strategies from the middle income trap. IZA Discussion Paper 8148.

Zenou, Y. (2009). *Urban Labor Economics*. Cambridge: Cambridge University Press.

5. Smart city for comprehensive urban management: concepts, impacts, and the South Korean experience

Yirang Lim

INTRODUCTION

Smart cities have gained a lot of attention from policymakers and international information and communication technology (ICT) vendors who seek innovation and opportunities. Smart city development is an opportunity to enhance urban competitiveness and increase efficiency in urban management mainly through ICT as well as innovation in management and decision-making. In general, smart cities have ICT infrastructure throughout the city where a massive amount of urban data is collected, processed, and shared allowing for efficient urban management. Traffic, weather, disaster, and emergency information is shared with citizens in real time. In an ideal situation, smart cities facilitate economic growth, especially in the ICT industry, enable citizens' active participation in decision-making processes, increase the quality of life through efficient public services, and protect the environment by reducing CO_2 emissions and energy consumption (Yigitcanlar and Han, 2009).

The early stage of smart city development was focused on implementing ICT infrastructures in selected urban sectors. For example, Smart City Adelaide cooperated with CISCO to implement smart lighting. Singapore has launched 'Smart Nation Singapore', focusing on transportation, home and environment, business productivity, health, and public sector services. Later, the smart city became a comprehensive urban development approach not only implementing ICT infrastructure but also concerning the overall quality of life and urban sustainability. For example, India launched a 'Smart Cities Mission' in 2015 to facilitate implementing 'smart solutions' that can provide core infrastructure, enhanced quality of life, and a sustainable environment. The European Commission launched the 'Horizon 2020 Energy' that focuses on environment-friendly transport and energy. It also contributes to urban governance, by inviting stakeholders into the decision-making process through various channels enabled by ICT. Moreover, sectoral ICT implementations are integrated into a broader management system. The emphasis of smart cities is still on technology, but the importance of human, social and institutional capital also receives attention (Batty et al., 2012; Hollands, 2008).

There are abundant research studies on the smart city concept. This chapter[1] contributes to existing literature with three main topics. The first is a discussion on the smart city concept, how it has emerged and evolved. The second is the impact of the smart city. Smart city development brings changes to the city and to citizens' lives. These changes are discussed from two opposing points of view: those of advocates and critics. Advocates argue that smart city development creates positive economic, environmental, social and governance impact. On the other hand, criticism concerns negative impacts such as privacy invasion. Finally, the third topic is empirical evidence of such impacts, whether positive or negative. We look at the South Korean case, where the government takes strong leadership in developing smart cities. Comparing smart cities and non-smart cities in terms of impacts provides insight into the achieved impacts.

SMART CITY CONCEPT

The term 'smart city' became famous in the late 2000s, after IBM's 'smarter planet' project (Baron, 2012). Their project claims that becoming smart is being sustainable and efficient, linking smartness with sustainability (Söderström et al., 2014). The idea spread widely to revitalize the economy that had been hit badly by the global financial crisis of 2008. Smart cities can be an option to attract educated and skilled people as well as global businesses that can contribute to urban competitiveness (Harrison and Donnelly, 2011; Lopes, 2017; Richter et al., 2015; White, 2016).

The term 'smart city' went viral recently, but the use of advanced technology and data in urban management has been around quite a long time. Similar concepts include intelligent city, information city, ubiquitous city (U-city), or digital city, which all point to the opportunity of exploiting technology in urban development and management (Nam and Pardo, 2011). The technology is mainly ICT that connects people and urban environments including infrastructure and public services (Harrison and Donnelly, 2011). What makes a city smart depends on how we define 'smartness' (Cocchia, 2014). Smartness so far is equivalent to advanced technology, hence techno-driven urban management is the core idea in the smart city (Dirks and Keeling, 2009; Harrison and Donnelly, 2011; Washburn et al., 2009; Zygiaris, 2013). However, in a broader sense smartness also refers to smart strategies that are not necessarily related to technology but facilitate efficient resource use (Caragliu et al., 2011; Giffinger et al., 2007; Zygiaris, 2013).

Some definitions describe the characteristics of the smart city concept (see Table 5.1). Commonly recognized characteristics are: (1) networked infrastructure such as business services, housing, leisure, lifestyle services and ICT; (2) business-led neoliberal urban development; (3) emphasis on social inclusion and equitable urban growth; (4) high-tech and creative industries and culture; (5) social and relational capital that can be represented as regional absorptive capacity; and (6) social and environmental sustainability (Caragliu et al., 2011).

The definitions describe what smart city has to be (feature), what it brings to the city (impacts), and what it tries to achieve (goals) (Lim et al., 2019a). Most commonly mentioned features are ICT infrastructures, smart citizens, social capital as well as institutional capacity. This shows that smart cities are not only technology-driven urban management methods but also acknowledge the social and governance domains that emphasize innovative relations among citizens, institutions and the private sector. The impacts of smart city development are innovation and collaboration in the decision-making process. It fosters the generation of innovative ideas to increase efficiency and collaboration among stakeholders including citizens. The goals of smart cities are normative, which are sustainable development and quality of life. Sustainable development often means urban competitiveness or economic growth while not jeopardizing the environment. The definitions also internalize the positive impacts of smart city development (Lim et al., 2019a).

Distinctive features of the smart city concept are innovation and collaboration. Innovation is a new idea or process in organizational production (Gil-Garcia et al., 2016; Hall, 2011). It is a key component of the smart city because it is the place where innovation occurs (Afzalan et al., 2017; Gil-Garcia et al., 2016; Kraus et al., 2015). Innovation in the smart city takes many forms, such as technological innovation (Ojasalo and Kauppinen, 2016), process innovation in urban management (Schuurman et al., 2012), organizational innovation in governance (Errichiello and Marasco, 2014), and urban innovation in general (Caragliu and Del Bo, 2019). Technological innovation is related to ICT use in smart cities. ICT corporations such as IBM and Accenture define technological innovation as the use of big data and analytics, cloud computing, machine-to-machine communication, sensors, and intelligent software (Van den Buuse and Kolk, 2019). These enable companies to produce new goods and services and therefore increase productivity. Thus, the smart city fosters entrepreneurship in ICT and knowledge-intensive industry (Tranos and Gertner, 2012).

Decision-making in the smart city involves various stakeholders, especially emphasizing citizen engagement. This is considered as a process innovation, which includes citizens in identifying the problem and finding the solution (Schuurman et al., 2012). At the same time, the smart city itself is considered

Table 5.1   *Definitions of smart city*

Source	Definition	Keywords
Giffinger et al. (2007: 11)	"A Smart City is a city well performing in a forward-looking way [...] built on the 'smart' combination of endowments and activities of self-decisive, independent and aware citizens."	Forward-looking, citizens
Caragliu et al (2011: 66)	"The label 'smart city' should, therefore, point to clever solutions allowing modern cities to thrive, through quantitative and qualitative improvements in productivity."	Clever solutions, productivity
Zygiaris (2013: 218)	"Cities prioritize their urban innovation ecosystems from their traditional urban character to innovative 'green', 'smart', 'intelligent', and 'innovating', aiming towards environmental and social sustainability."	Innovation, sustainability
Hall et al. (2000: 1)	"The vision of 'Smart Cities' is the urban center of the future, made safe, secure, environmentally green, and efficient because all structures [...] are designed, constructed, and maintained making use of advanced, integrated materials, sensors, electronics, and networks which are interfaced with computerized systems comprised of databases, tracking, and decision-making algorithms."	Environmentally green, efficient, computerized systems
Dirks and Keeling (2009: 9)	"A smarter city is one that uses technology to transform its core systems and optimize the return from largely finite resources."	Technology, optimize
Toppeta (2010: 4)	"Smart cities are those that are combining ICT and Web 2.0 technology with other organizational, design and planning efforts to de-materialize and speed up bureaucratic processes and help to identify new, innovative solutions to city management complexity, in order to improve sustainability and 'livability'."	Technology, innovative solutions, sustainability, liveability
Debnath et al. (2014: 49)	"In general, a smart city is characterized by its ICT infrastructures, facilitating an urban system which is increasingly smart, inter-connected, and sustainable."	ICT infrastructure, sustainable

as an innovation (Walravens et al., 2014). Smart clusters and living labs facilitate innovation for a better urban environment and quality of life (Komninos et al., 2013; Kraus et al., 2015). Smart clusters and living labs focus on new technologies or new measures to tackle wicked urban problems. Provision of an open learning environment can lead to economic benefits. Access to information and knowledge inspires people, which leads to innovative ideas (Gil-Garcia et al., 2016; Komninos et al., 2013; Kraus et al., 2015). These ideas create value through product or process innovation (Hall, 2011).

In conclusion, the smart city aims to achieve urban sustainability with high quality of life (Dirks and Keeling, 2009; Toppeta, 2010). Although there is no unified definition, the concept is evolving around implementing advanced technology for urban management and development. Several studies provide an overview of definitions (e.g. Cocchia, 2014; Nam and Pardo, 2011; Trindade et al., 2017). The definitions include requirements, performance and goals of smart cities which are closely associated with positive impacts. The commonly acknowledged feature of the smart city concept is the use of ICT in urban management. ICT paves the way to innovation and collaboration so that smart cities can provide efficient and optimized solutions to urban problems.

ADVOCATES OF SMART CITY DEVELOPMENT

Advocates of smart city development emphasize positive impacts. Typical positive impacts include economic, social and governance, and environmental benefits (Lim et al., 2019a). Economic benefits are increasing urban competitiveness, productivity, and support of sustainable economic development. Social benefits include reducing the inequality gap and facilitating social development. In the governance aspect, smart cities provide a platform where citizens can actively engage in the decision-making processes through ICT which increases democracy and transparency. Environmental benefits are protecting the environment by reducing CO_2 emissions and energy use. All in all, smart cities are expected to deliver a wide range of benefits to urban sustainability.

For sure, smart cities create economic benefits because the project itself attracts massive investment for ICT infrastructure. That is why international ICT vendors actively publicize smart city solutions. For them, smart cities are a marketing strategy that promotes the companies' products and services (Zanella et al., 2014). According to several forecasts[2] the smart city market is expected to grow more than US$1.2 trillion by 2020. For the city itself, a smart city can offer a brand as modern and future-oriented, thereby attracting investments and people. That way, the city can enhance its competitiveness. Using ICT infrastructure, real-time data on traffic, energy consumption, air quality and security are utilized to react promptly to problems. Smart cities can optimize resource use to reduce CO_2 emissions and administration costs while providing better public services to citizens (Sarma and Sunny, 2017). At the same time, human capital, which is a core element of smart cities, can contribute to economic development (Caragliu et al., 2011; Richter et al., 2015).

Social benefits of smart city development are related to intangible assets of the city such as quality of life and social capital (Lim et al., 2019a). Increasing quality of life is a common goal of cities and smart city development often includes this goal in its conceptual definition. Quality of life in general means people's physical and mental well-being and satisfaction (Hagerty et al., 2001). The smart city provides citizen-centric (consumer-oriented) public services that can increase objective indicators of quality of life, represented as urban amenities (Lee and Lee, 2014; Plessis and Marnewick, 2017; Pokric et al., 2014). However, subjective quality of life such as relationships with family and friends, emotional well-being, and feeling part of the community is difficult to relate directly with smart city development because these are rooted in citizens' priorities and subjective perspectives. ICT changes the lifestyle and relationship among people at a personal level and this is hard to measure or observe. However, in general, smart cities can increase the material quality of life by providing efficient public services and eventually people's well-being.

Social capital is both a key factor in and the result of smart city development (Lim et al., 2019a). Social capital is regarded as a combination of the software of a smart city and human and institutional capital (Hollands, 2008). At the same time, smart cities provide digital infrastructures where people can build new relationships and trust, and shared norms (Mandarano et al., 2010). This can benefit both individuals and community which increases social capital and encourages participation (Dempsey et al., 2011). The smart city is an opportunity to empower citizens and promote equality, social inclusion, and development by freely provided public information. Empowered citizens build stronger social capital that can increase information sharing, capacity to deal with unexpected problems, and facilitate effective decision-making and collective work (Mandarano et al., 2010). Social capital increases when technologies connect people, enabling them to share experiences and knowledge (Afzalan et al., 2017; Hollands, 2015). Inevitably, smart city citizens need to have the ability to exploit ICT infrastructure (Stratigea, 2012).

Smart cities offer an open environment where people can freely express their opinions and exchange ideas which enables active citizen participation (Sajhau, 2017; Yigitcanlar, 2015). For example, in South Korea, the government launched 'epeople.go.kr' where people can file complaints, report issues such as illegal parking, and suggest policies. The South Korean government also launched a direct communication platform, 'e-petition (www1.president .go.kr/petitions)' where people bring up social issues and the government gives direct reactions when the petition gathers over 20,000 signatures from citizens within a month. Active participation is desirable for democratic and transparent governance. In smart cities, collaboration, citizen participation and transparent decision-making are enabled by technological, human, social and institutional capital (Afzalan et al., 2017; De Wijs et al., 2016; Nam and Pardo,

2014; Wiig, 2015). Citizens' participation whereby people's opinions are heard contributes to the equal and just city (Gil-Garcia et al., 2016; Komninos et al., 2013; Sajhau, 2017; Zygiaris, 2013). However, whether smart city development contributes to an increase in social capital, citizen participation and empowerment, equality, or justice is not yet empirically proven (Lim et al., 2019a).

Environmental sustainability can be perceived as protecting the natural environment (prevent people using natural resources) and altering human behaviour (alternative energy production and less consumption). The former is not unique to smart city development because protecting the natural environment has been practised in traditional urban planning such as green belts and zoning regulation. Smart cities are more related to the latter aspect, by promoting renewable energy use and reducing energy consumption. ICT enables real-time data on energy use, traffic and waste collection so that resource use can be optimized. An efficiency increase was reported in multiple case studies especially in the transportation sector (Sarma and Sunny, 2017; Welde, 2012; White, 2016). The introduction of GPS can trace transport data to reduce congestion and CO_2 emissions (Snow et al., 2016). Also, people can participate in daily energy reduction such as using energy-efficient home appliances, recycling and using eco-friendly goods.

CRITICISM OF SMART CITY DEVELOPMENT AND NEGATIVE IMPACTS

The criticism of smart city development is associated with the negative effects of ICT applications (Lim et al., 2019a). Kitchin (2014) pointed out concerns associated with smart cities: (1) big data produced and used in smart cities should be examined to see whose interests they serve; (2) not all urban problems can be quantified and solved through technological solutions; (3) smart cities are highly dependent on technology developed by private companies which marketizes urban governance that eventually profits private organizations, increases the possibility of a monopoly of these corporates, and eliminates cities' uniqueness because of a 'one-size-fits-all' approach to the smart city; (4) a smart city is vulnerable when the software is down; (5) data collection in smart cities generates issues on privacy invasion and restricting the freedom of speech. These concerns can be categorized into two.

First are problems related to private corporations providing ICT solutions. The interest of private corporations may not be in line with public benefits, and can disregard the 'uniqueness' of each city. Private corporations aim to produce a profit (Zanella et al., 2014), which may come at a social cost. Also, one-size-fits-all solutions may not work in every city because some urban problems and characteristics cannot be quantified or subjected to technological solutions. Since ICT infrastructure requires massive investment, it can divert policy priority from existing problems (Grossi and Pianezzi, 2017). Unlike the argument that technology enables participation in decision-making processes, criticisms point towards automated decision-making processes based on big data and algorithms which may exclude citizens. Too much emphasis on technology can lead to a digital divide and increased inequalities (Chourabi et al., 2012). Instead of enhancing public participation and social inclusion, the digital divide and an unequal distribution of technology may increase polarization and inequality. The business-oriented tendency may lead to economic and social polarization and inequality in employment, housing and neighbourhoods (Hollands, 2008). Socially marginalized groups are easily overlooked. The pro-business, pro-educated and skilled people, and pro-advanced technology approach can enlarge the gap between haves and have-nots when the benefits of developing smart cities are not distributed equally (Wolfram, 2012).

The digital divide can be observed not only in the social and economic status of people but also in the urban fabric. Smart cities require their citizens to be smart also. This means people who cannot exploit smart services provided by smart devices (i.e. smartphones, tablets) can be excluded. This exploitation ranges from a simple act such as sending emails and searching for information on the internet via a smartphone or computer to more complicated work such as creating a smartphone application or computer program. Millennials, who were born and raised with ICT, are already used to doing these things daily. However, the older generation, especially those not used to technology, can be excluded from the decision-making process. Not only age but also socio-economic differences can create a digital divide (McAllister et al., 2005). People with technology can easily access job information and have a better chance of getting a job but people who do not may experience a longer period of unemployment. To prevent further gaps, inclusive policy intervention is needed.

The second category of problems relates to privacy invasion and freedom of speech and is related to the first problem. Because private corporations provide technology, personal data comes into private hands. ICT infrastructure gathers and uses personal data which may violate privacy (Angelidou, 2017). For example, CCTV and collection of GPS data can assist in emergency response or arrest of criminals but citizens are not free from the surveillance. Although smart cities provide a platform where people can openly disclose their political opinions, people may feel uncomfortable when it can be traced back to an individual. This may discourage freedom of speech.

Current so-called smart cities are labelled 'smart' because they have ICT infrastructure and public services using advanced digital technology (Söderström et al., 2014). These 'self-congratulatory' smart cities are problematic because technology is seen as a panacea for every urban problem and promotes one-size-fits-all solutions which neglect local characteristics (Hollands, 2008). Smart cities put too much emphasis on the technology, at the expense of human capital with knowledge (not data) able to interpret and make proper decisions for cities (Söderström et al., 2014).

EMPIRICAL EVIDENCE OF IMPACTS: EXPERIENCE OF SOUTH KOREA

South Korea has been promoting smart city development since the early 2000s. Smart cities can be categorized into a first and second wave. First-wave smart cities are Ubiquitous cities (U-cities) that focus on implementing ICT infrastructure in transportation and security surveillance sectors. According to Korea Land and Housing Corporation which is in charge of national smart city development, 42 administrative cities implemented U-city projects from 2009 to 2013. Second-wave smart cities have advanced from U-cities, acknowledging the smart city concept has evolved towards comprehensive urban management. The government promoted using the term 'smart city' instead of 'U-city'. Second-wave smart cities still emphasize ICT infrastructure, but provide more smart services including public administration, health and welfare, culture and tourism, and real-time facility management. Twelve administrative cities have been appointed as second-wave smart cities. In total, the government initiated smart city projects in 54 cities and 107 cities remain as non-smart cities.

These 54 smart cities are highly developed cities, where population numbers and densities are high. As shown in Figure 5.1, second-wave smart cities are concentrated in the upper left side, which is Seoul and the metropolitan area. Also, the figure shows an overlap between the highly populated area and smart cities. A large population number indicates the likely existence of highly educated and skilled people to facilitate smart city development in community initiatives. High density eases the implementation of ICT infrastructure. Also, these cities have financial resources which the local governments can use for the projects. These urban characteristics constitute the inherent smartness of the city (Lim et al., 2019b).

The empirical study assesses the performance of smart cities and compares them with that of non-smart cities. The performance variables account for positive and negative impacts for four dimensions of sustainability: economy, environment, social, and governance. Table 5.2 shows the specific performance variables. The data set is established 2018 to compare the before and after of smart city development. Figure 5.2 visualizes the scores in each city type in 2008 and 2018.

The results show that second-wave smart cities perform better than first-wave or non-smart cities in most variables. These advanced smart cities expanded

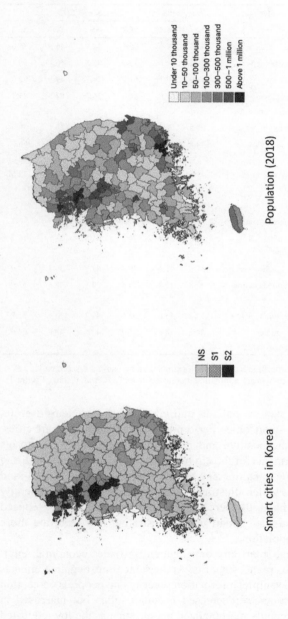

Population (2018)

Smart cities in Korea

Note: NS: Non-smart cities; S1: first-wave smart cities; S2: second-wave smart cities.

Figure 5.1   Smart cities and population in Korea

Table 5.2   Variables and score of smart city performance

Dimensions	Performance variables	Score 2008			Score 2018		
		NS	SC1	SC2	NS	SC1	SC2
Economy	GRDP per capita	44.1	45.0	60.1	44.7	46.3	56.6
	Local income tax per capita	39.2	54.8	72.8	38.5	56.1	76.1
	Number of patents	44.9	49.1	61.7	44.7	49.5	62.0
	Businesses and employment in knowledge intensive industries	37.3	64.6	84.6	36.7	64.3	85.7
Environment	Electricity consumption per capita	54.5	54.9	51.2	54.2	56.1	56.9
	CO_2 emissions in the industrial sector	44.3	58.3	63.7	44.3	63.8	66.6
	Participation in environmental protection	47.0	58.7	75.4	46.8	58.1	79.6
Social	Satisfaction in life	51.1	41.7	29.1	49.3	45.6	49.6
	Perception of economic status	52.6	47.2	47.3	39.9	58.5	75.7
	Employment rate of socially marginalized groups	58.8	39.3	20.1	61.8	33.9	16.7
	Perception of information security	47.0	41.1	30.4	57.8	30.1	14.9
Governance	Citizen participation via online participatory tools	49.3	45.7	55.5	50.1	48.3	52.9
	Number of citizen initiatives	52.2	43.0	33.6	49.7	55.8	55.2
	Perception of government's transparency and democracy	44.8	58.6	77.9	47.4	48.3	64.6

Note: The performance score is normalized from the original data by using a z-score and converted to percentile. The variables are adopted and adjusted from Lim et al. (2020), Figure 1 Smart City Impact Index.

to 'soft' infrastructures such as policies and civil initiatives (Neirotti et al., 2014). Also, first-wave smart cities performed better than non-smart cities. Table 5.3 summarizes the positive and negative impacts. Positive impacts indicate improved performance of the city while the negative impacts indicate the opposite. For example, local income tax per capita increased in first- and second-wave smart cities which illustrates that people's income has generally increased. On the other hand, the perception of information security reduced in both first- and second-wave smart cities, illustrating that there are more concerns about privacy violation.

The findings show that smart city development provides economic, environmental, social and governance benefits. At the same time, negative impacts were also observed. For example, information security and people's perception of transparency and democracy decreased in smart cities but increased in non-smart cities. Also, socially marginalized people such as the low-educated

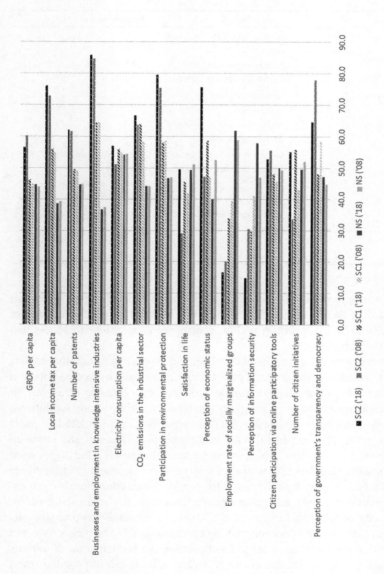

Figure 5.2   Performance scores of smart and non-smart cities

Table 5.3   Empirical evidence on positive and negative impacts of smart city development from South Korean example

Dimensions	Positive impact	Negative impact
Economy	Increase in local income tax per capita	–
	Increase in businesses in knowledge-intensive industries	
Environment	Reduction in electricity consumption	–
	Reduction in CO_2 emissions in the industrial sector	
Social	Increase in satisfaction on life	Decrease in employment of low-educated
	Increase in satisfaction on income level	Decrease in perception of information security
Governance	Increase in the number of citizen initiatives	Decrease in perception of transparency
		Decrease in perception of democracy

Source: Lim et al. (2020).

had fewer opportunities in the job market due to lack of digital education or devices. In theory, smart cities offer more information on the job market (Ménascé et al., 2017), but in reality, people need the ability to access and utilize the information.

In South Korea, the government regulates and supervises smart city projects in order to restrict the influence of private corporations and overcome potential social costs. Top-down and pre-made strategies can enhance efficiency in project implementation, but this rigidity can hinder a variety of urban solutions. Bottom-up and citizen-initiated projects may not be directly related to smart technology, but they can identify the real problems in the city and come up with innovative solutions. Public, private, academic and civil initiatives need to work together for desirable results of smart city development (Yigitcanlar et al., 2018). Not only civil society but also private firms, educational organizations, research institutes, and government agencies are important stakeholders in smart city development (Snow et al., 2016). To encourage community participation, planning and decision-making processes need to be democratic and collaborative (Snow et al., 2016). To encourage the participation of various stakeholders, smart cities can create an overarching brand to promote smart products or services developed by the stakeholders (Snow et al., 2016).

CONCLUDING REMARKS

Smart cities are expected to achieve sustainable urban development. Especially, smart cities are expected to increase economic productivity, reduce administrative costs of public services, and provide a more pleasant living environment (Caragliu et al., 2011; Neirotti et al., 2014; Zanella et al., 2014). The positive results are widely emphasized in the literature (Lim et al., 2019a); however, smart city development can divert policy priority from urgent urban problems such as poverty and unemployment (Afzalan et al., 2017; Hollands, 2015; McNeill, 2015). Cities have limited financial, human and institutional resources and smart cities can divert the resources away from where they are needed. Smart city development can be a tempting vision for leaders because it promises visible outcomes. For example, the Chinese and Indian governments strive to plan and develop smart cities but critics argue they are neglecting the urban poor, housing deficit, and high unemployment rate issues (Datta, 2015; Söderström et al., 2014). To critics, smart cities are marketing schemes of international ICT vendors (Hollands, 2008; Söderström et al., 2014). It is important to identify who benefits from what in smart city development. The fact that smart cities use technical, human, social and institutional capital can either facilitate social development or increase the digital divide and inequality.

These positive and negative impacts of smart city development have implications for developing countries. Developing countries are interested in smart cities because they want to increase efficiency in public service delivery, leading to a higher quality of life and promoting inclusive decision-making that takes into account the needs of vulnerable people (Tan and Taeihagh, 2020). For example, the Indian government planned to build 100 smart cities in 2015 (Datta, 2015). Smart cities can be perceived as both an opportunity and a threat for developing countries. For example, e-government can contribute to tackling corruption because open public information creates a transparent environment (Afzalan et al., 2017). On the other hand, the lack of financial, institutional and technological capacities are major challenges (Tan and Taeihagh, 2020; Vu and Hartley, 2018). Especially, institutional capacity is important because smart city development needs a clear and sound execution strategy (Vu and Hartley, 2018). Smart cities require vast financial and technological investments and without a clear strategy, those investments can be wasted, which would have been used for other issues like poverty, housing and unemployment (Datta, 2015; Söderström et al., 2014). Smart cities seem to be a panacea for urban problems, but the leadership needs specific goals, master and execution plans, and appropriate regulations.

South Korean smart cities can be a benchmark for developing countries. South Korea initially started smart city development with hardware (ICT infrastructure) and moved on to software (programs and governance). South Korean smart cities aim to offer a high-quality living environment by offering smart urban services. ICT infrastructure connects people, infrastructure and institutions so that they can share real-time data and information. Especially, first-wave smart cities (U-cities) implement transportation and security services that influence the everyday life of citizens and eventually affect the quality of life and citizen involvement (Lim et al., 2019b). For developing countries, improving infrastructure is a priority as well. Since implementing ICT infrastructure is not enough for a city to become a smart city, mature smart cities need collaborative governance that includes all actors. In South Korea, smart cities developed in populated and economically advanced cities. If this should be the case in developing countries, it may increase the gap between rich and poor regions. To avoid the negative impacts while maximizing the positive ones, political and civil efforts are required (Hollands, 2008; Yigitcanlar et al., 2018).

NOTES

1. The contents are based on the two published articles (Lim et al., 2019a, 2019b) and one forthcoming work (Lim et al., 2021) which are part of the author's PhD trajectory.
2. There are several private market research results about smart cities. Global Industry Analysts, Inc. predicted the global market of the smart city will be US$1.2 trillion by 2020 in their Global Smart Cities Market (MCP-7080) published in February 2016 (http://www.strategyr.com/MarketResearch/Smart_Cities_Market_Trends .asp). Also, Technavio estimated the CAGR (Compound Annual Growth Rate) will be about 20 per cent by 2020 in their Global Smart Cities Market 2016–2020 report published in September 2016 (https://www.technavio.com/report/global -machine-machine-m2m-and-connected-devices-global-smart-city-market-2016 -2020). Another report from Frost & Sullivan estimated its market to be US$1.565 trillion by 2020 in November 2014 (https://ww2.frost.com/news/press-releases/ frost-sullivan-global-smart-cities-market-reach-us156-trillion-2020).

REFERENCES

Afzalan, N., Sanchez, T. W. and Evans-Cowley, J. 2017. Creating smarter cities: Considerations for selecting online participatory tools. *Cities* 67, 21–30.
Angelidou, M. 2017. Shortcomings to smart city planning and development: Exploring patterns and relationships. *TeMA (Online)* 10, 77–93.
Baron, M. 2012. Do we need smart cities for resilience? *Journal of Economics and Management* 10, 32–46.
Batty, M., Axhausen, K. W., Giannotti, F., Pozdnoukhov, A., Bazzani, A., Wachowicz, M., Ouzounis, G. and Portugali, Y. 2012. Smart cities of the future. *European Physical Journal Special Topics* 214, 481–518.

Caragliu, A. and Del Bo, C. F. 2019. Smart innovative cities: The impact of smart city policies on urban innovation. *Technological Forecasting and Social Change* 142(C), 373–383.

Caragliu, A., Del Bo, C. and Nijkamp, P. 2011. Smart cities in Europe. *Journal of Urban Technology* 18, 65–82.

Chourabi, H., Nam, T., Walker, S., Gil-Garcia, J. R., Mellouli, S., Nahon, K., ... Scholl, H. J. 2012. Understanding smart cities: An integrative framework. In *2012 45th Hawaii International Conference on System Sciences*. IEEE, 2289–2297. https://scienzepolitiche.unical.it/bacheca/archivio/materiale/949/urbana,%202016 -17/smart/S.pdf.

Cocchia, A. 2014. Smart and digital city: A systematic literature review. In R. P. Dameri and C. Rosenthal-Sabroux (eds.), *Smart City*. Cham: Springer, 13–43.

Datta, A. 2015. A 100 smart cities, a 100 utopias. *Dialogues in Human Geography* 5, 49–53.

De Wijs, L., Witte, P. and Geertman, S. 2016. How smart is smart? Theoretical and empirical considerations on implementing smart city objectives: A case study of Dutch railway station areas. *Innovation: The European Journal of Social Science Research* 29, 424–441.

Debnath, A. K., Chin, H. C., Haque, M. M. and Yuen, B. 2014. A methodological framework for benchmarking smart transport cities. *Cities* 37, 47–56.

Dempsey, N., Bramley, G., Power, S. and Brown, C. 2011. The social dimension of sustainable development: Defining urban social sustainability. *Sustainable Development* 19, 289–300.

Dirks, S. and Keeling, M. 2009. *A Vision of Smarter Cities: How Cities Can Lead the Way into a Prosperous and Sustainable Future*. New York: IBM Institute for Business Value.

Errichiello, L. and Marasco, A. 2014. Open service innovation in smart cities: A framework for exploring innovation networks in the development of new city services. *Advanced Engineering Forum* 11, 115–124.

Giffinger, R., Fertner, C., Kramar, H., Kalasek, R., Pichler-Milanovic, N. N. and Meijers, E. 2007. *Smart Cities: Ranking of European Medium-Sized Cities*. Final Report, Centre of Regional Science, Vienna University of Technology.

Gil-Garcia, J. R., Zhang, J. and Puron-Cid, G. 2016. Conceptualizing smartness in government: An integrative and multi-dimensional view. *Government Information Quarterly* 33, 524–534.

Grossi, G. and Pianezzi, D. 2017. Smart cities: Utopia or neoliberal ideology? *Cities* 69, 79–85.

Hagerty, M. R., Cummins, R., Ferriss, A. L., Land, K., Michalos, A. C., Peterson, M., Sharpe, A., Sirgy, J. and Vogel, J. 2001. Quality of life indexes for national policy: Review and agenda for research. *Bulletin of Sociological Methodology* 71, 58–78.

Hall, B. 2011. Innovation and productivity. NBER Working Paper, No. 17178. Cambridge, MA: National Bureau of Economic Research.

Hall, R. E., Bowerman, B., Braverman, J., Taylor, J., Todosow, H. and Von Wimmersperg, U. 2000. The vision of a smart city. Presentation at the 2nd International Life Extension Technology Workshop Paris, France, September.

Harrison, C. and Donnelly, I. A. 2011. A theory of smart cities. Presentation at the 55th Annual Meeting of the ISSS-2011, Hull, UK.

Hollands, R. G. 2008. Will the real smart city please stand up? Intelligent, progressive or entrepreneurial? *City* 12, 303–320.

Hollands, R. G. 2015. Critical interventions into the corporate smart city. *Cambridge Journal of Regions, Economy and Society* 8, 61–77.

Kitchin, R. 2014. The real-time city? Big data and smart urbanism. *GeoJournal* 79, 1–14.

Komninos, N., Pallot, M. and Schaffers, H. 2013. Special issue on smart cities and the future internet in Europe. *Journal of the Knowledge Economy* 4, 119–134.

Kraus, S., Richter, C., Papagiannidis, S. and Durst, S. 2015. Innovating and exploiting entrepreneurial opportunities in smart cities: Evidence from Germany. *Creativity and Innovation Management* 24, 601–616.

Lee, J. and Lee, H. 2014. Developing and validating a citizen-centric typology for smart city services. *Government Information Quarterly* 31, S93–S105.

Lim, Y., Edelenbos, J. and Gianoli, A. 2019a. Identifying the results of smart city development: Findings from systematic literature review. *Cities* 95, 102397. https://doi.org/10.1016/j.cities.2019.102397.

Lim, Y., Edelenbos, J. and Gianoli, A. 2019b. Smart energy transition: An evaluation of cities in South Korea. *Informatics* 6, 50. https://doi.org/10.3390/informatics6040050.

Lim, Y., Edelenbos, J. and Gianoli, A. 2021. What is the impact of smart city development? Empirical evidence from the Smart City Impact Index. Forthcoming.

Lopes, N. V. 2017. Smart governance: A key factor for smart cities implementation. In *2017 IEEE International Conference on Smart Grid and Smart Cities*, ICSGSC 2017, 277–282.

Mandarano, L., Meenar, M. and Steins, C. 2010. Building social capital in the digital age of civic engagement. *Journal of Planning Literature* 25, 123–135.

McAllister, L., Hall, H., Partridge, H. and Hallam, G. 2005. Effecting social change in the "smart city": The West End Connect Community Project. In C. Bailey and K. Barnett (eds.), *Social Change Research in the 21st Century*. Brisbane: Queensland University of Technology, 1–16.

McNeill, D. 2015. Global firms and smart technologies: IBM and the reduction of cities. *Transactions of the Institute of British Geographers* 40, 562–574.

Ménascé, D., Vincent, C.-E. and Moreau, M. M. 2017. Smart cities and new forms of employment. *Field Actions Science Reports* 2017, 16–21.

Nam, T. and Pardo, T. A. 2011. Conceptualizing smart city with dimensions of technology, people, and institutions. In *Proceedings of the 12th Annual International Digital Government Research Conference: Digital Government Innovation in Challenging Times*. ACM, 282–291.

Nam, T. and Pardo, T. A. 2014. The changing face of a city government: A case study of Philly311. *Government Information Quarterly* 31, S1–S9.

Neirotti, P., De Marco, A., Cagliano, A. C., Mangano, G. and Scorrano, F. 2014. Current trends in smart city initiatives: Some stylised facts. *Cities* 38, 25–36.

Ojasalo, J. and Kauppinen, H. 2016. Collaborative innovation with external actors: An empirical study on open innovation platforms in smart cities. *Technology Innovation Management Review* 6, 49–60.

Plessis, H. du and Marnewick, A. L. 2017. A roadmap for smart city services to address challenges faced by small businesses in South Africa. *South African Journal of Economic and Management Sciences* 20. https://doi.org/10.4102/sajems.v20i1.1631.

Pokric, B., Krco, S. and Pokric, M. 2014. Augmented reality based smart city services using secure IoT infrastructure. In *Advanced Information Networking and Applications Workshops (WAINA), 28th International Conference on Advanced Information Networking and Applications*. IEEE, 803–808.

Richter, C., Kraus, S. and Syrjä, P. 2015. The smart city as an opportunity for entrepreneurship. *International Journal of Entrepreneurial Venturing* 7, 211–226.

Sajhau, P. 2017. IBM: Building sustainable cities through partnerships and integrated approaches. *Field Actions Science Reports* 16, 52–57.

Sarma, S. and Sunny, S. A. 2017. Civic entrepreneurial ecosystems: Smart city emergence in Kansas City. *Business Horizons* 60, 843–853.

Schuurman, D., Baccarne, B., De Marez, L. and Mechant, P. 2012. Smart ideas for smart cities: Investigating crowdsourcing for generating and selecting ideas for ICT innovation in a city context. *Journal of Theoretical and Applied Electronic Commerce Research* 7, 49–62.

Snow, C. C., Hakonsson, D. D. and Obel, B. 2016. A smart city is a collaborative community: Lessons from smart Aarhus. *California Management Review* 59, 92–108.

Söderström, O., Paasche, T. and Klauser, F. 2014. Smart cities as corporate storytelling. *City* 18, 307–320.

Stratigea, A. 2012. The concept of 'smart cities': Towards community development? *Netcom: Réseaux, communication et territoires.* https://journals.openedition.org/netcom/1105.

Tan, S. Y. and Taeihagh, A. 2020. Smart city governance in developing countries: A systematic literature review. *Sustainability* 12, 899. https://doi.org/10.3390/su12030899.

Toppeta, D. 2010. The smart city vision: How innovation and ICT can build smart, "livable", sustainable cities. The Innovation Knowledge Foundation. http://www.thinkinnovation.org/file/research/23/en/Toppeta_Report_005_2010.pdf.

Tranos, E. and Gertner, D. 2012. Smart networked cities? *Innovation: The European Journal of Social Science Research* 25, 175–190.

Trindade, E. P., Hinnig, M. P. F., da Costa, E. M., Marques, J. S., Bastos, R. C. and Yigitcanlar, T. 2017. Sustainable development of smart cities: A systematic review of the literature. *Journal of Open Innovation: Technology, Market, and Complexity* 3, 11.

Van den Buuse, D. and Kolk, A. 2019. An exploration of smart city approaches by international ICT firms. *Technological Forecasting and Social Change* 142, 220–234.

Vu, K. and Hartley, K. 2018. Promoting smart cities in developing countries: Policy insights from Vietnam. *Telecommunications Policy* 42, 845–859.

Walravens, N., Breuer, J. and Ballon, P. 2014. Open data as a catalyst for the smart city as a local innovation platform. *Communications & Strategies*, Special Issue: Smart Cities, 15–33.

Washburn, D., Sindhu, U., Balaouras, S., Dines, R.A., Hayes, N. and Nelson, L. E. 2009. Helping CIOs understand "smart city" initiatives. *Growth* 17, 1–17.

Welde, M. 2012. Are smart card ticketing systems profitable? Evidence from the city of Trondheim. *Journal of Public Transportation* 15, 133–148.

White, J. M. 2016. Anticipatory logics of the smart city's global imaginary. *Urban Geography* 37, 572–589.

Wiig, A. 2015. IBM's smart city as techno-utopian policy mobility. *City* 19, 258–273.

Wolfram, M. 2012. Deconstructing smart cities: An intertextual reading of concepts and practices for integrated urban and ICT development. https://pdfs.semanticscholar.org/3053/7dcc1a785e968caf1660d8a3932a1c5c868d.pdf.

Yigitcanlar, T. 2015. Smart cities: An effective urban development and management model? *Australian Planner* 52, 27–34.

Yigitcanlar, T. and Han, J. H. 2009. Managing ubiquitous eco cities: Telecommunication infrastructure networks, technology convergence and intelligent urban management systems. Unpublished paper.

Yigitcanlar, T., Kamruzzaman, M., Buys, L., Ioppolo, G., Sabatini-Marques, J., da Costa, E. M. and Yun, J. J. 2018. Understanding 'smart cities': Intertwining development drivers with desired outcomes in a multidimensional framework. *Cities* 81, 145–160.

Zanella, A., Bui, N., Castellani, A., Vangelista, L. and Zorzi, M. 2014. Internet of things for smart cities. *IEEE Internet of Things Journal* 1, 22–32.

Zygiaris, S. 2013. Smart city reference model: Assisting planners to conceptualize the building of smart city innovation ecosystems. *Journal of the Knowledge Economy* 4, 217–231.

6. How sustainable, green and smart eco-cities deal with water issues

Meine Pieter van Dijk

INTRODUCTION

Water is one of the key issues in urban management. Because of climate change, cities can expect more or less rain, higher sea levels and more runoff in the major rivers. The traditional Integrated Water Resources Management (IWRM) approach tends to be replaced by more Adaptive Water Management techniques (Van Dijk and Blokland, 2016). The latter approach aims to adapt water management to climate change, which requires mobilizing stakeholders in a governance structure and using modern technological options and information technology. The problem is how to link the adaptive governance structures to existing urban management and governance structures in a systematic way.

Climate change challenges cities. Cities can expect heat waves (Zhang et al., 2019a), less rain or more rain, and certainly more volatility (IPCC, 2018). Hence it is necessary to pay more attention to managing water in cities, which may suffer from flooding (Jakarta), or droughts (Johannesburg) or both (Beijing). We will separate the issue of providing drinking water from the challenge of dealing with surface water.

The main question of this chapter is: Which approaches and interventions contribute to the ability of water management to adapt to climate change and which lessons can be drawn from successful examples of urban water management that can inform other rapidly urbanizing cities in emerging economies to achieve sustainable urban development? The study finds that many interventions used under the different approaches are similar, while governance structures used in the case of sustainable, green and smart eco-cities tend to be different.

APPROACHES TO DEAL WITH URBAN WATER ISSUES

An approach implies an underlying analysis of the issue at stake and coherent ideas about the solution. The urban planning, urban management and urban governance paradigms were distinguished in Chapter 1 and different approaches and concepts were mentioned, such as the green and the smart city concepts.

Here we focus on the green, sustainable and eco-cities concepts, in combination with the smart cities concept. Combining the latter with the eco-cities concept results in the smart eco-cities concept as the third concept to be analysed. For each approach we analyse the technical interventions and their governance structure. For governance we specifically assess the stakeholders working with local and national governments in the decision process and in particular the private sector.

In the case of water related issues in urban areas, adaptive water management usually implies improved water management and assuring the supplying of clean drinking water, proper sanitation services and water for commercial use. A common strategy is to store water to prevent floods and to use the surplus in times of water shortages. In the green cities and eco-cities concept the landscape and the waterscape are also considered to be important. Different urban projects focus on achieving zero carbon emissions and several cities have as an objective CO_2 emissions reduction, which would also have consequences for wastewater treatment, which usually produces a lot of CO_2. Smith Morris (2011) shows how in the 'New urbanism' in England, CO_2 reduction played an important role.

The green cities concept has been promoted by the Asian Development Bank (ADB). It intends to make cities greener, more environmentally friendly and liveable. It also gives attention to water management.

The United Nations' Habitat programme and others have pushed the sustainable cities approach (UN Habitat, 2018). The Sustainable Cities Programme (SCP) is a joint UN-HABITAT/United Nations Environment Programme (UNEP) capacity-building and institutional strengthening facility, with the goal of ensuring environmentally sustainable local development and to fully realize the vital contributions that urban areas make to overall social and economic development. The SCP promotes good environmental governance at all levels to support local and national partners to adopt environmental planning management processes and integrate good practice into national policy and legal frameworks. However, sustainability has many aspects – such as the environment, economic and financial sustainability, and social and institutional sustainability – and does not just concentrate on water management issues.

Cities are under pressure to become more competitive and more ecological. The eco[2] cities concept (Suzuki et al., 2010) combines the two approaches. It helps cities with two ambitions: to achieve greater ecological and economic sustainability. Our research originally focused on eco-city dimensions only (Van Dijk, 2011), but this chapter combines this approach with the desire to be a smart city. The eco-city concept only later broadened its meaning by including water management. It promotes using environmental technologies for water and energy management to make the eco-city's life support systems become closed loop systems.

Smart eco-cities (Van Dijk, 2018) are about managing flows of information in an integrated way. The information may concern traffic, people, pollution, products, services and the water flowing in and out of the city. Developing smart eco-cities starts with defining what a city wants to achieve. Smart eco-cities aim to innovate water related services to improve water quality, water quantity management and water governance, by using artificial intelligence to analyse data from sensors in a computer network and using information provided by the population.

Cities have introduced policies and programmes to deal with issues like climate change, congestion and pollution. In this chapter an overview will be given of the interventions that have been made in the green, the sustainable and the smart eco-cities approach, such as: closing the water cycle (suggested by the Switch city of the future project; Butterworth et al., 2011); reducing greenhouse gas emissions; waste minimization and integrated waste management; and developing integrated infrastructure and transport policies. Other ways of using urban water differently are heat exchange systems using underground water, rainwater harvesting systems and the separation of grey and brown water. Cities are improving the runoff of water and the capacity to store the rain or sewer water temporarily, for example through water absorption beds, natural and/or concrete reservoirs. Alternatively infiltration-by-design helps to recharge urban aquifers and mitigate floods. Cities may choose between promoting cisterns, rooftop gardens, retention ponds and permeable pavements to reduce runoff.

Adaptive water management also looks at different infrastructural options and different modes of transportation, some of which are more sustainable than others. The choice between different options is often conditioned by history, culture and climate. Water for transportation is often at the losing end, but some cities encourage sustainable transportation by introducing shared means of transportation, and encouraging alternative forms of transportation including the use of existing rivers and canals. The chapter will limit itself to assessing to what extent the approaches and interventions provide an integrated solution to urban water challenges, given the increased complexity of urban challenges due to for example climate change.

THREE DIFFERENT APPROACHES BUT SIMILAR URBAN INTERVENTIONS

For water management the relevant approaches mentioned in Chapter 1 are sustainable cities (UN Habitat, 2018), green cities (Lindfield and Steinberg, 2012) and the smart city concept (Hajer and Dassen, 2014). We include the last category under the smart eco-city concept, whereby we define smart as making use of information technology to build a smart city. Criteria used for the Smart Cities Awards that are given each year are: dealing differently with mobility, IT infrastructure, water management, renewable energy (solar or wind), waste reduction and reuse, safety, cultural development, globalization and governance. Smart cities emphasize the importance of innovations, such as the digital town hall and using IT for other purposes. There are three types of smart city definitions (Van Dijk, 2018):

- Emphasizing the technology, the *use of the internet of things* for all kinds of problems.
- Stressing *transition and adaptation* to rapid changes, by pooling knowledge, sharing best practices and considering different initiatives to tackle challenges faced (innovative planning).
- Pointing to different ways of managing cities, focusing on *managing the flows* and using ICT and geographical information systems to do that in an integrated way.

These three approaches are compared in Table 6.1, by providing the definition, the objectives, the role of different stakeholders, the environmental ambitions, and the solutions proposed.

Other researchers have emphasized the importance of other concepts for urban water issues, such as the resilient city concept (OECD, 2018), the pure eco-cities concept (Bhatnagar, 2010), and in the Chinese case the sponge city concept (Li et al., 2017). In the sponge city concept the idea is to involve the private sector, although this has not happened much in Chinese cities (Liang et al., 2020). Other approaches not discussed in this chapter are promoting the circular economy (Yong et al., 2009), or creating clean, healthy and/or vibrant (in economic terms) cities. These are concepts that do not necessarily focus on water or water related issues, but may still be relevant to deal with other urban issues.

Table 6.2 summarizes solutions and interventions that are being used. The subsequent sections will relate these to the three approaches.

Table 6.1   *Different approaches to urban water management*

Question	Green cities	Sustainable cities	Smart eco-cities
What is the definition?	Making cities greener, more environmentally friendly and liveable	Cities going for sustainability and good quality of life	Eco-cities focus on the social and living environment
What are the objectives to be achieved?	Achieving more environmentally friendly cities	Building sustainable and liveable cities	Building an eco-city in which it is pleasant to live
What is the role of different stakeholders?	Focus on the role of the private sector	City planners play an important role	Motivated individuals
Environmental ambition?	Looks at people, profit and planet	Different types of sustainability concepts	More green, less polluted, and integrated
Possible solution?	Concept is pushing the green economy approach	Balance economic and environmental sustainability	A different type of planning is suggested and water landscaping
Relevant references	Lindfield and Steinberg (2012) for the ADB	UN Habitat (2018); UNDP (2014)	Bhatnagar (2010); Wong and Yuen (2011)

Table 6.2   *Solutions and interventions for different urban water issues and examples*

Possible solutions	Interventions	Examples
Promoting attitudinal changes	Provide information about climate change adaptation	Van Dijk and Hao Li (2015)
A different type of planning is suggested	Involving stakeholders and issue oriented	Wong and Yuen (2011)
Closing the water cycle	Linking drinking water and surface water management	Singapore, in Butterworth et al. (2011)
Dealing with flooding and increasing water storage	Providing adequate infrastructure and sensors	Rotterdam (2016)
Improving the quality of water (details in Table 6.3)	Options: wetlands use, separating grey water, etc.	Butterworth et al. (2011)
Improved drainage, infiltration and slower runoffs (Table 6.4)	More drains, infiltration places and using vegetation	Liang et al. (2020)
Water and energy nexus	Alternative wastewater treatment	Liang and Van Dijk (2009)
Partnerships with the private sector	For management, technology or financial reasons	Van Dijk (2016)
Policies, subsidies and incentives	Providing selected policy support	Yong et al. (2009)

After summarizing the methodological approach the possible solutions will be explained in more detail.

METHODOLOGICAL APPROACH

This chapter is a literature review of three approaches and interventions which are currently being pushed. The interventions especially consider technologies and governance models. Examples will be used from Europe and Asia. The approaches will be compared at the conceptual level and the level of the activity, so as to indicate the strong and weak points of the interventions.

The different approaches for urban water management are listed in Table 6.1 and interventions to solve the issues in Table 6.2. The research questions are: What do the three approaches look like? Which interventions have been undertaken by the government or different actors and what can we learn from them? Using case studies from Chinese, Southeast Asian and European cities, the study will ask for each intervention:

1. What is the issue to be addressed?
2. What has been done so far?
3. What is the governance structure?
4. Is the intervention a success?
5. Is there a good source of information on the experience with this intervention?

The initiatives can be taken at the national, regional, city, district neighbourhood, building and household level and this implies the importance of multilevel governance structures. There are ecological buildings, ecological villas, blocks of houses, or apartment buildings with common heating/cooling systems or a grey water reuse facility. We want to study the importance of urban management, governance structures and policies to develop these interventions at these different geographical levels.

INTERVENTIONS IN URBAN WATER MANAGEMENT

Promoting Attitudinal Changes: Climate Change Adaptation, Working on Resilience

What is the issue to be addressed? De Jong (2016) defines urban resilience as "The ability to learn, plan, and recover from the hazards to which [cities] are exposed". We can add to the complexity of urban resilience by including the notion of sustainability. Resilience is the measure of the ability of an ecosystem to absorb changes, persist, and return to its equilibrium after a temporary disturbance. A vulnerability index measures the lack of resilience (Zhang et al., 2019b). This vulnerability assessment, which addresses climatic threats, provides a holistic understanding of the susceptibility to climate change that could facilitate adaptation to climate change in the future.

What has been done? In the case of the Rotterdam Climate Initiative (2017), cities have incorporated disaster resilience preparation activities in their urban plans. Often these cities invest in disaster-resilient infrastructure and work on disaster preparedness. The emphasis is on building infrastructure, sometimes at the expense of organizing a governance structure. The governance dimensions also include policies, laws and regulations in support of disaster risk mitigation and climate change adaptation. Part of good governance is promoting awareness-raising and providing training and education on these issues.

What is the governance structure for achieving attitudinal changes? Given citizens are the first stakeholders suffering from disasters, awareness-raising, training and providing basic education on these issues is crucial. The potential victims have to be involved before flooding or drought starts. At the citizens' level, developing capacities and building networks complements the government's efforts to improve infrastructure. Governance structures of multiple stakeholders enable collaboration in transforming cities into disaster-resilient cities, which are prepared for the consequences of climate change. Resilience also depends on the city's ability to coordinate governance structures following a disaster. In the Resilient City programme launched by the Rockefeller Foundation (2015) indicators are used to assess the ability to learn, plan, and recover from the hazards to which these cities are exposed.

What are the adaptation mechanisms in the urban areas and to what extent do urban actors pursue these strategies successfully? The example of Singapore is striking. In Singapore the government deals with the water cycle process in an integrated way, whereby the costs and charges are integrated in one bill for the customers. The water utility in Singapore has functioned well for a long time, although it was only a municipal department, not even corporatized to separate its finance from the regular municipal finance. However, the authorities did not interfere. Singapore's adaptive water management aims to close the urban water cycle. In Singapore no water gets lost between the resource, the use for drinking water and the treatment and reuse of wastewater. This is the work of NEWater company. The city uses a desalination plant using reverse osmosis technology for the process of transforming sea water into drinking water, if additional water is necessary in the closed urban water cycle. Getting the population to accept this new approach, which provided independence from other suppliers of water, required an attitudinal change, which required high profile political support.

A Different Type of Planning

What is the issue to be addressed? Adaptive water management requires preparedness for disasters. Different types of planning can be discussed for each of the different approaches. However, the case of the eco-city concept is illustrative. In that approach it has been suggested that it is necessary to develop: "an ecological approach to urban design, management and towards a new lifestyle" (Wong and Yuen, 2011: 3). The focus should be on the urban metabolism or a different way of dealing with the cycles of energy, water, waste and pollution.

Adaptive water management deals with waste in a different way, for example because waste can block drains, or because waste causes health hazards (Isunju et al., 2011). Hence, solid waste minimization and integrated waste management are important (Oduro-Kwarteng and Van Dijk, 2017).

What has been done? Wong and Yuen (2011) emphasize in their book on eco-city planning the importance of urban management by highlighting the urgency of planning of eco-cities, taking into account the need to deal with water issues and the possible use of water for water scaping (defined as landscapes that incorporate water). They reframe the challenge as making water part of the landscape. Beautiful examples can be found in cities like Nanjing and Shanghai.

What is the governance structure? Planning in many countries is a government-initiated process. The challenge is to involve other stakeholders. Wong and Yuen (2011) mention several successful examples and their book is a good source of information on eco-city planning.

Dealing with Flooding

What is the issue to be addressed? Many cities face flooding during the rainy season. This problem is often aggravated due to climate change. Governments may not have the funds and private sector involvement may be possible. Van Dijk (2016) analyses plans to build a dyke around Jakarta to protect the city from flooding, using mainly private sector stakeholders.

What has been done? Cities are improving the runoff of water, using infiltration and water collection systems. It is also possible to utilize ground-water refill. There are several examples of infiltration-by-design (in Beijing; Butterworth et al., 2011). This helps to recharge urban aquifers, mitigate floods, and let city surfaces breathe. As a European example of a resilient city, Rotterdam in the Netherlands has drawn attention, through its investments in infrastructure after being partially flooded in the 1950s. It has built a sluice to protect it from sea level rise and created polders for temporarily storing drinking water upstream in case there is too much water coming from the river, or if it became too polluted for human consumption. The capacity to store rainwater temporarily has been extended also in many other cities in Europe.

What is the governance structure and success? Rotterdam stipulated that the local water board and water utility would work together. The governance structure comprises public–public cooperation between the original water board for the area, the drinking water company and the municipal council. Internationally Rotterdam is one of the first members of the Rockefeller Foundation's 100 Resilient Cities Initiative (RCI). Rotterdam's climate initiative combines climate change mitigation and adaptation. This has made Rotterdam one of the leading cities addressing climate change and building a resilient city (Rotterdam, 2016). The city is working on climate change mitigation and adaptation strategies by constantly learning from the latest scientific knowledge and practical experiences. The integrated approach of RCI helped the stakeholders to jointly build the integrated long-term vision of Rotterdam as a Climate Proof City by 2025. Supportive of this and an elaboration of this vision is the Resilience Strategy which Rotterdam released in 2016 (Rotterdam Climate Initiative, 2017). The Resilience Strategy underscored seven goals geared towards a holistic vision in achieving a resilient city (see also OECD, 2018).

Improving the Water Quality

What is the issue to be addressed? The quality of drinking and surface water is sometimes a problem. In the case of closing the water cycle, residues of drugs and all kinds of chemicals may end up in the water and make it unfit for human consumption or use.

What has been done? Table 6.3 presents different ways to improve the quality of surface water in cities, emphasizing the use of new technologies and providing references for further details.

What is the governance structure and the success? Tianjin in the north of China was faced with the problem of a polluted river. Achieving eco-city status required a major cleaning up initiative. The flagship eco-city project of Tianjin is now located 45 km from the city and is developed in cooperation with Singapore and partially financed under the Global Environmental Facility (GEF). Dunn and Jamieson (2011) evaluated it in terms of the relation between eco-city development and sustainable tourism. The objective of the project is to develop an economically sustainable, socially harmonious, environmentally friendly and resource conserving city. Total investment is expected to reach 30 billion Yuan, while China and Singapore each control half of this investment. It is largely located on unusable land, which makes the investment less sensitive to outside critique.

Table 6.3   Different ways to improve the quality of surface water

Technological options to improve the quality of surface water	Technology used	Relevant reference
Traditional wastewater treatment	Large scale centralized or smaller scale decentralized units	Liang and Van Dijk (2009)
Natural wastewater treatment, for example using a wetland	Natural processes	Butterworth et al. (2011)
Separating brown and grey water, in the house, but also in the neighbourhood	Reserving one pipe in the house or road for that purpose, next to a drinking water, a sewer (the black water) and a drainage pipe	Liang and Van Dijk (2012)
Allowing wastewater reuse for urban agriculture	Providing a light treatment	Butterworth et al. (2011)

The story of the Sino-Singapore Tianjin eco-city is well documented (UNDP, 2014). A joint working committee was established to study the major challenges in achieving a harmonious and environmentally friendly city. An eco-city management committee has been set up by the Tianjin municipal government. Tianjin has learned from experimental economic reforms and resulting business growth in the Binhai new area, the coastal area of Tianjin. From the landscape point of view the use of surface water in the design of the city is beautiful. There are canals and lakes, which fit into the road plan. Also its location near the sea makes it an attractive waterscape. However, the beautiful eco-city at 45 km from Tianjin is far from the polluting port city of Tianjin, where more action should have been taken to assure a different approach to urban water management and the supply of good quality water.

Drainage, Infiltration and Slower Runoffs

What is the issue to be addressed? Volatile rains cause peaks in runoff water. Floods mean there is not enough water absorption capacity, no way to store the water temporarily, or there is not enough capacity for letting the water infiltrate the soil. It is necessary to promote slower runoffs and new ways of storing water temporarily.

What has been done? The Chinese authorities have developed the 'sponge city' concept, to slow, spread, sink, and store runoff. A definition provided by a consultancy firm assisting the city of Wuhan to deal with water is: a sponge city is the collective denominator for a number of smart solutions to capture the water in other parts of the city to prevent flooding of the low lying parts of the city (reported in *Nieuwe Rotterdamse Courant*, 9 January 2019). Cities in

Table 6.4   Water related activities in Zhuanghe sponge city, summer 2018

Improvement	Technology used
Innovative water drainage	Separate drains for wastewater and surface runoff water
Building an underground reservoir	Levelling off peaks in the supply of wastewater and surface runoff water
Innovative water penetration	Reduce surface runoff water and refill aquifer
Permeable concrete, asphalt parking places using plastic to reinforce the soil	Promote aquifer refill and reduce runoff water
Planting grass around houses and building roof gardens	Technology for water supply and drainage
Collecting rainwater	Rainwater harvesting technologies (Liang and Van Dijk, 2011)

the programme are improving the runoff of water and the capacity to store the rainwater temporarily. The activities listed in Table 6.4 were carried out in the framework of the project in Zhuanghe (near Harbin), which we studied as an example of the sponge city approach.

Many cities are improving the runoff of water and the capacity to store rainwater temporarily. Zhuanghe and Tianjin city have created water absorption beds. Infiltration-by-design helped to recharge the aquifer in Beijing, while also mitigating flooding. Other cities choose between cisterns, rooftop gardens, retention ponds and permeable pavements to reduce half to nearly all runoff. The efforts were studied in the Switch project and can be called Water-Sensitive Urban Design (WSUD in Australia), Low-Impact Development (LID in North America) or Sustainable Urban Drainage Systems (SUDS in Europe; Butterworth et al., 2011).

Water and Energy Nexus

What is the issue to be addressed? Water contains energy, if only in terms of the nutrients available in it. The water–energy nexus considers wastewater as an asset, because of its potential to generate energy in a wastewater treatment plant in the form of heat or biogas.

What has been done? Very little has been done to recover the energy to date, despite the opportunity to use the energy contained in (waste) water. Available technologies range from producing biogas during wastewater treatment to using the heat produced in the process for heating or cooling buildings.

What is the governance structure? Liang and Van Dijk (2009, 2012) give examples of decentralized and centralized wastewater reuse systems. The latter article puts it in the context of creating eco communities in Beijing. They conclude that it is important to achieve integration of disparate initiatives in a framework of urban management.

Partnerships with the Private Sector

What is the issue to be addressed? The government is often unable to conduct all activities itself and instead partners with private sector initiatives. This often takes the form of a public–private partnership (PPP), whereby use is made of the complementary skills of the public sector and the private stakeholders.

What has been done? Harnaschpolder in the Netherlands is an urban waste-water plant financed and built by the private sector, which brings in private finance and the latest technologies.

What is the governance structure and the success? The Water Board is a public partner in the project but the technology, investments, operation and maintenance have all been outsourced to private parties in the consortium. The formula chosen is a Design, Build, Finance and Operate (DBFO) model, where the private sector designs, builds, finances and operates the facility for a period of 30 years, while the cities concerned have signed off-take contracts with the private party for the output produced.

Urban Water Policies: Incentives and Subsidies, or Taxes as Disincentives

What is the issue to be addressed? Besides producing the right quantity and quality of water, water in cities may help cooling buildings in the summer and heating buildings in the winter. Malpractices such as the overuse of water require discouragements through taxes or other disincentives, while other policies provide incentives for appropriate behaviour, or subsidies for the necessary investments.

What has been done? It is important to distinguish different types of policies to achieve green, sustainable, or smart eco-cities: general policies, subsidies, planning requirements and demand management policies, energy related and other activities. Examples are:

- General policies at the national level to promote water conservation or avoid flooding. Policies at the city level to improve urban drainage and water storage.
- Subsidies at the national level to raise awareness for the issues, subsidies for adapting buildings (separating grey and brown water for example) and at the city level subsidies can be given for decentralized treatment of grey water.

Table 6.5   *Main emphasis concerning governance in the different concepts discussed*

Criteria	Sustainable cities	Green cities	Smart eco-cities
Role of government	Coordinating	Initiating	Facilitating, creating the conditions
Multi-layer governance?	Multiple levels of government	Multiple involvement of stakeholders	Multiple layers of governance
Achieve coordination	By developing an overall strategy	The initiatives tend to be less coordinated	Using information technology

- Planning requirements at the national level can promote closing the water cycle. Not providing building permits for lower lying areas of the city is an important policy measure for cities at risk of flooding.
- Demand management policies at the national level may target water and energy and at the local level the authorities can help to make available the necessary devices.

What is the governance structure and the success? The aim is to close the energy and water cycles so that nothing gets lost. In the smart eco-city of the future the attention will require managing the flows smartly, taking the interactions into account. Smart ecological cities require integration of sectors, such as water and energy, water and urban agriculture and water consumption by industries or households.

GOVERNANCE OF SUSTAINABLE, GREEN AND SMART ECO-CITIES

As far as the governance of the three discussed concepts (sustainable, green and smart eco-cities) is concerned the priorities concerning water related activities are known but the concepts remain relatively vague on how they should be governed.

We nevertheless find some differences in governance between the three approaches. The findings are summarized in Table 6.5, showing how governance is taking shape in the different concepts, which in practice leads to similar water related interventions.

The sustainable city concept mainly pays attention to the involvement of government structures at the city and local levels. It emphasizes environmental planning and capacity building of national and local governments and as such fits best in the urban planning paradigm. The green city concept also emphasizes planning, but not just environmental planning as in the case of the sustainable cities concept. The emphasis is also on involving the private sector as a stakeholder and as such it fits well in the urban management paradigm (Wong and Yuen, 2011).

Only the smart eco-cities concept pays more attention to involving all stakeholders and their organizations through newly created governance structures at different levels. In summary the smart eco-city concept emphasizes the involvement of all stakeholders, while in the green and sustainable cities concepts the initiative is often expected to be taken by the national and local government, eventually with the private sector. Hence the smart eco-cities concept fits best in the urban governance paradigm, where resources of different stakeholders are being combined.

CONCLUSIONS

This chapter has reviewed how changes in water management enable cities to deal with climate change. The challenge is to achieve better coordination of different actors and activities to deal with water. The approach chosen to deal with a particular urban water issue largely depends on the challenges faced and the objectives a city wants to achieve. In that light, we discussed three approaches, which have somewhat different objectives and integrate interventions in different ways. If the emphasis is on the environment, then sustainable cities may be the right approach. If the emphasis is on the use of IT, a smart eco-city approach may be more appropriate. The different approaches deal differently with water management issues and only the sustainable city paradigm follows the classical integrated water resources management approach. The green and smart eco-city concepts are more in favour of an adaptive water management approach, which means trying to focus on the most important issues together with the relevant stakeholders. Three other points where they are different are the governance, planning of the operation and maintenance cost (often overlooked) and the involvement of the private sector, often considered a risk, rather than an opportunity (Liang et al., 2020).

We found that while the approaches differ, in practice the activities undertaken are often very similar. We discussed different interventions that have been used in Asian and European cities. Successful interventions require appropriate technological solutions, local governance structures and a system to assure the operation and maintenance costs can be paid, preferably through cost recovery mechanisms. We find a large number of technological options, which may perform well if used for the right purpose at the right scale. It is concluded that a combination of different stakeholders with several interventions and policy instruments is needed to achieve adaptive water management dealing in the right way with urban water issues. The initiative does not have to come from national or local governments. Project developers and private individuals can also take the initiative. These stakeholders can be incentivized to do so.

We found at the local level that the focus is often on one issue. The different approaches discussed may lead to sectoral approaches, for example concerning sustainable drinking water supply, without looking at waste or water management. One relevant question is how might the projected changes in rainfall affect climate change adaptation policies in the concerned cities?

Efforts to create urban environmental sustainability in Asian cities and one European city were analysed and the question was to what extent these cities have followed a certain approach and were they successful? In terms of expected solutions most approaches look at the government. Only in the case of eco-cities is there more space from the beginning for involving all kinds of stakeholders. There is a need for more awareness raising concerning what other stakeholders and in particular households can do to achieve a better living environment and how to create new governance structures to deal with the more important water issues, where stakeholders other than the national state can play a role.

Ideally the city would follow a system approach to assess the interaction between the different components distinguished so far. Objectives concerning justice such as equality and equal access are important, while also managing urban risks. All decision making should be sustainability-based, integrating social, economic, environmental and cultural considerations as well as compact, transit-oriented urban form principles. Such decision-making processes should be democratic, inclusive, empowering and aimed at engendering hope. In practice sectoral interests may hinder a system approach.

Coordination could take place in the framework of urban management, but the emphasis should be on involving stakeholders in decision making and implementing sectoral initiatives, facilitating their initiatives at the city, neighbourhood (many initiatives should be taken at the neighbourhood level; information dissemination activities about green opportunities can enable these initiatives), building and household level.

The eco-city approach also raises the ethical issue of how to deal with poorer people, who cannot afford the additional efforts. It is a challenge to pay special attention to the role of poor people in all these concepts. It helps if the governance structure is decentralized. Different actors can then play a role, for example the project developers can sign for a certain approach and the relevant people can receive subsidies for specific activities. Citizens can be promoted to engage in rainwater harvesting projects or build facilities for the separation of grey and brown water. Finally, it is possible to introduce demand management, to limit the consumption of water.

It is not useful to impose one model to deal with all water issues, but we can learn from other cities. Governance structures should bring different stakeholders together. It is not easy to develop the right governance structures. It is important to create an enabling environment allowing for private initiatives, whereby the government regulates them and ensures accountability.

We learned that cities in practice often focus on one or two elements of a concept and are not really following an integrated approach. Secondly, some cities wanted to be eco-cities in the 1990s and are trying to become sponge cities now (Zhuanghe), or smart cities (Shenzhen and Beijing), where they were eco-cities before (all three). This has to do with the support received from the national level. The impression in China is that cities move from one government financed project to another, without bothering too much about the name of the intervention or the sustainability of their investments after the end of the projects.

REFERENCES

Bhatnagar, M. (ed.) (2010). *Eco-Cities: Perspectives and Experiences.* Hyderabad: Icfai University Press.

Butterworth, J., McIntyre, P. and da Silva Wells, C. (2011). *Switch in the City: Putting Urban Water Management to the Test.* The Hague: IRC.

De Jong, M. (2016). Sustainable urban and infrastructural development in China: Why intergovernmental relations are the key. Inaugural Address, Delft University of Technology.

Dunn, J. and Jamieson, W. (2011). The relation between of sustainable tourism and eco-city development. In T.-C. Wong and B. Yuen (eds.), *Eco City Planning: Policies, Practice and Design.* Berlin: Springer, 93–109.

Hajer, M. and Dassen, T. (2014). *Smart about Cities: Visualizing the Challenge for 21st Century Urbanism.* The Hague: PBL Netherlands Environmental Assessment Agency.

IPCC (2018). Global Warming of 1.5°C. https://www.ipcc.ch/sr15/.

Isunju, J. B., Schwartz, K., Schouten, M. A. C., Van Dijk, M. P. and Johnson, W. P. (2011). Socio-economic aspects of improved sanitation in slums: A review. *Public Health*, 125, 368–376.

Li, H., Liuqian Ding, Minglei Ren, Changzhi Li and Hong Wang (2017). Sponge city construction in China: A survey of the challenges and opportunities. *Water*, 9, 594. doi:10.3390/w9090594.

Liang, X., Liang, Y., Chong C. and Van Dijk, M. P. (2020). Implementing water policies in China: A policy cycle analysis of the Sponge City Program using two case studies. *Sustainability*, 12. doi:10.3390/su12135261.

Liang, X. and Van Dijk, M. P. (2009). Financial and economic feasibility of decentralized wastewater reuse systems in Beijing. *Water Science and Technology*, 61, 1965–1973.

Liang, X. and Van Dijk, M. P. (2011). Economic and financial analysis on rainwater harvesting for agricultural irrigation in the rural areas of Beijing. *Resources, Conservation and Recycling*, 55, 1100–1109.

Liang, X. and Van Dijk, M. P. (2012). Beijing: Managing water for the eco city of the future. *International Journal of Water*, 6, 270–290.

Lindfield, M. and Steinberg, F. (2012). *Green Cities*. Manila: Asian Development Bank.

Oduro-Kwarteng, S, and Van Dijk, M. P. (2017). Regulatory environment for private sector involvement in solid waste collection in Ghana. *International Journal of Environment and Waste Management* (IJEWM-40948), 20. https://doi.org/10.1504/IJEWM.2017.086026.

OECD (2018). Resilient cities. http://www.oecd.org/cfe/regional-policy/resilient-cities.htm.

Rockefeller Foundation (2015). *The City Resilience Framework*. New York: Rockefeller Foundation.

Rotterdam (2016). *Rotterdam Resilience Strategy: Ready for the 21st Century*. Consultation document. 100 Resilient Cities. http://lghttp.60358.nexcesscdn.net/8046264/images/page/-/100rc/pdfs/strategy-resilient-rotterdam.pdf.

Rotterdam Climate Initiative (2017). Climate adaptation. http://www.rotterdamclimate initiative.nl, accessed 21-9-2018.

Smith Morris, E. (2011). Down with ECO-towns! Up with ECO-communities, or is there a need for model eco-towns? A review of the 2009–2010 Eco-town proposals in Britain. In T.-C. Wong and B. Yuen (eds.), *Eco City Planning: Policies, Practice and Design*. Berlin: Springer, 113–130.

Suzuki, H., Dastur, A., Moffatt, S., Yabuki, N. and Maruyama, H. (2010). *Eco² Cities: Ecological Cities as Economic Cities*. Washington, DC: World Bank.

UNDP (2014). *Sustainable and Liveable Cities: Towards Ecological Civilization*. China National Human Development Report 2013. Beijing: United Nations Development Programme.

UN Habitat (2018). Sustainable cities programme. Nairobi United Nations Habitat Programme. http://www.fukuoka.unhabitat.org/programmes/detail04_03_en.html.

Van Dijk, M. P. (2011). Three ecological cities, examples of different approaches in Asia and Europe. In T.-C. Wong and B. Yuen (eds.), *Eco City Planning: Policies, Practice and Design*. Berlin: Springer, 31–51.

Van Dijk, M. P. (2016). Financing the National Capital Integrated Coastal Development (NCICD) project in Jakarta (Indonesia) with the private sector. *Journal of Coastal Zone Management*, 19, 5. doi:10.4172/2473-3350.1000435.

Van Dijk, M. P. (2018). Smart eco cities are managing information flows in an integrated way: The example of water, electricity and solid waste. In M. Dastbaz, W. Naude and J. Manoochehri (eds.), *Smart Futures: Challenges of Urbanization and Social Sustainability*. Berlin: Springer, 149–169.

Van Dijk, M. P. and Blokland, M. W. (2016). Introduction and reflection on benchmarking for the delivery of water and sanitation services to the urban poor. In M. P. Van Dijk and M. W. Blokland (eds.), Special issue: Benchmarking for the delivery of water and sanitation services to the urban poor, *International Journal of Water*, 10, 109–121.

Van Dijk, M. P. and Hao Li (2015). Climate change policies and adaptive behaviour of farmers in southern China. *Review of Economic Anthropology*, 35, 155–175.

Wong, T.-C. and Yuen, B. (eds.) (2011). *Eco City Planning: Policies, Practice and Design*. Berlin: Springer.

Yong, G., Qinghua, Z., Doberstein, B. and Fujita, T. (2009). Implementing China's circular economy concept at the regional level. *Waste Management*, 29, 996–1002.

Zhang, M., Huan, W., Wei, J. and van Dijk, M. P. (2019a). Assessing heat wave vulnerability in Beijing and its districts, using a three dimensional model. *International Journal of Global Warming*, 17, 297–314.

Zhang, M., Zelu Liu and Van Dijk, M. P. (2019b). Measuring urban vulnerability to climate change using an integrated approach: Assessing climate risks in Beijing. *PeerJ*, 7, e7018. http://doi.org/10.7717/peerj.7018.

7. Urban commons in emerging economies

Rudina Toto, Marija Ćaćić, Zvezdina Ivanova, Peter Nientied and Katarzyna Stachowiak-Bongwa

INTRODUCTION

Collaborative management and governance in the city, conceptualized within the framework of the *urban commons* (UC), has generated renewed attention. Definitions vary, but all affirm that UC consists of people (commoners / UC's community), a resource, and interaction around the UC otherwise defined as *commoning* (social practices and governance rules) (Dellenbaugh and Schwegmann, 2017; Marella, 2017). Umeå School of Architecture (2015) defines UC as "a space of social interaction, where resources are collectively owned or shared between or among communities' populations. These resources are said to be *held in common*." Bauwens and Niaros (2017: 5) call them "a shared resource, which is co-owned and/or co-governed by its users and/or stakeholder communities, according to its own rules and norms." Commons are not new; they have existed for centuries through communities' collective action in governing forests, pastures, fisheries and irrigation systems, among other shared resources (Ostrom, 1990, 1999; Schlager, 2004; Toto, 2019). These traditional natural commons, or common pool resources (CPR), are important to commoners' livelihood, and depletable if overexploited (Ostrom, 1990). Thousands of CPR governance cases around the world reveal scale dependencies and features (so-called design principles) present in robust CPRs, opposing Hardin's (1968) popular argument of the *tragedy of the commons*, particularly for small-scale commons. A nested system of CPR governance is, according to Ostrom (1999), beneficial for achieving robust and sustainable commons at larger scales.

Building on CPR scholarship, research attention has expanded from traditional commons to, amongst others, urban commons. UC differ as they are not necessarily imperative for livelihood, are often contested for land use, and may signify development and power struggles over space. The extent of their openness differs. Cross-sectoral collaboration and related property systems also vary – most UC are enabled and operated in collaboration with local authorities (Parker and Johansson, 2011).

This chapter focuses on urban open spaces for public use. These spaces are considered as commons, or shared resources, as they relate to communities and social interaction, and can be governed through formal and informal rules. Open spaces vary from urban squares and parks to neighbourhood playgrounds. The goal of this chapter is to develop insights that could help urban governments appreciate and make use of commons-based modalities by exploring the concept and practices of urban open spaces as UC. Furthermore, by investigating concrete cases, this chapter contributes to broader efforts of establishing empirical research on evidence-based approaches to transforming places and fuelling discussions on open public space and its governance (Brain, 2019). Our UC research has been carried out in four cities in four formerly socialist countries in Central and Eastern Europe (CEE). Various open spaces have been examined through the lens of UC, revealing existing practices, challenges, as well as future potentials and suggestions for balancing private and public interests in urban governance and increasing cities' liveability.

Management complexity in cities is increasing, with a multitude of actors having various perspectives on problems and self-organized solutions. This also applies to open spaces. Planners and city managers often conceive management of open spaces as a routine, local government task. However, open spaces exhibit a variety of property rights arrangements, which can engender controversial social interactions in these spaces and render their design and maintenance so complicated that dealing with them in a sustainable way necessitates community involvement, and sometimes leadership. Local governments often fail in proper policing and maintenance, leading to the dehumanization of open space (Ondrejicka et al., 2017). Many cities have witnessed the emergence of community/actors' groups as centres of decision-making, involved in governing and adding value to open spaces (Boamah, 2018; Berardo and Lubell, 2016). These centres of decision-making are formed around a shared resource (the open space) and govern it by developing resilient systems in the city. The more these centres interact amongst themselves and with local governments in a polycentric network of governance interactions (Boamah, 2018; McGinnis, 2011; Ostrom 1999), the greater the ability of the urban system to respond to shocks and disturbances (Finka and Kluvankova, 2015). However, local governments often fail to appreciate community initiatives as they 'disturb' established governance. This reaction signifies a limited management perspective. Therefore, the question for this chapter is to explore whether urban commoning is or can be complementary to urban governance. Urban governance is understood as a broader framework for city making and city liveability, while UC is understood as community-led, networked governance.

ARE UC IN CEE SPECIAL?

While traditional commons have been studied in CEE (Hribar et al., 2018; Tomašević, 2018; Toto, 2019; Vameşu et al., 2018), UC has received limited attention so far. Ondrejicka et al. (2017) and Poklembová et al. (2012) discuss UC from a spatial viewpoint. Łapniewska (2017) has examined grassroots initiatives in Poland, while Borčić et al. (2016) have discussed community gardens in the socialist and post-socialist eras in Zagreb. Post-socialist cities have some features of UC. First, open common spaces are deemed as public spaces. Public in this sense stands for collective, a concept with a somewhat negative connotation in the region for being linked to the state and to imposed collective work (Grabkowska, 2018). Second, since the transformation of communist systems to democratic and market systems in the early 1990s, the private sector has been leading city development all over CEE (Aliaj et al., 2010; Hirts, 2014). This, along with the often-troublesome development of a new public sector after 1990 – characterized by slow response, corruption, and a failure to deliver basic facilities – has impacted civic culture (Svirčić-Gotovac, 2016; Toto, 2019). A third feature is the layout of cities, based on communist planning perspectives, that has often allowed for (sometimes extreme) infill of public open space, resulting in densification, infrastructure problems, and space scarcity. Urban governments have been permitting this infill, eager to support private sector-led development and address land restitution/compensation issues resulting from land reprivatization.

The relevance of this chapter, however, is not limited to CEE. Similarly, the above-mentioned challenges are not unique to CEE. As Iaione (2016: 2) states, "Urban public spaces are perceived as nobody's or local public authority's places, rather than everybody's places, like commons." Indeed, the theme of UC and open spaces should be relevant for cities in the Global South and the Global North. Many UC practices can be found in the Global South (Kuttler and Jain, 2015; Shareable, 2018), in the form of urban actions and activism, as well as more customary commons practices. They are, however, not perceived as UC, but as remnants of the past (Borčić et al., 2016).

GOVERNANCE OF URBAN COMMONS

Contrary to Hardin's (1968) point in 'The tragedy of the commons', and his predecessors (Obeng-Odoom, 2016), Ostrom (1990, 1999, 2010) redefined the commons as well-regulated and resilient systems, which are not inherently subject to a tragedy of overuse. Ostrom explored the conditions under which

Table 7.1   Bundle of rights for commons

	Authorized entrant	Authorized user	Claimant	Proprietor	Owner
Access	X	X	X	X	X
Withdrawal		X	X	X	X
Management			X	X	X
Exclusion				X	X
Alienation					X

Source: Ostrom (2003); Schlager and Ostrom (1992).

people have incentives to conserve common-pool resources, and showed that natural CPRs are not bound to end in failure. Collectively governed resources can work to serve individual, as well as collective purposes (Acheson, 2011). There are eight design principles that robust cases of commons governance share. These principles include clear boundaries, fair distribution of costs and benefits, collective choice arrangements for governing the resource, monitoring and graduated sanctioning, conflict resolution, minimal recognition of rights to organize, and nested enterprises in a polycentric system of interactions, and constitute the features of resilient governance for the commons (Ostrom, 1990, 1999).

Ostrom developed a theory of collective action in which "a group of principals can organize themselves voluntarily to retain the residual of their own efforts" (1990: 25). Commons can have a variety of self-organized arrangements shaping socio-ecological interaction. Important in Ostrom's writing is the notion of *subtractability* – building on the idea that appropriators are rivalrous and the use of the resource units diminishes what is left for others (Borch and Kornberger, 2015), and that it is not possible, or very costly to *exclude* others from accessing the resource system (Ostrom, 1990; Schlager, 2004). For subtractable goods, depletion can occur due to imbalanced withdrawal versus replenishment rate; for non-excludable goods, the free-rider problem can arise (Ostrom, 1990; Toto, 2019). The property system for the commons is envisioned as a bundle of rights, not merely as legal ownership (Schlager and Ostrom, 1992), where rights (Table 7.1) define the *boundaries* of the system.

For Ostrom (1990) CPRs are natural or man-made, the latter encompassing urban commons, such as squares, streets, bridges and parking spaces. Ostrom acknowledged the existence of non-subtractive resources, such as knowledge, which have different dimensions (Hess and Ostrom, 2007). On the other hand, viewing public open spaces as UC, where more users add to the value of the resource by enjoying it (Kohn, 2004) is interpretable in terms of subtractability. Thus, these spaces are not diminishable over time, but can suffer from overcrowding and may encompass natural resources (i.e. ecosystems) that are depletable. In addition, "rights, obligations and restrictions attributable to each of the stakeholders who use and enjoy such spaces" (Boydell and Searle, 2014: 324) become obscured if divisibility is not considered. But UC are diverse (Hess, 2008); parking spaces where more cars means less space, or streets where increased traffic volume hampers the flow of traffic, are clearly divisible.

For public open spaces, free-riding has a different meaning: "In the city, the commons is an inherently relational phenomenon … usage and consumption practices are a constitutive part of the production of the urban commons: in fact, consuming the city is nothing but the most subtle form of its production" (Borch and Kornberger, 2015: 7–8). Two significant issues for urban commons are abuse from overuse (Lee and Webster, 2006), and maintenance over free-riding. UC often have vague social and property rights boundaries.

Public open space as UC goes beyond the 'ownership – accessibility – divisibility' discourse. Open public space is a created artefact as a means for humans to make cities liveable and satisfy individuals' fundamental rights of city appropriation through social processes (Marella, 2017; Williams, 2018). This differs from natural resources, which exist in a biocentric fashion. Public open space is a social system, where everyone feels represented, and can achieve his or her social and political ambitions. Local governments may hold the legal status of property owner but cannot control all uses. While the bundle of ownership rights, accessibility and divisibility, and governance rules apply to UC in ways similar to CPRs, there is the alternative view of rights (beyond property) to the city (Harvey, 2008; Lefebvre, 1972). This concept classifies public open space as UC, regardless of the quantity of rights from the ownership bundle.

Another critical aspect for public open space is the system of values that users and commoners attribute to it. These can be examined in two directions: (i) the land-use mixture between natural ecosystems and artificially created landscape (impermeable, concrete) in a single place/square; and (ii) the high presence of non-utilitarian values, which lowers the chances for commodification of public open space. In both cases, values are difficult to quantify and map. Ecosystem services provided by the natural landscape of the UC have unknown boundaries in terms of who can benefit from them. This is also true for the utility derived from the UC (in contrast to a CPR), where direct beneficiaries can be easily defined and the *rationality* discussion is highly valid (Łapniewska, 2017). Non-utilitarian values are various and differ per user group, particularly between those residing in and outside of the city. However, the connection of people to public open space, regardless of location, is strengthened by these values and to socio-political accomplishments in and over the space, which are defining features of the city as a space for collaboration and human interaction. Hence, regardless of the property status and the

Table 7.2   Dimensions of UC

Dimension	Description
Drivers	Historically shared/used resource, socio-political interaction, land-use and design approach, new social practices, appropriation of the city.
Boundaries	Broad variety of distribution of (property) rights, benefits and costs, and user pool. Often ambiguous.
Governance	Community – commoners, local government as partner, informal and constitutional rules, challenges; community-led network governance.
Values	Resilience and sustainability of the resource, equity, utility, self-realization and identity, spirituality, socialization, and education.

Source: Based on Ostrom (1990); Foster (2016), Dellenbaugh (2015), Boamah (2018) and Brain (2019).

respective governance model, this connection is perhaps the strongest factor in defining the commoning potential for public open space, and therefore its status as a UC (Marella, 2017; Williams, 2018).

Interaction with and use of the UC creates social and economic value in the city and a greater sense of community. The more consolidated the social ethics, the higher the efficacy of collective governance of public open spaces (O'Brien, 2012). As Holst (2016: 75) writes: "the city is the source which interrelates people and their vital environments in multiple and often inter-twined ways so that the crucial question for the citizen of the modern age is more about living in vital and humane urban environments". This act of live-able city-making is inspired by people and goes beyond 'cold' and 'rational' urban management tools, to incorporate dialoguing, networking, individual experiences of place-crafting, and memories of what was or has to be shared in a city's resources.

Enright and Rossi (2018) identify two main approaches to UC. The first is a neo-institutional strand inspired by Ostrom's work. It is influential in the public sphere and within mainstream collaborative economies. Examples include Foster and Iaione (2019), Iaione (2015) and Foster (2016). The second is the neo-Marxist strand, broadened here to the activist strand, with a critical urban studies perspective, looking at both the defence of the commons and the production of alternative communal economies outside of capitalism. Examples include Dellenbaugh (2015), Ramos (2016), Stravides (2016) and Shareable (2018). In academic research, various angles of the critical approach can be found, including the spatial (Moss, 2014; Pelger et al., 2017), feminist (Huron, 2015), regulatory and property angle (Garnett, 2012; Williams, 2018).

UC's diversity is related to functions and use of the resource, scale, rights/ boundaries, actors and the complexity of their interactions (see Table 7.2). Differences between governing a community garden or neighbourhood open space on the one hand, and an urban road or parking lot on the other seem obvious. In the vision of urban collaborative governance of Foster and Iaione (2019), complexity requires that all actors who have a stake in the commons be part of an autonomous centre of decision-making as co-partners, or co-collaborators – preferably coordinated or enabled by the public authority. The state facilitates or enables citizen-led commoning, synonymous with proposals regarding a *partner state* (Ramos, 2016). Hence, UC governance is an element of network governance in the city, where the presence of rules (informal or constitutional) and stakeholders' decision-making autonomy define the robustness of the UC and its ability to produce liveable cities (Shutina, 2019).

OPEN SPACES IN FOUR CEE CITIES

Methodology

Open spaces offer a challenging case for studying UC in the frame of urban governance. UN Habitat (2015: 15) states that, "A prosperous city offers a profusion of public goods and develops policies and actions for a sustainable use of, and equitable access to, *the commons*, such as public space." In approaching open spaces as UC, social capital can be connected to a specific space (Foster, 2006; Holst, 2016), allowing for co- and participatory design (Colding and Barthel, 2013; Parker and Schmidt, 2017), and responsible and resilient handling of the city's spatial resources. It takes into account everyone who contributes to the city's creation and participates in its experience (Pelger et al., 2017).

Three typologies of open spaces (large, city scale; intermediate; and neighbourhood scale, 17 spaces in total) were studied through the lens of UC in four cities: Podgorica (Montenegro), Tirana (Albania), Stara Zagora (Bulgaria), and Szczecin (Poland). The choice of cities was made to represent capitals and secondary cities. UC dimensions as indicated in Table 7.2 were linked to features to be explored: drivers of spatiality and standards, use/functions and social practices/interaction; boundaries – which for the sake of this research consist of ownership rights and the user pool; governance and rules; prevailing values; challenges (overcrowding or abandonment); free-riding and lack of maintenance; and commoners and commoning potential. Commoning potential is understood as common interest for commoning and social bonding; ownership rights and users' distance from the open space; governance mechanism; values; and space appropriation. A mixed-methods approach was used to build the cases, consisting of: a literature review; desk study of legislation and planning documentation; expert knowledge; visual, on-site observations three times per day seven days a week over the course of three weeks distributed over a two-month period; and interviews with experts and commoners.

Contextualization

The case study cities are located in four countries that shared a communist period (1944–1989/90), varying from milder Titoism in former Yugoslavia (which included present-day Montenegro), to more isolated and harsh Stalinism in Albania, with regimes in Bulgaria and Poland falling in between. Poland and Bulgaria joined the European Union (EU) in 2004 and 2007 respectively. Montenegro and Albania are candidate countries, with Montenegro already negotiating accession to the EU (Table 7.3).

Tirana and Podgorica are both capital cities. Tirana has approximately 790,000 inhabitants within the municipality (Municipality of Tirana, 2016) while Podgorica has approximately 186,000 (Municipality of Podgorica, 2014). Both cities' populations grew after 1990, but Podgorica shows a steadier increase (approximately 42 per cent since 1991), compared to the rapid and uncontrolled urbanization of Tirana with almost 400 per cent population growth (since 1991). From a spatial perspective, Podgorica has preserved its modernist urban structure, with vast public spaces incorporated in new developments. The city has signs of ill-development at the cost of public space. Most of Tirana's urban developments have taken place either on previous public space, or as new (informal) suburbs on former agricultural land. Most developments have occurred in the absence of formal planning, characterized by energy and chaos, scarce public infrastructures, and increasing environmental pollution (Aliaj et al., 2010).

Stara Zagora is a centrally located, intermediate town in Bulgaria, with about 151,000 residents in 1991, 138,000 inhabitants in 2011, and an estimated 136,000 in 2017 (City Population, 2017). Rapid growth during the early communist period is contrasted by low birth rates, migration to Sofia, and emigration abroad after the socio-political regime change. Main urban management issues include uneven distribution of government resources for maintenance and new developments, with a focus on the city centre. Szczecin is a regional capital in Western Poland and a port city with about 413,000 inhabitants in 1991 and 404,000 in 2017 (GUS, 2018; Statistical Office Szczecin, 2004, 2012). Szczecin has benefited from its close location to Germany and from Poland's EU accession, but lags behind in comparison to other Polish cities. Economic development, traffic, and environmental issues are key urban management concerns.

Drivers Affecting Spatiality and Use

Each space studied has a particular origin and value in the history of each city's urban tissue, which defines drivers for commoning and affects the spatiality and use of these spaces (see Figures 7.1 and 7.2). The central squares

Table 7.3   *UC open space typologies in each city and respective areas in m²*

UC open space typology	1. Central square	2. Intermediate space	3. Neighbourhood	
Cities			Functional UC	Non-functional
Tirana	1. Scanderbeg (40,000)	2. '1 km Park' (35,000)	3. Pocket Park (1,400)	4. Neighbourhood Square (1,800)
Podgorica	5. Independence (15,000)	6. The Unnamed Square (4,000)	7. Tuški Put (1,700) 8. Block IX (1,000)	9. Maxim Building (2,500)
Stara Zagora	10. City Hall (2,850)	11. Banya Piperka Park (9,750)	12. Trite Chuchura 40 (1,200)	13. Kazanski 28 (440)
Szczecin	14. Solidarity Plaza (9,600)	15. Flowers Boulevard (10,800)	16. Sciegiennego 1 – backyard (300)	17. Libelta street a/b/c (450)

of Tirana and Podgorica convey history, symbolism, and identity since the establishment of both cities. Yet, due to historical events, symbolism and identity values become debatable. Scanderbeg Square is the central meeting point of Tirana's radial street system and an unavoidable pedestrian space. It is the 'celebration place' of a unique surrounding urban and architectural heritage, where the square itself suffers from a 'wiped-out' past (Nientied and Aliaj, 2019). The square is a place claimed by everyone in Tirana and is used as a political medium to either bring citizens together for fostering (imposed) common purposes, or to indoctrinate the crowd through the power of the void. Podgorica's Independence Square is a rather monumental space intended for social gathering and integration. It is a symbol of political perseverance, and is the central node of the orthogonal grid of the first urban modernist tissue of the city, Nova Varoš – the administrative and socio-cultural centre. Both Tirana's and Podgorica's squares have gone through controversial urban renewal programmes.

Stara Zagora's City Hall Square dates back to the 1980s and was added to the original location of the city hall building from the masterplan of Libor Bayer for the reconstruction of Stara Zagora after the big fire of 1877 (Georgiev, 1986). The square is the main event venue in the city, hosting all national holiday celebrations, concerts, and political activities. It was meant as a social gathering space, but currently has no other functions besides circulation when there are no events. It lacks atmosphere and utilities to make it attractive for the public. Szczecin's Solidarity Plaza is relatively new, but with an intense recent history and offers a perfect spot in the city for political manifestations. Before the Second World War, there were houses and a theatre on the plaza (destroyed by bombardments). In 1970, it became the arena of a major social

Source: Author.

Figure 7.1　The central squares in each city: Tirana (left) and Podgorica (right)

Source: Author.

Figure 7.2   *The central squares in each city: Stara Zagora (left) and Szczecin (right)*

protest against the socialist government, brutally suppressed by the army. The protest did add to the identity of the plaza and the city, however, and led to the creation of the Solidarity Movement in 1980. The current appearance of iconic architecture, constructed between 2005 and 2006, pays tribute to victims of the 1970 protest, to the Solidarity movement, and to earlier cultural traditions through the Philharmonic Hall (built next to the Plaza, on the same spot as the pre-war Concert Hall).

The intermediate spaces in the cities studied differ. The '1 km Park' in Tirana is a former military aerodrome runway in west Tirana's suburb. After 1990 it turned into a neglected open space, surrounded by new residential buildings, until it was redeveloped into an urban park in 2010. The project preserved the linear character of the runway, avoiding fragmentation and introducing a series of functional events along the park. Similarly, in eastern Podgorica the Unnamed Square constitutes the only recognizable public space. The square is mostly a green area, surrounded by residential and mixed-use buildings along a main boulevard. It suffers from poor maintenance. In Stara Zagora, the Banya Piperka Park (former site of canning factory Piperka, 1923) is centrally located and was reconstructed and transformed into the city's bath ('banya') with a new park in the 1960s (Yankova, 2015). The park, currently surrounded by residential buildings and a hybrid public building, receives poor maintenance and attracts fewer users compared to other green spaces in the city. In Szczecin, the Flower Boulevard was a parade ground before the Second World War. After the war its status dwindled and the square became a place popular for its flower market and cafés. To improve the aesthetics of the place, the municipality replaced the market with a tiled alley and glass pavilion in 2010, the latter serving as a Tourist Information Point. The square is now used as a pedestrian thoroughfare, but is otherwise mostly empty, except when fairs are organized.

The neighbourhood open spaces share similarities with the intermediate spaces in terms of size, use, and physical features. Tirana's neighbourhood spaces represent two cases of physically open and partially closed squares. Both have open access to users, but the Pocket Park is an internal yard, frequented mostly by residents of the surrounding building block, while the Neighbourhood Square is one of the few public spaces inherited from the communist city period that has not been invaded by new development. The latter is being used as a mixed space for parking, playground, sport facilities, green area, and walking. In Podgorica three such spaces were selected to include Block IX in the city centre. Block IX is a common property with limited access. This space has planned green landscape elements and is well maintained. The Tuški Put inner yard on the other hand has open access, is well-maintained, and is a popular public space for the neighbourhood. Maxim space in Podgorica was developed in 2005 as the semi-atrium of a building block for about 5,000 inhabitants. This space, with an impermeable floor, is poorly maintained and used exclusively as a walking passage. At times, children use the space. A few power generators and two large ventilation openings for the underground parking lot are the only elements to refract the void. In Stara Zagora, the neighbourhood spaces of Kazanski and Trite Chuchura were built as public spaces for the surrounding communist residential blocks. However, they have experienced contrasting fates. Trite Chuchura, a popular meeting place for the neighbourhood, is a partially green space owned by the government but unofficially managed and maintained by the residents of the adjacent block. Kazanski 28 used to be a semi-green site with a children's playground, a small café, and a vegetable stall, but has been sold to a private investor, who is building another residential building on the plot (without public space). In Szczecin, the neighbourhood open space Sciegiennego was created by the municipal project Green Backyards, which turned an empty and completely paved yard into a green area with pergolas, roses, a small pond, and benches. The backyard was revitalized based on a plan that was democratically chosen by residents and financially supported by the municipality for 75 per cent of the costs. In Libelta Street the residents, tired of having to drive to their homes and garages through a muddy path, established a neighbourhood committee, collected money, and pushed the municipality into action for levelling and paving the road, by gaining the political support of a few councillors.

Boundaries, Governance, Values and Commoning Potential

In all four cities, most of the open spaces are public property of the respective municipalities. Exceptions are two small neighbourhood squares in Podgorica held in common by the residents; one in Tirana shared between the residents and the developer; and one in Stara Zagora, which is municipal property but soon to be privatized. Szczecin is the only city where users clearly consider the open spaces as urban commons, even though the property belongs to the municipality. For Stara Zagora, commoning potential is observed in Trite Chuchura, while in Podgorica and Tirana, only the small neighbourhood squares (two in each city) are considered as UC by their users. However, this is a broad definition and residents show different levels of bonding with the respective spaces, or willingness to pay for common maintenance. For instance, though Block IX (Podgorica) is commonly owned and access to potential external users is prohibited, relations between users (residents) are weak and they vaguely declare a common interest to the space, delegating maintenance to a private company. In the case of '1 km Park,' some bonding and common concerns are present among specific stakeholder groups, such as shop and café owners, who directly bear the consequences of unattractive public space through fewer clients. In Szczecin, neighbourhood residents are willing to pay for maintaining the open space while in Stara Zagora, users' bonding and willingness to pay, in both Trite Chuchura and Banya Piperka Park, is limited to specific groups.

The boundaries of these spaces are defined by the pool of users and commoners, and consist of the present property relations/rights and commoning. Hence, the user pool varies between 'unmeasurable' for central squares (city-level spaces), to 155 families for one neighbourhood square. A distinction is made between users and commoners, assuming that users merely have access rights, which they use occasionally, and have no emotional connection or involvement in the space's management regardless of interaction occurrences. Commoners may have at least one more right (Table 7.1), or have a sense of place attachment and *appropriate* the respective space as 'theirs' because it has significance for their life.

The central squares in Podgorica and Tirana, though different in physical size, share purpose and count the whole city as their respective user pool. Temporary users include tourists. It is almost impossible to distinguish users from commoners within the cities' resident populations. In the intermediate spaces, the user pool encompasses residents of the neighbourhood, occasional and regular passers-by, owners of commercial activities and their clients, and distinct user groups from other neighbourhoods, who choose that particular space for leisure. In Tirana and Podgorica, the presence of the latter category of users is also linked to insufficient open public areas in neighbourhoods. The case of Stara Zagora is quite the opposite; there are sufficient public spaces in the city centre, and City Hall Square and Banya Piperka Park are not popular due to a lack of atmosphere and utilities. Szczecin also has sufficient open and leisure space in the city centre, such as the main park, the river with boulevards for walking, and the castle, among other spaces. Solidarity Plaza's user pool is regional and international as the Philharmonic Hall acts as a magnet for musical and architectural tourism. As for all neighbourhood open spaces, most of the users and commoners are residents and children from the surrounding building blocks. Users of the commercial activities (if present) also frequent the space, together with some individuals (mostly elderly living nearby) who find the amenities of the respective spaces comfortable and easily accessible.

Local governments are responsible for the governance of central squares and intermediate spaces in all cities. In Tirana, the municipality benefits from a national by-law governing public space, which defines space creation and management rules for various typologies, users' rights, and opportunities for public–private partnerships. However, there are no legal prerogatives or rules on commons. In Poland, new interventions in main public spaces are mandated to come out of national or international architectural competitions organized by the Polish Architects Society. They must be accepted by the Monuments Conservator and comply with the city's Master Plan. In Podgorica and Stara

Zagora such approaches are still in formation, though city plans are to be followed. In all cities, most of the present cases of resident initiatives are fuelled by individuals or non-governmental organizations, though in Szczecin the municipality has played a major role in implementation. Municipal regulations are dissimilarly applied; in the central squares and intermediate public spaces special permits are needed for activities and interventions; the neighbourhood open spaces benefit from more freedom, since most of them are out of the governmental focus for monitoring and maintenance.

Conventional municipal management for central squares and intermediate spaces is appreciated by citizens. As people do not know one another, they prefer not to participate in governance platforms, or pay temporary fees for a specific space improvement, because of either low trust in government, or fear of free-rider behaviour. This contrasts with the large array of values that people attach to the larger spaces such as central squares. In all cities, values such as symbolism, identity, historical ties, spiritual connection, socialization, and cultural development are attached to the main squares. Independence Square in Podgorica has limited identity values due to transformations. In Stara Zagora, the square was designed as an open void in front of the city hall building, without street furniture or greenery. People perceive it more as a continuation of the boulevard than as a place of special significance. As described above, Szczecin's and Tirana's squares are loaded with significance.

For intermediate and small user pool spaces, the presence of non-utilitarian values is subject to the place that each space holds in the historical formation of the urban fabric, and to the degree of consolidation in each neighbourhood. When spaces have been built recently, residents mostly search for direct utility and socialization values. When spaces have historical significance, even if hidden by a lack of maintenance or invisible to outsiders, cognitive development, equity, and identity are present. This is less the case in Tirana's and Stara Zagora's selected spaces, due to the very dynamic and unprecedented urban transformation of the urban core, the population mix, and/or historical city layers being erased.

Urban commoning is much more present in neighbourhood (small user basin) open spaces. At the neighbourhood scale it is possible to observe public open spaces with and without commoning. However, a small-basin UC resembles a robust CPR more than a central square or intermediate space does, even when the latter is well maintained and significantly valued by citizens. In the UC of Podgorica and Tirana, commoners' rights vary from proprietor to owner, on the bundles of rights scale. Citizens follow both constitutional and informal management rules. In Podgorica, commoners living in the respective residential blocks define 'house rules' based on social housing legislation and informally agreed upon quality criteria, and display them in the commonly shared open spaces. In Tuški Put, open access to any user besides owners is allowed. Therefore, full compliance with house rules is far from being achieved. However, residents 'enjoy' the increased presence of users from the surrounding neighbourhood, even outside of predefined leisure hours, because this makes the square more vivid, pleasant, and safe. In contrast, Block IX protects its space by prohibiting external users from accessing it. It does not benefit from a potentially enhanced atmosphere deriving from its use, representing a case of gating or enclosure of the commons (Lee and Webster, 2006).

The Pocket Park in Tirana is also 'open access' and attracts users beyond the mere community of commoners (owners). During 2015–16, a local NGO supported the commoners' initiative to redesign and revive their common space. Initially, there was no bonding among residents, nor between them and the open space though they were sharing ownership. The local NGO noticed a lack of trust among the residents, but also a collective willingness for an external actor (preferably not local government) to promote self-organization, and a readiness to contribute (also financially) to improvements in the open space, as long as there was an external guarantor and the municipality was monitoring the process and covering a part of the expenses. Working with the community to overcome all three barriers, the NGO brought forward a successful model of cooperation. Besides resulting in improved open space for public use, it also nurtured a UC case. The challenge lies in managing the occasional overcrowding effect imposed by students (free-riders) of a nearby school, who sometimes have lunch on the site and leave behind waste.

The Maxim Building in Podgorica and the Neighbourhood Square in Tirana do not reveal urban commoning. The former is poorly maintained and represents a 'meaningless void', where residents as authorized users express not having any incentive for renewal or self-governance of the space. Neighbourhood Square may have more potential as UC; the Municipality has built a sports facility and residents fear losing the square because they feel that the limited local maintenance funds may be diverted towards investments for other public open spaces. However, as long as they do not want to bear any cost, they are space consumers rather than appropriators. In Stara Zagora, the two neighbourhood spaces show different pictures: Trite Chuchura is a popular neighbourhood meeting space. It is municipal property but de facto managed by the residents of the adjacent block. Kazanski 28 will cease to exist as it was sold to a property developer. The two cases in Szczecin – Sciegiennego and Libelta Street – show a significant involvement of residents, including substantial financial contributions in partnership with the municipality to make the space green and more attractive.

DISCUSSION

This chapter explores three typologies of public open space in seventeen case studies across four cities, focusing on their UC dimensions, including the presence and potential of urban commoning. Based on these cases, a positive relationship is observed between the size of the user/commoner pool and their property rights on the one hand (defined as boundaries), and the number of values attributed to the space on the other. However, the same relationship is not necessarily present between boundaries and commoning. More commoning is present in the smaller user groups and the spaces that are perceived as less important. More property rights alone also do not guarantee commoning. It is people's bonding and shared values that produce social interaction and engagement over the space. Table 7.4 provides a summary of findings for the three typologies of public open spaces.

Central squares embody a large range of values and have national importance. People feel connected to central squares and consider them as landmarks. However, this commoning energy is not reflected in commoning practices. The user pool is very large, commoners' property rights are limited to access and withdrawal, and it is difficult for people to deal directly with the abuse of space. Furthermore, people feel it is more effective to assign management to local government instead of employing several community forums with prolonged decision-making and action. Central squares are typical cases for urban management, where constituencies transfer responsibilities to the government, though with a significant risk factor for irresponsible and non-transparent local government decision-making, which is often politicized or used ideologically. The central squares explored in this chapter are usually managed through an urbanism perspective with no discussion of rights or city appropriation. As a result, commoning tends to end up in cases of activism, where the solution for any specific issue is not equally embraced by all users/commoners. Finally, in the central squares, the property rights perspective is not directly or vividly present in the discourse when important decisions are to be taken.

Intermediary spaces are often the subject of conflicting spatial activities and interests. Residents look forward to comfortable, intimate, secure and shared open spaces but other more distant circles of (occasional) users may hamper these feelings. Commoning is achievable, but not as a unique and holistic approach. Rather, commoning should be seen as community-based participation in public space development, complementary to other conventional urban management modalities.

Neighbourhood open spaces seem to have more commoning presence and potential, since residents and other stakeholders are close, can develop social bonding, and can monitor the space. Ownership rights are more clear, though

Table 7.4   *Open space typologies compared across UC dimensions and potential*

Dimensions	Features summarized	Open spaces as UC		
		Central	**Intermediary**	**Neighbourhood**
Drivers	Size, function, history, appropriation	Large size; central locations; mixture of functions	Large to medium size; various locations; mixture of functions	Medium to small size; neighbourhood location; specific functions
		Several historical stages of design and creation; places for public gathering	Newly created of part of the urban tissue; places for socializing in the neighbourhood	Newly created as part of the urban tissue; places for socializing in the neighbourhood
Boundaries	User pool	The whole city	Surrounding neighbourhoods, local businesses, and occasional passers-by	The neighbourhood and occasional users
	Boundaries	Legal ownership with local government (LG)	Legal ownership with LG	Mixed cases (from LG to residents to developers)
		Access and withdrawal, regulated occasional management	Access and withdrawal, partial management for specific sites within the area	Access, withdrawal, management and in one case exclusion and alienation
Governance	Rules, LG involvement, payments and penalties, civil society	Constitutional rules, payment through taxes and occasional donations, civic society present	Constitutional rules, payment through taxes and occasionally direct contributions, civic society present	Informal and constitutional rules, users manage, payments through taxes and direct contributions, NGOs very involved
	Challenges	Free-riding is present and lack of atmosphere can threaten governance	Lack of maintenance and free-riding	Abuse and free-riding. Lack of maintenance and abandonment can threaten in a few cases

Dimensions	Features summarized	Open spaces as UC		
		Central	Intermediary	Neighbourhood
Values	Values (commoners hold)	All values present	Mostly utility values present, but spiritual, socialization, and ecological services may also be present	Mostly utility values, occasionally also historical ties, socialization, and ecological services
Potential	Bonding, common interest, willingness to contribute, social norms pertaining to space	Interested to contribute in kind; norms mostly linked to identity and symbolism. No willingness to pay as long as taxes are paid. Bonding with the space but no bonding between users	Interested to contribute in kind; societal ethics as the social norm; low bonding with the space and between users	Interested to contribute in kind and cash; bonding with the space and between users is present, with some exceptions. Social norms vary between cases

sometimes alienation rights do not belong to the residents. The governance approach is mostly grassroots. In addition to the spatiality of the user pool and their ownership rights, one can observe a temporal factor that affects people's connection to space in all three typologies. In the neighbourhood squares, time and identity are factors that define bonding among users and between users and the space. In newly established neighbourhoods, bonding sometimes develops rather fast out of the need for connection and action over the space as a common interest; or it can take time for people to get to know each other.

CONCLUSIONS

The academic literature on public open space as urban commons is not well developed as yet and it is therefore difficult to draw conclusions that can be generalized. There is agreement in the literature about UC as social systems, where robustness and sustainability depend not only on property rights and governance rules, but on a fuller understanding of the system of values attached by users/commoners to specific open public spaces. Shared values should be strong (even if they are only utility values) and commoners should develop bonding, based on trust, for the governance of the UC to work efficiently. Therefore, in UC, the governance discussion should embrace management approaches that reflect both ownership rights and human well-being.

Based on a definition of UC as a shared resource which is co-owned and/or co-governed by its users/commoners, a model with four dimensions was used:

drivers, boundaries, governance, and values. In the empirical sections, this model proved to be adequate. Communities and the urban resource are starting points to make the most out of open spaces in cities – unlike many approaches that take public management as a starting point and then promote forms of participation. In a UC approach, local governments are facilitators of community processes and therefore provide an alternative to public sector regulation of private sector management. Various users attach values to a resource even though UC boundaries are ambiguous, driving them to engage and interact. Such processes require community-led governance and interaction with authorities.

Every so often, local governments do not consider user groups and their values and impose challenges or barriers for UC to develop. Sometimes, communities need local governments to initiate urban requalification, or third parties to induce them into commoning. This is especially relevant for situations with new communities, cases with limited place attachment, or cases of ongoing urbanization and (perceived) distance from consolidated urban cores (Šarović, 2016). Even in such cases, a strong sense of community and established social norms (O'Brien, 2012) constitute key factors for conceiving of enduring urban commons as instruments for the governance of urban open spaces.

In this chapter, UC of former socialist CEE cities were discussed. UC are relevant for other regions too, particularly for the Global South where UC have been discussed to a much lesser extent than for cities of the Global North. On the management of public space, UN Habitat (2015: 89) states that "With the right knowledge and resources, community groups can become more actively involved, particularly in underused or neglected spaces, either by managing the space themselves or by licensing or leasing the space from the local authority and taking ownership of it for the benefit of the community." Whether licensing or leasing is the right instrument is unclear, but the point is that communities can take care of their environment in an institutional relationship with local government and other stakeholders. Since many cities in the Global South have imperfect local authorities, ample opportunities can be created to improve urban conditions if local authorities acknowledge their own limitations and see UC as an alternative to public management.

Hence, from an urban governance perspective, local governments should stimulate rather than suppress communities to initiate the commoning of public open spaces as resources, as it enhances a sense of ownership, responsibility, and environmental stewardship. A UC approach to central squares, as argued, seems impracticable due to the user pool's scale and complexity. This is not a law; for example, New York's Central Park is run by the Central Park's Conservancy Organization, a non-profit formed in 1980 by a group of concerned citizens.

Cities are open access systems. Hence, free-riding that results from over-crowding and a lack of user inclusion in open space maintenance could easily become a challenge for UC of any level and typology. Crowding that does not lead to overuse and space depletion adds value to open spaces and improves their atmosphere. The challenge lies in the abuse and abandonment perceived as a risk that is strongly related to a lack of maintenance and free-riding behaviour. The presence of free-riders may inhibit the willingness and readiness of residents/commoners to initiate commoning practices.

For UC to develop at neighbourhood and intermediate levels, local governments should be much more receptive to citizens' initiatives and even invite them to participate as a way of enabling local development. In most of the cases studied in this chapter, local governments are hindering rather than facilitating commoning practices. Local governments with modernist approaches insufficiently acknowledge that 'traditional' social practices could well be applied and adjusted to communities' situations, and that encouragement of commoning or custodianship (Radywyl and Biggs, 2013) enhances the liveability of the city.

REFERENCES

Acheson, J. 2011. Ostrom for anthropologists. *International Journal of the Commons*, 5(2), 319–339.

Aliaj, B., Dhamo, S. and Shutina, D. 2010. *Between Energy and the Vacuum*. Tirana: Co-PLAN & POLIS University.

Bauwens, M. and Niaros, V. 2017. *Changing Societies through Urban Commons Transitions*. P2P Foundation in cooperation with Heinrich-Böll-Stiftung.

Berardo, R. and Lubell, M. 2016. Understanding what shapes a polycentric governance system. *Public Administration Review*, 76(5), 738–751.

Boamah, E. F. 2018. Polycentricity of urban watershed governance: Towards a methodological approach. *Urban Studies*, 55, 3525–3544.

Borch, C. and Kornberger, M. (eds.). 2015. *Urban Commons: Rethinking the City*. London: Routledge.

Borčić, L. S., Cvitanovic, M. and Lukić, A. 2016. Cultivating alternative spaces: Zagreb's community gardens in transition – from socialist to post-socialist perspective. *Geoforum*, 77, 51–60.

Boydell, S. and Searle, G. 2014. Understanding property rights in the contemporary urban commons. *Urban Policy and Research*, 32, 323–340.

Brain, D. 2019. Reconstituting the urban commons: Public space, social capital and the project of urbanism. *Urban Planning*, 4(2), 169–182.

City Population. 2017. *Bulgaria: Major Cities*. http://citypopulation.de/Bulgaria-Cities .html?cityid=2751 [accessed 15 February 2019].

Colding, J. and Barthel, S. 2013. The potential of 'Urban Green Commons' in the resilience building of cities. *Ecological Economics*, 86, 156–166.

Dellenbaugh, M. (ed.). 2015. *Urban Commons: Moving Beyond State and Market*. Basel: Birkhäuser Verlag AG.

Dellenbaugh, M. and Schwegmann, M. 2017. Actors of urban change from an urban commons perspective. *Actors of Urban Change: Urban Commons, Urban Change Talk Newspaper*, Issue 3, 15–17.
Enright, T. and Rossi, U. 2018. Ambivalence of the urban commons. In K. Ward, A. E. Jonas, B. Miller and D. Wilson (eds.), *The Routledge Handbook on Spaces of Urban Politics*. Abingdon: Routledge, 35–46.
Finka, M. and Kluvankova, T. 2015. Managing complexity of urban systems: A polycentric approach. *Land Use Policy*, 42, 602–608.
Foster, S. R. 2006. City as an ecological space: Social capital and urban land use. *Notre Dame Law Review*, 82(2), 527–582.
Foster, S. R. 2016. The city as a commons. *Yale Law & Policy Review*, 34(2), 282–349.
Foster, S. R. and Iaione, C. C. 2019. Ostrom in the city: Design principles and practices for the urban commons. In D. Cole, B. Hudson and J. Rosenbloom (eds.), *Routledge Handbook of the Study of the Commons*. London: Routledge, 235–255.
Garnett, N. S. 2012. Managing the urban commons. *University of Pennsylvania Law Review*, 160, 1995–2017.
Georgiev, G. 1986. The war for liberation 1877–1878. In P. Beron (ed.), *Encyclopedic Reference Guide*. Sofia: s.n., 54–55.
Grabkowska, M. 2018. Urban space as a commons in print media discourse in Poland after 1989. *Cities*, 72, 122–129.
GUS. 2018. *Wojewodztwo zachodniopomorskie. Podregiony, powiaty i gminy – Zachodniopomorskie Voivodship. Subregions, Powiats, Gminas.* http:// szczecin.stat.gov.pl/publikacje-i-foldery/roczniki-statystyczne/wojewodztwo -zachodniopomorskie-2018-podregiony-powiaty-gminy,7,18.html [accessed 20 January 2019].
Hardin, G. 1968. The tragedy of the commons. *Science*, 162, 1243–1248.
Harvey, D. 2008. The right to the city. *New Left Review*, 53, 23–40.
Hess, C. 2008. Mapping the new commons. Paper presented at the 12th Biennial Conference of the IASC, Governing Shared Resources: Connecting Local Experience to Global Challenges. University of Gloucestershire, Cheltenham, 14–18 July.
Hess, C. and Ostrom, E. (eds.). 2007. *Understanding Knowledge as Commons: From Theory to Practice*. Cambridge, MA: MIT Press.
Hirts, S. 2014. The post-public city: Experiences from post-socialist Europe. Globalizing Architecture: Flows and Disruptions, refereed proceedings of the 102nd Annual Conference of the Association of Collegiate Schools of Architecture, 123–129.
Holst, J. 2016. From common land to urban commons: Accessing the city through the squares. In D. Barrado, J. Fernandez-Santos and J. L. Casero (eds.), *Open Sourcing, Investigación y Formanción Avanzada en Acquitectura*. Universidad San Jorge, 69–76.
Hribar, M. Š., Kozina, J., David, B. and Urbanc, M. 2018. Public goods, common-pool resources, and the commons: The influence of historical legacy on modern perceptions in Slovenia as a transitional society. *Urbani Izziv*, 29(1), 96–109.
Huron, A. 2015. Working with strangers in saturated space: Reclaiming and maintaining the urban commons. *Antipode*, 47(4), 963–979.
Iaione, C. 2015. Governing the urban commons. *Italian Journal of Urban Law*, 7(1), 170–221.
Iaione, C. 2016. The CO-city: Sharing, collaborating, and commoning the city. *American Journal of Economics and Sociology*, 75(2), 1–44.
Kohn, M. 2004. *Brave New Neighborhoods: The Privatization of Public Space*. London: Routledge.

Kuttler, T. and Jain, A. 2015. Defending space in a changing urban landscape: A study on urban commons in Hyderabad, India. In M. Dellenbaugh, M. Kip, M. Bieniok and M. Schwegmann (eds.),*Urban Commons: Moving Beyond State and Market.* Berlin: Bauverlag Gütersloh, 72–90.

Łapniewska, Z. 2017. (Re)claiming space by urban commons. *Review of Radical Political Economics*, 49(1), 54–66.

Lee, S. and Webster, C. 2006. Enclosure of the urban commons. *GeoJournal*, 66(1–2), 27–42.

Lefebvre, H. 1972. *Le Droit à la Ville Suivie de Espace et Politique.* Paris: Éditions Anthropos.

Marella, M. R. 2017. The commons as a legal concept. *Law Critique*, 28, 61–86.

McGinnis, M. D. 2011. Networks of adjacent action situations in polycentric governance. *The Policy Studies Journal*, 39(1), 51–78.

Moss, T. 2014. Spatiality of the commons. *International Journal of the Commons*, 8(2), 457–471.

Municipality of Podgorica. 2014. *Prostorno Urbanistički Plan Glavnog Grada – Podgorice – do 25 Godine (Spatial Urban Plan of Capital City – Podgorica, till 2025).* http://podgorica.me/db_files/Urbanizam/PUP/pup.pdf [accessed 10 February 2019].

Municipality of Tirana. 2016. *TR030: Plani i Përgjithshëm Vendor i Bashkisë Tiranë (General Local Territory Plan of Tirana Municipality).* Tirana: Municipality of Tirana.

Nientied, P. and Aliaj, B. 2019. The public in search of identity: New symbolism in urban spaces – a study of central squares of Balkan capitals. In M. Finka, M. Jaššo and M. Husár (eds.), *The Role of Public Sector in Local Economic and Territorial Development: Innovation in Central, Eastern and South Eastern Europe.* Cham: Springer EAI, 203–237.

Obeng-Odoom, F. 2016. Property in the commons: Origins and paradigms. *Review of Radical Political Economics*, 48(1), 9–19.

O'Brien, D. T. 2012. Managing the urban commons: The relative influence of individual and social incentives on the treatment of public space. *Human Nature*, 23(4), 467–489.

Ondrejicka, V., Finka, M., Husar, M. and Jemecny, L. 2017. Urban space as the commons: New modes for urban space management. IOP Conference Series: Earth and Environmental Science 95, 052004.

Ostrom, E. 1990. Design principles of robust property rights institutions: What have we learned? In G. K. Ingram and Y. Hong (eds.), *Property Rights and Land Policies.* Cambridge, MA: Lincoln Institute of Land Policy, 25–51.

Ostrom, E. 1999. Design principles and threats to sustainable organizations that manage commons. Workshop in Political Theory and Policy Analysis. Bloomington: Indiana University.

Ostrom, E. 2003. How types of goods and property rights jointly affect collective action. *Journal of Theoretical Policies*, 15(3), 239–270.

Ostrom, E. 2010. Beyond markets and states: Polycentric governance of complex economic systems. *American Economic Review*, 100(3), 641–672.

Parker, P. and Johansson, M. 2011. The uses and abuses of Elinor Ostrom's concept of commons in urban theorizing. Paper presented at the International Conference of the European Urban Research Association (EURA) 2011 – Cities without Limits, 23–25 June, Copenhagen.

Parker, P. and Schmidt, S. 2017. Enabling urban commons. *CoDesign*, 13(3), 202–213.

Pelger, D., Kaspar, A. and Stollman, J. 2017. *Spatial Commons: Urban Open Spaces as Resource*. Berlin: Universitätsverlag der TU Berlin.

Poklembová, V., Kluvánková-Oravská, T. and Finka, M. 2012. Sustainable management of urban public spaces: Lessons from commons governance. *Terra Spectra STU, Planning Studies: Central European Journal of Spatial and Landscape Planning*, 4(2).

Radywyl, N. and Biggs, C. 2013. Reclaiming the commons for urban transformation. *Journal of Cleaner Production*, 50, 159–170.

Ramos, J. M. 2016. *The City as Commons: A Policy Reader*. Melbourne: Commons Transition Coalition.

Šarović, R. 2016. Suburbanizacijski procesi i kvalitet života u podgoričkoj mreži naselja. In *Tranzicijska preobrazba glavnih gradova, Zagreba i Podgorice, kao sustava naselja*. Zagreb: Institut za društvena istraživanja u Zagrebu, 41–65.

Schlager, E. and Ostrom, E. 1992. Property-rights regimes and natural resources: A conceptual analysis. *Land Economics*, 68(3), 249–262.

Schlager, J. M. 2004. Common-pool resource theory. In R. F. Durant, O. Florino and R. O'Leary (eds.), *Environmental Governance Reconsidered*. Cambridge, MA: MIT Press, 145–176.

Shareable. 2018. *Sharing Cities, Activating the Urban Commons*. Mountain View. CA: Shareable.

Shutina, D. 2019. *Territorial Rescaling for Polycentric Governance: The Case of Albania*. Tirana: Polis University.

Statistical Office Szczecin. 2004. *Podstawowe tendencje w rozwoju demograficznym wojewodztwa zachodniopomorskiego wraz z nowa prognoza ludności na lata 2003–2030 (Basic Tendencies in Demographic Development of Zachodniopomorskie Voivodship and the new Population Prediction for 2003–2030)*. http://bip.um .szczecin.pl/files/B39751FDF2CD457C95986F90F52FC7AF/urzad_statystyczny .pdf [accessed 20 January 2019].

Statistical Office Szczecin. 2012. *Raport z wynikow w wojewodztwie zachodniopomorskim. Narodowy Spis powzechny ludnosci I mieszkan 2011 (Report on Results in the Zachodniopomorskie Voivodship. National Population and Housing Census 2011)*, Chapter V, p.40, table 2. http://szczecin.stat.gov.pl/publikacje-i-foldery/spisy -powszechne/raport-z-wynikow-w-wojewodztwie-zachodniopomorskim-nsp-2011 ,15,1.html [accessed 20 January 2019].

Stravides, S. 2016. *Common Space: The City as Commons*. London: Zed Books.

Svirčić-Gotovac, A. 2016. Postsocijalistička transformacija Zagreba i Podgorice kao glavnih gradova. In *Tranzicijska preobrazba glavnih gradova, Zagreba i Podgorice, kao sustava naselja*. Zagreb: Institut za društvena istraživanja u Zagrebu, 7–25.

Tomašević, T. 2018. *Commons in South East Europe: Case of Croatia, Bosnia & Herzegovina and Macedonia*. Zagreb: Institute for Political Ecology.

Toto, R. 2019. Forest commons as a model for territorial governance. In M. Finka, M. Jaššo and M. Husár (eds.), *The Role of Public Sector in Local Economic and Territorial Development: Innovation in Central, Eastern and South Eastern Europe*. Cham: Springer EAI, 97-130.

Umeå School of Architecture. 2015. http://www.arch.umu.se/en/research/research -projects/interdisciplinary-development-projects/urban-commons/ [accessed 16 August 2018].

UN Habitat. 2015. *Global Public Space Toolkit from Global Principles to Local Policies and Practice*. Nairobi: UN Habitat.

Vameşu, A., Barna, C. and Opincaru, I. 2018. From public ownership back to commons: Lessons learnt from the Romanian experience in the forest sector. In P. Bance (ed.), *Providing Public Goods and Commons. Towards Coproduction and New Forms of Governance for a Revival of Public Action.* Liège: CIRIEC, 55–74.

Williams, M. J. 2018. Urban commons are more than property. *Geographical Research*, 56(1), 16–25.

Yankova, K. 2015. Why an area in Stara Zagora is called "Piperka"? https://www.zarata.info/zashto-rajon-v-stara-zagora-se-naricha-pi/ [accessed 12 February 2019].

8. Knowledge and skill transfer in Addis Ababa's light-rail transport

Taslim Adebowale Alade and Alberto Gianoli

INTRODUCTION

The efficiency and effectiveness of a light-rail transport (LRT) system is linked to the interactions and strategies of urban multi-actors, who may enable the transfer of knowledge and skills (Bressers et al., 2016). Developing an LRT system in a context with different socio-economic, environmental and technical characteristics (Cheng and Huang, 2013) requires adequate transfer of knowledge and skills. This chapter analyses this important issue in relation to the Addis Ababa LRT.

The adoption and implementation of a sustainable LRT requires appropriate strategies embedded in knowledge and skills to take into account local complexities and peculiarities (Drejer, 2002). These strategies need procedures which are also rooted in multi-actor interaction processes (Bressers et al., 2016). The multi-actor interaction process is dynamic and complex, and requires a robust connective capacity (Edelenbos et al., 2013) amongst the concerned multi-actors within the context of infrastructural policy implementation and adaptation. However, as interaction processes are human actions, all these effects flow through the main characteristics of the urban actors involved (Bressers and Klok, 1988). The absence of adequate strategies and transfer processes among relevant actors may lead to the failure of infrastructure projects and consequent substantial negative effects on public budgets and quality of life.

Scholars within the technological-capability school of thought argue that developing economies should not linger in a stagnant mode as receivers of technologies transferred from the Global North (Fu et al., 2011, Bhaduri, 2016). Rather, these economies must embark on appropriate innovation and knowledge acquisition measures towards the adaptation and integration of the transferred technologies (Bhaduri, 2016).

Against this background, the chapter aims to address the following research question: How were knowledge and skills transferred from Chinese to

Ethiopian urban actors in relation to the Addis Ababa LRT? The lessons learnt from the Addis Ababa experience are relevant for other sub-Saharan urban areas planning to adopt LRT systems. In addition, the Addis Ababa experience may show policy and decision makers in urban areas the relevance of effective strategies to transfer skills and knowledge within the broader context of urban management and governance.

After introducing the theoretical framework and the methodological approach that have guided the study, the chapter discusses the empirical data and analysis, and then provides conclusions and recommendations.

THEORETICAL FRAMEWORK

The conceptual model representing the relationships between urban-actor interactions and processes, which enable the transfer of knowledge and skills, is explained in this section. The dependent variables are represented as knowledge and skills, while the interactions between multinational corporations (MNCs) and the Ethiopian Railway Corporation (ERC) and these actors' strategies represent the independent variables.

Urban-Actor Processes Based on Interactions

Urban-actor interaction is defined in this context as the multi-stakeholder group collaborations between the ERC and the Chinese consortium as a type of MNC. These collaborations have defined roles, based on the nature of collaboration, types of roles and level of commitment (Alade et al., 2019). These collaborations vary broadly in terms of their size, goals, membership and actions (Fadeeva, 2005).

The main goal of the multi-actor interactions from the MNC supplying the LRT innovation is to provide the LRT receiving country with reasonably fast and low-cost access to resources, knowledge and skills that are complementary to its fundamental capabilities. While transaction costs are important, the actual benefits result from the exchange, dissemination and outsourcing of complementary capabilities and knowledge during the multi-actor interaction (Ernst and Kim, 2002; Kim, 1998).

The multi-actor interactions can be categorized as follows:

1. The nature of collaborations, which include formal negotiations and stakeholder dialogues, networking, multi-partner projects and information sharing, reasoned argumentation to foster mutual understanding, which in turn requires trust and transparency in the use of terms (Sarkis et al., 2010).

2. The types of roles played during the adoption process and implementing the service innovations (Fadeeva, 2005), such as: (i) Coordinator by providing rules for checks and balances; (ii) Financier based on concession types; (iii) Technical research and development (R&D) or expert organization providing technical up to date innovative ideas for better decision-making in the adoption of innovation.
3. Level of involvement which may be very active, active, slightly active, or passive.

The Addis Ababa LRT system was governed by the Engineering Procurement and Construction (EPC) Turnkey Contract, signed September 2009, which included a loan agreement signed June 2011, and the project commenced on 31 January 2012 (Bogale, 2018). The EPC is a project delivery method that defines the roles and responsibilities of multi-actors. The contractor in this case was the Chinese Railway Engineering Corporation (CREC) for construction and maintenance and the Shenzhou Metro Group (SMG) for operations. The contractor is responsible for delivering the whole LRT from the design stage to the final product. Thus, the employer, in this case the ERC, requests for tender that consists of the required performance and capacities from the contract in its employer requirement (Ayalew, 2015).

Three multi-actors were involved in the governance of this project delivery: the owner/employer (the Addis Ababa city government), the employer representative (ERC) and the contractors (CREC and SMG) (Yeo and Ning, 2002). In general, the EPC contract has advantages, such as reduced project delivery time, clearly divided roles and responsibilities, fixed price for the owner against inflation rates, and reduced workload due to multi-actors. The disadvantages of EPC are the difficulty for the owner to identify the scope of work to be done because the design does not get completed before the bidding, the pre-tender stage costs are higher, and the owners' ability to control the project is limited (Costa and Pimentel, 2009).

Urban-Actor Processes Based on Motivation, Cognition and Resources

Urban-actor processes are the interactions and strategies developed by the multi-actors, and they need to display a sufficiently strong combination of motivations, cognitions and resources to facilitate the adaptation of the process (Bressers, 2004; Owens, 2008). Motivations provides the motive or rationale behind actors' actions, giving the actors the purpose to act. Cognition builds on the understanding, reasoning and awareness of facts by the actors on how best success can be achieved. Resources provide actors with the ability to perform individually and with power during the interaction with other actors (Bressers et al., 2016).

There are mutual relations amongst the three key actor characteristics (Bressers et al., 2016). Every change in one of the three has effects on the other two. Usually motivation is mentioned first, although it is often valuable to start with how the actors perceive reality and the difficulties involved, and whether beneficial information is available about the context of relevant technology, social, economic and geographical conditions, as a precondition for motivation. Actors also need resources, and the obtainability of those resources is guaranteed to impact the actors' motivation, for example a deficiency of essential resources generates a low self-effectiveness assessment (Bandura, 1986).

On the other hand, we understand that knowledge is power; information can aid strategic purposes and therefore can be used as a basis of power. The gathering and processing of data is also an activity that needs resources. The three factors of motivation, cognition and resources not only determine, but in turn are determined by the actions and interactions that occur in the process.

Motivations

The motivation to act in certain ways during multi-actor interaction is embedded in actors' own values and goals (Bressers et al., 2016). In addition, self-interest, as mentioned in various economic theories, has a vital role to play, although more selfless values can directly provide noble self-goals (Gatersleben and Vlek, 1998).

External influence can also be a motivating factor, while personal-effectiveness evaluation plays a very significant role as a motivation factor (Bandura, 1986). This personal-effectiveness evaluation is significant because it provides the multi-actors with a yardstick to judge whether their chosen behaviour or actions are within or beyond their capacity. If beyond their capacity, it leads to a de-motivational effect, which reveals part of the relationship between motivation and the availability of resources (Bressers et al., 2016).

Cognitions

In policy sciences, the 'argumentative turn' highlights that knowledge is produced in multi-actor interactions, and given meaning by actors, who themselves are facilitated by frames of reference (Fischer and Gottweis, 2012). These frames of references are termed cognitive maps (Axelrod, 1976) or frames (Schön, 1983; Schön and Rein, 1994; van Hulst and Yanow, 2016), as well as policy core beliefs (Sabatier and Jenkins-Smith, 1999).

Cognitions are not so much realistic information, but more interpretations of genuineness, which are influenced by frames, filters, and interactions amongst multi-actors. A component of these frames is related to boundary decisions, which are ideas about what is part and what is not part of a contextual situation at hand (Bressers and Lulofs, 2010).

These various cognitions can identify the challenges at hand or components of a project that need to be solved, or the time frames that are significant, such as short-term results as against contributing to a long-term vision, or in terms of important levels and scales, as rooted in a higher level or larger scale of addressing problems. Dissimilarities in boundary decisions among the different multi-actors during interaction processes can have a major impact on their interaction in the process (Bressers et al., 2016).

Resources
Resources available to actors are vital in multi-actor interactions and important in the multi-actor relationship setting as a source of power (Bressers et al., 2016). Resources are assets that public and private actors can use to support their actions. The significance and importance of resources is dependent on the actions an actor wants to perform.

In this regard, possessing resources that other actors need to access for their required activities offers a source of power. Ordinarily, power is to an extent an outcome of acknowledgement to an actor by other actors. However, when this acknowledgement is not supported by real resources, it is weak whenever it is discovered.

The resources that are the basis for these powers include finance, skilled personnel, consensus and time. The ability of actors to use these resources is conditioned by formal, legal and institutional rules (Klok, 1995; Knoepfel et al., 2011). Therefore, the dependency of an actor on the resources of another actor predicts the balance of power. Similarly, in contextual interaction theory, it is not only formal powers that count, but also powers based on various kinds of important and required resources.

Transfer of Knowledge and Skills

Knowledge and skills transfer is interpreted in this context as the absorptive capacity developed by the ERC during the transfer of LRT from the MNCs. Absorptive capacity depends on an existing knowledge base or know-how, most of which is tacit knowledge, and the intensity of commitment or effort (Cohen and Lavinthal, 1990). Absorptive capacity in terms of knowledge transfer is directed at catching up with advanced industrial countries (Fu et al., 2011), and on how to use the technology that has been provided by the advanced countries in order to continue its use in a sustainable manner.

Absorptive capacity for new knowledge and the nature of knowledge required identifies that there is a need for tacit and explicit knowledge for innovation, to be codified and transferred from one context to another, which would make its adoption easier (Adler et al., 2003; Aubert and Hamel, 2001; O'Neil et al., 2002).

The process of local capability formation (Ernst and Kim, 2002) relates to the research especially with regards to the absorptive capacity as a result of knowledge and skills transfer, which are categorized into *explicit* and *tacit* knowledge (Polanyi, 1962).

Explicit knowledge means knowledge that is codified in formal, systematic language, i.e. encoded knowledge. It is the type of knowledge that can be stored, combined, transmitted, and retrieved with relative simplicity via various devices, in form of blueprints.

Tacit knowledge is knowledge that is difficult to codify and communicate. It is knowledge that can only be communicated through commitment, action and participation in a context and locality. Tacit knowledge is dependent on experience, i.e. people obtain it through imitation, practice and observation. Its diffusion needs apprentice-type training and face-to-face interaction. Diverse kinds of tacit knowledge are related to different aspects of organizational activities and with different degrees of complexities in transferring it.

Therefore, an organization that is systematically able to reframe, capture, identify, interpret, recodify, reframe and share a new knowledge base, connecting it with its own current knowledge platform, putting it into suitable use, is better able to adapt innovations, especially those that include technologies (Barnsley et al., 1998, Ferlie et al., 2001).

The prerequisites for absorptive capacity are the organization's current knowledge and skills foundation, particularly the availability of tacit, i.e. un-codifiable knowledge, pre-existing associated technologies, its learning culture, and proactive governance directed toward sharing knowledge (Barnsley et al., 1998, Ferlie et al., 2001; Zahra and George, 2002).

Furthermore, for effective knowledge conversion to become productive learning, two important elements are needed, namely: an existing knowledge base or know-how, most of which is tacit knowledge, and the intensity of commitment or effort. Cohen and Lavinthal (1990) refer to this as absorptive capacity. How fast and successfully the local innovation receiving organization internalizes and converts transferred knowledge into its own capability through learning will be largely dependent on its absorptive capacity and ability to utilize the transferred knowledge (Ernst and Kim, 2002). Nevertheless, the intensity of effort decides the speed of knowledge conversion.

The theoretical framework in Figure 8.1 shows the urban-actor processes, depicting the interactions and strategies between the multi-actors, which enables the transfer of knowledge and skills.

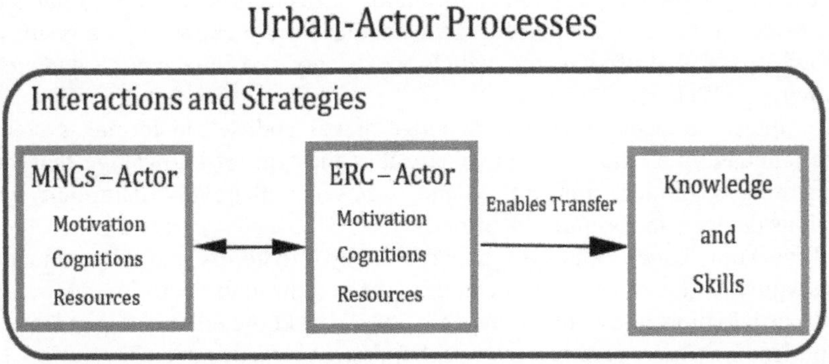

Urban-Actor Processes

Source: Conceptual idea of theoretical framework is partly adapted from elaboration of the layers of context in contextual interaction theory and structural governance (Bressers, 2009).

Figure 8.1   Theoretical framework

Relationship between Interactions and Strategies of Urban-Actor Processes, Knowledge and Skills

The MNCs and ERC actor processes in the case study took place as a form of multi-actor interaction because ERC interacted with many departments within the city comprising other LRT related city authorities and with MNCs. The MNCs' interactions took place between CREC and SMG and ERC.

These interactions and strategies were embedded in the motivation, cognition, and resources of the multi-actors, which enabled the transfer of knowledge and skills among ERC and MNCs. These transferred knowledge and skills fostered a viable and functional LRT in the long run for the LRT receiving corporation and city – ERC in Addis Ababa. Other MNCs interacting between the ERC and the Chinese consortium were consultants hired by the ERC, such as the Italferr, an MNC from Italy and SweRoad, an MNC from Sweden. Italferr and SweRoad were also part of the employer representative of ERC, to support ERC with their strategies during interactions with the MNCs from China, because the ERC had less knowledge of LRT requirements since it was the first time that LRT was being implemented as a form of public transport.

METHODOLOGY

This section explains the single case study research strategy, using a mixed method of qualitative and quantitative approach.

This research employed a mixed method using both qualitative and quantitative approaches in the single case study of Addis Ababa city. Mixed methods research provides instruments for researchers to study complex phenomena within their contexts (Baxter and Jack, 2008), and enables the researcher to explore entities or organizations, and investigate complex relationships, interventions, programmes and communities (Yin, 2003), which supports the deconstruction and subsequent reconstruction of various phenomena.

The qualitative method entails a two-step approach:

1. Pilot interviews using open-ended questions as a pre-test – which was carried out in 2015.
2. This was followed by two rounds of in-depth interviews using semi-structured questions. The first round took place in 2015 and second round in 2017.

The quantitative approach entailed the use of a survey questionnaire for a total of 254 passengers. These 254 respondents comprised passengers along the North–South (N–S) line (16.9 km) and the East–West (E–W) line (17.35 km). The quantitative approach built on the findings of a qualitative focus group discussion with six respondents. This discussion was based on semi-structured survey questions that were intended to get feedback on the real situation on the ground, which is essential in testing and restructuring the final survey questionnaire in the context of events for LRT passengers in Addis Ababa.

The sampling method used was purposive sampling which was selected because it was based on the characteristics of the population as LRT experts, LRT passengers and the objectives of the study. The target population for the survey included Ethiopians (Addis Ababa LRT experts working with ERC) and Chinese (LRT experts from CREC and SMG) for the qualitative approach, while the quantitative approach sample comprised the LRT passengers. The analysis instrument which was used to code the data gathered for the qualitative approach was the Atlas-TI software, while the Statistical Package for the Social Sciences (SPSS) was used for the quantitative approach.

FINDINGS

This section explains the empirical results deduced from the analysis of data acquired based on the concepts, variables and indicators, and includes the answer to the research question.

Multi-Actor Processes

The multi-actor interaction processes entail interactions and strategies, which comprise *motivation, cognitions* (Bressers, 2009) and *resources* (Klok, 1995; Knoepfel et al., 2011).

Motivation

The motivation at play during the multi-actor interactions between the MNCs from China and the ERC from Addis Ababa is embedded into the MNCs and ERC shared values and goals. These are *road congestion reduction, modal shift to LRT* and *affordable transport* for the ERC of Addis Ababa city.

Road congestion reduction for now shows a 21% (153,405 passengers) modal shift from Anbessa city buses to LRT, which is a comparable mode of transport based on affordable fares for passengers (Alade et al., 2020a).

For the MNCs from China, the motivations are *monetary gains* through contractual obligations, levels of *trust built* from the quality provision of LRT and its positive effects, and to provide a better platform to penetrate other potential city clients around the globe in transition to LRT.

Affordable transport

The new LRT was able to cater for the transport needs of the bottom of pyramid (BoP) through the provision of an affordable ticket fare price and structure. This fare structure provided by the multi-actors for the passengers is a zoning system of 2, 4 and 6 Ethiopian ETB.[1] The 2-ETB fare is for short distance passengers travelling within a restricted zone of a few LRT stops. The 4-ETB fare is for intermediate distance passengers. The 6-ETB fare is for long and end-to-end distance passengers.

Out of 254 total passengers as respondents, 68% of the passengers perceived this ticket fare as affordable (just OK), 22% perceive it as very affordable, while 10% perceive it as expensive (not affordable). This brings the total percentage of passengers perceiving the ticket pricing as affordable to 90%, thus fulfilling the target for the low-income passengers at the BoP, to increase accessibility and foster inclusion.

Monetary gains and trust

Although the MNCs representing the Chinese consortium to some extent shared the same motive with their ERC counterparts on congestion reduction, affordable transport and modal shift to the LRT, the Chinese consortium also had a strong motive for monetary gains for their MNCs and as a source of foreign direct investment (FDI) to China.

In addition, the Chinese consortium was motivated to build a high level of trust with the ERC, as an aftermath of knowledge sharing, knowledge transfer, and quality LRT provision, which provides the positive effects of affordable fare, gradual modal shift, and congestion reduction. This built trust over time is likely to foster the trust of other cities in transition to LRT in Africa and across the globe, especially when cities like Addis Ababa are able to demonstrate self-sufficiency in its operation and maintenance of the LRT after knowledge transfer from the Chinese. This will serve as a source of attraction to other cities to emulate.

As confirmed by a top Chinese LRT manager, this motive for monetary gain and trust can also be observed from the Chinese investment in other African countries on various infrastructural projects, embedded in China's policy plans to harness the rapidly growing market value in Africa's infrastructural sector, and provide quality infrastructure and profitable bilateral relationships between the countries.

Cognitions

An absorptive capacity framework is embedded into the ERC's knowledge and skills framework which is further analysed below. This absorptive capacity framework is divided into three, namely: *types of knowledge transfer structure, knowledge transfer ratio plan*, and *type of knowledge transfer streams* (Alade et al., 2020a).

In terms of absorptive capacity, the ERC had less capacity to maintain the LRT infrastructure, due to the sophistication (complexity) of the LRT system. Therefore, in this regard there was a strong emphasis on knowledge transfer in the contract agreement between the ERC, CREC and SMG, and this was incorporated from the start of the LRT project and is categorized as one of the main key performance indicators.

Transfer of knowledge varies, depending on how the LRT receiving organization organizes its tacit knowledge to assimilate and effectively use the explicit knowledge, using various capacity building structures.

The knowledge transfer in our case study took place mostly between the ERC directors, mid- to low-level experts and the Chinese consortium experts. The technical knowledge shared by the Chinese consortium represents explicit knowledge codified in formal, systematic language, i.e. encoded knowledge, in various forms of documented manuals of operation, instruction and concepts organized in digital formats provided to ERC. An example is the taking over of the LRT driving from the Chinese just six months after the start of operation, because of continuous observation, face-to-face apprentice training, imitation and practice as a tacit form of knowledge acquired by the ERC.

A structural framework to acquire the knowledge was set up through different strategies, on the basis of a knowledge transfer ratio plan consisting of:

- First year – Ethiopians (ET) 30%, Chinese (CH) 70%: This depicts that in the first year, the knowledge transferred from CH to ET will be at a ratio of ET 30% and CH 70%.
- Second year – ET 40%, CH 60%: This ratio means by the second year, there should be an improvement from 30% to 40% for ET, while the Chinese counterparts are also releasing responsibilities to the Ethiopians more than in the first year from 70% to 60%.
- Third year – ET 60%, CH 40%: The third year shows that slightly more than half of knowledge is now transferred to the Ethiopians.
- Fourth/fifth year – ET 100%: By the fourth and fifth years, it is expected that there should be 100% knowledge transfer to the Ethiopians.

The progress from October 2015 of this was actualized as the knowledge transfer in 2017 resulted in 296 personnel as Ethiopians and 117 Chinese, and human power improved after one year with good inputs – 100% Ethiopian LRT drivers were already driving the LRT, 100% of the operations control centre was managed by the ERC locals, and 100% of the finance, human resource and security departments were managed by the ERC locals. Some components of the operations and maintenance department were still building more capacity, aiming to reach 100% by the fifth year.

Medium- and long-term training
Training programmes in China, Ethiopia, and other parts of the world, with a planned learning curve for all LRT processes and phases were provided. Approximately 600 ERC staff were sent for training to prepare for construction and operation, some of whom were sent to China, parts of Europe and some trained locally and on the job during the construction and operation phase. However, 70% out of the 600 ERC were trained outside before the commencement of the LRT project and the Chinese at times only needed to fill in gaps where the ERC staff trainee fell short. As an example, out of the 600 Ethiopian personnel, 20 people were trained in China on signalling components, and some of the technicians and engineers that needed retraining were retrained in the short term.

Nineteen mainstream and certifiable positions in operation and maintenance
The knowledge transfer was divided into different components of training, which is embedded in all stages with a specific number of trainees. Examples of operational positions include: control centre, information dispatcher, power dispatcher, and operation dispatcher. Maintenance positions include:

sub-signalling, communication, rolling stock, construction of the infrastructure, human resources department, security department commercial centre, transport centre, driving department, operation control centre, etc.

Pairing of every Chinese manager by Ethiopians in the main departments
An example here is when a Chinese manager in the procurement, finance, operations, and maintenance departments also had an Ethiopian manager working side by side as the local manager. In this way, the Ethiopians could learn on the job quickly, by working alongside the Chinese to see what is done every day, asking questions and getting clarity of understanding and purpose.

Resources

Resource management in light-rail transport
Resource management in light-rail involves how limited resources are managed and optimized to achieve expected outcomes during production of goods or provision of services to the target audience (Pisoni et al., 2017).

Time resource management
Time resource management was achieved in the following phases of time periods of the light-rail project:

1. Design phase period: This is characterized by ERC's timely interaction with city level authorities, such as Addis Ababa's road authority, city water and electricity companies, city telecommunication provider, etc., to incorporate their activities and assets with the needs of the LRT. In addition, and very importantly, it was necessary to resolve third-party issues arising from the private and public owned assets along the LRT routes.
2. Construction phase period: Multi-actors' interaction between ERC and other MNCs – CREC, SMG, Sweroad and Italferr – was facilitated by ERC to construct the components of the LRT in a timely fashion. This was also managed using the stakeholder dialogue method, having some of the steering committee members involved at every main construction stage. This ensured that most contracts of different phases were approved as quickly as possible, not exceeding any of the stipulated periods for construction.
3. Operation phase period: The structured absorptive capacity aided a timely technology knowledge transfer, which ensured that only Ethiopians were driving the LRT after six months of starting the operation. In addition, major parts of operation and maintenance were handled solely by the Ethiopians between two and three years after operation. This saved Addis Ababa city a significant amount of money, which would have been used

to pay the Chinese in foreign currency, costing more as extra expenses, if the locals were not technically empowered within the right period of LRT adaptation.

Technical knowledge (human resource) management
In acquiring light-rail technology transferred from China, ERC used tacit knowledge as a form of absorptive capacity to structure its knowledge transfer to acquire the Chinese explicit knowledge. Frugality, i.e. doing more with less resources was achieved in human resources, as extra cost was avoided in extending the five year concession to the Chinese, via appropriate knowledge gap filling by the Ethiopians, who received technical training a few years before, during and after the operation of the LRT.

Finance management
Using the limited available finance in Ethiopia, and a part borrowed as a loan from China, Addis Ababa city controlled the use of this resource through the efficient use of human resources and time. Frugality in these two areas helped expenditure to be deployed more effectively, avoiding the need for more loans, which might have been required if completion was delayed and inflation set in, which would have affected counterpart funding and costs for components of the rolling stock. Prudent financial management saved costs in the present and future adaptation of LRT in Addis Ababa. As mentioned by a top director, "We did not have any reason to spend more than we budgeted for. This is because all components of the LRT were done within time, avoiding any form of significant inflation of foreign currency for our counterpart funding and we have 50% of our workers who have presently taken over the LRT operations and maintenance, paid in our local currency."

Nature of Interactions, Types of Negotiations and Levels of Involvement

The multi-actor interactions that took place within the LRT adaptation processes between the Addis Ababa and Chinese counterparts focused on their roles, types of negotiations during the design, construction and operation phases, key performance indicators (KPIs), and resource management (financial, time and human).

Nature of interactions and types of negotiations
The project involved formal negotiations, voluntary agreements, stakeholder dialogue, multi-partner projects, information sharing, and reasoned argumentation to foster mutual understanding, all of which required trust and transparency in the use of terms (Sarkis et al., 2010).

The ERC used mainly stakeholder dialogues and government intervened with formal negotiations when the Addis Ababa city administration was facing challenges with other stakeholders. For example, as mentioned by an ERC expert using the stakeholder dialogues, "We don't need to go back and forth, the federal government representatives in the steering committee are already aware of the technical and non-technical decisions the ERC is proposing, so we have their support for approval and funding by the government, which becomes easier and moves faster."

The stakeholder dialogues further provided better understanding by avoiding top-down communication, through the engagement of related top government officials' positions from the bottom, i.e. *bottom-up approach*. This ensured a smoother process, saving time, and fostering faster LRT implementation. Seventy per cent of the 17 respondents during the second and third round semi-structured interviews from ERC supported the claim that their dialogues with other multi-actors were more stakeholder dialogues than formal negotiations.

To minimize risk and cost during the operations, the Chinese consortium assumed responsibility for any cost resulting from a component failure or revenue shortage during construction (building) and operation.

Levels of involvement

Levels of involvement may be categorized as very active, active, slightly active or passive. The Addis Ababa city administration, ERC and Chinese consortium were very active multi-actors, because the LRT was implemented within the city of Addis Ababa, which required interacting with many other actors, such as utility companies.

The ERC also performed the role of an intermediary between the city multi-actors and the Chinese consortium, as the Chinese consortium was a client of ERC and needed ERC to facilitate several issues, such as right of way, security matters, demolitions and resettlements, utility relocations, etc.

The federal government played an active role, by financing the LRT counterpart funding and seeking loans from EXIM bank as a guarantor for the country. The government also provided rules for checks and balances, especially from the Chinese consortium, such as fare regulation to avoid overcharging the LRT commuters, quality control of rolling stock provided and adherence to KPIs, such as knowledge transfer. Other multi-actors playing active roles were the consultants hired by the ERC, such as Italferr and SweRoad. Thus, no actor fell into the range of slightly active or passive levels of involvement.

These negotiations at the national level and roles at the city level were successful because a steering committee comprised of both national and city officials coordinated these processes together, providing a good level of constant situation awareness of stages involved in the implementation processes. This avoided delays and unnecessary bureaucracy due to fewer communication gaps.

How Were Knowledge and Skills Transferred from Chinese to Ethiopian Urban Actors?

The ERC structured how the knowledge and skills were transferred from the Chinese to Ethiopian urban actors, using a well-structured absorptive capacity, and their tacit knowledge to acquire the Chinese explicit knowledge.

Furthermore, it is pertinent to highlight that interaction processes between the multi-actors were part of a symbiotic relationship in terms of decision-making processes, which are sensitive to the local skills, decision process initiatives and context-specific knowledge (Bhaduri et al., 2018), from ERC in Addis Ababa.

Therefore, knowledge and skills transfer occurred not only from the Chinese consortium to the ERC, but also vice versa. Interaction processes in regard to the local skills of ERC also provided benefits to the MNCs and multi-actors, to better understand the context situation at hand, which only ERC understood initially.

In relating these research findings to its theoretical framework, we see that the MNCs and ERC urban multi-actors interacted using strategies such as stakeholder dialogues in negotiations and structured absorptive capacity, considering their motivation, cognition and resources, which positioned each actor with roles mainly created by the structured absorptive capacity of ERC. These roles created by ERC's structured absorptive capacity enabled an adequate level of knowledge transfer and skills in specific areas, such as design, planning, operations, and maintenance of the LRT despite its failure in a few aspects of the LRT implementation.

CONCLUSIONS AND RECOMMENDATIONS

We conclude with two subsections. First we summarize the main lessons learnt from the success of the structured absorptive capacity of the ERC and the relative failures encountered during the LRT implementation. Then we offer recommendations on how to govern the transfer of urban knowledge and skills.

Lessons Learnt from LRT Knowledge Transfer from China to Ethiopia

To a large extent, the structured absorptive capacity by the ERC to acquire knowledge and skills from the Chinese consortium was the main determinant for knowledge and skills transfer between ERC and the Chinese consortium.

In this regard, it can be argued that the tacit knowledge demonstrated by ERC, using different efforts to acquire these skills and knowledge and their initial knowledge base, facilitated the adequate acquisition of the explicit knowledge provided by the Chinese. This tacit knowledge used the knowledge transfer structure, knowledge transfer ratio plans and streams, and other unique approaches to knowledge transfer, such as the pairing of each ERC departmental head with the Chinese.

This chapter further demonstrates that the transfer of skills and knowledge from the Chinese to ERC within one to five years can be described as adequate, because of ERC's proactive structure of absorptive capacity, which aimed at acquiring 100% of the skills and knowledge; and the willingness of the Chinese to release their skills and knowledge to the ERC with limited hindrances, such as language barrier, city and culture contexts.

On the other hand, two main relative failures or challenges occurred, despite these emulative achievements by the ERC. The first is the non-functional electronic ticketing system on board the LRT, which could not function as planned due to the high travel demand leading to a highly congested LRT, where passengers were unable to swipe their cards on the electronic device (Alade et al., 2020b). This failure led to the extra cost of constructing new emergency paper ticket shops at each of the 41 stations, employing ticket attendants, and paying extra to acquire the land to build these shops, due to resettlement costs for the original landowners (Alade et al., 2019).

The second was the inability to prevent 30% fare evasion by passengers (Alade et al., 2020b), which led to a lower cost recovery rate and impacted expected investment returns to pay loans acquired from China in the EPC contract. The ticket attendants on board the LRT during transit and before transit are very few as compared to the number of passengers, thereby encouraging fare evasion with limited enforcement to 'pay before ride' (Alade et al., 2019).

These failures stem from inadequacy in the cognitive understanding of the project and its frames related to boundary decisions, i.e. ideas about what is part and what is not part of the contextual situation at hand (Bressers and Lulofs, 2010). Thus, challenges may arise in a project that need to be re-assessed at a higher level or larger scale in order to solve such problems (Bressers et al., 2016).

It is also pertinent to note that despite the well-structured absorptive capacity, the aspect of hardware manufacturing of the LRT rolling stock, such as engine parts, still needs to be harnessed for knowledge transfer by the ERC in the long run, because for the moment it is only the Chinese that are responsible for this component.

However, the success of the LRT within just three years has led to a progressive modal shift from other motorized transport to the LRT; provision of more affordable transport as compared to other public transport; reduction in road congestion; gradual reduction in CO_2 emissions; and fostering of transit oriented development (TOD) (Alade et al., 2020b), which has to a reasonable extent overshadowed the relative failures or made the relative failures almost insignificant, as compared to the tangible success.

Furthermore, it can be argued that implementing the LRT in Addis Ababa for the first time became a learning by doing and doing by learning process, which has provided lessons learnt for knowledge transfer to the Chinese on how to avoid similar challenges in particular city contexts in the future. Similarly, the ERC learnt from the reasons for components failure in the LRT and how to adjust for improvements in the future LRT routes. The case study shows that what was needed for successful knowledge and skill transfer involved providing knowledge to both ERC and the Chinese consortium, using a decision-making process derived from knowledge of the setting or context gained from learning and experience, and this successfully combined both knowledge about the local context from ERC and technical knowledge from the MNCs (Bhaduri et al., 2018).

Recommendations

Governing the transfer of urban knowledge and skills can be achieved through a knowledge transfer policy and decentralized authority policy.

Knowledge transfer policy
The knowledge transfer policy direction is deduced considering the logical reasoning that there is no benefit in transferring the LRT innovation, without also transferring the knowledge of how best to operate and maintain it. In this regard, the cognitive process practised by Addis Ababa actors is a policy direction for other cities in transition to LRT to emulate. Thus, knowledge transfer policy directions can be formulated to include: types of knowledge transfer structure, knowledge transfer ratio plan, type of knowledge transfer streams, and multi-actors' processes of interactions and strategies. These should be incorporated into the adaptation agreement between the MNCs and light-rail city authorities from the inception before adaptation. Therefore, cities should enforce a structured technological transfer as one of their KPIs in their contract agreements with other multi-actors within the country and from abroad. This will guarantee the sustainable operation and maintenance of the light-rail rolling stock within bearable costs and will over time provide the platform for local production of light-rail soft- and hardware components. In addition, this can be complemented through documentation of knowledge transfer, from experienced staff through audio-visual means, to reduce brain drain of skilled labour in the transport sector and provide documented technical assistance to new and younger engineers and scientists.

Decentralized authority policy

This policy path is to provide a decentralized authority for the transport authorities, by providing them with total autonomy to perform, as observed in ERC of Addis Ababa. A decentralized authority in transport institutions will provide the benefit of innovative strategies through more robust infrastructure implementation models and stronger authority to deal with wicked transport problems. This is because a decentralized authority is characterized by a private sector system, but in this case with sound regulative functions in place to overcome inequalities among transport operators and passengers and reduce the bureaucracy of implementing transport projects. ERC enjoyed the autonomy to implement the light-rail system, and was given full control of responsibility to perform better.

NOTE

1. ETB: Ethiopian Birr, the Ethiopian national currency, with a current equivalence rate of 29 ETB to 1 USD.

REFERENCES

Adler, B., Kwon, S. and Singer, J. 2003. The "Six-West" problem: Professionals and the intraorganizational diffusion of innovations, with particular reference to the case of hospitals. Marshall School of Business, University of Southern California, Los Angeles. http://www.marshall.usc.edu/web/MOR.cfm?doc id=5561.

Alade, T., Edelenbos, J. and Gianoli, A. 2019. Adapting urban light-rail transport to the African Context: A process conducted by transport authorities and Chinese rail corporations in Addis-Ababa, Abuja, and Lagos. *Urban Science*, 3(4), 109. https://doi.org/10.3390/urbansci3040109.

Alade, T., Edelenbos, J. and Gianoli, A. 2020a. Frugality in multi-actor interactions and absorptive capacity of Addis-Ababa light-rail transport. *Journal of Urban Management*, 9(1), 67–76.

Alade, T., Edelenbos, J. and Gianoli, A. 2020b. A sustainable approach to innovation adoption in light-rail transport. *Sustainability*, 12(3), 1262. https://doi.org/10.3390/su12031262.

Aubert, B. and Hamel, G. 2001. Adoption of smart cards in the medical sector: The Canadian experience. *Social Science & Medicine*, 53(7), 879–894.

Axelrod, R. (ed.). 1976. *Structure of Decision: The Cognitive Maps of Political Elites*. Princeton: Princeton University Press.

Ayalew, B. 2015. Systems engineering approach for Addis Ababa light railway project from the employer perspective. Master's dissertation, Addis Ababa University, Addis Ababa Institute of Technology School of Mechanical and Industrial Engineering Railway Engineering. http://etd.aau.edu.et/bitstream/handle/123456789/16178/Biniyam%20Ayalew.pdf?sequence=1&isAllowed=y.

Bandura, A. 1986. *Social Foundations of Thought and Action: A Social Cognitive Theory*. Englewood Cliffs, NJ: Prentice Hall.

Barnsley, J., Lemieux-Charles, L. and McKinney, M. 1998. Integrating learning into integrated delivery systems. *Health Care Management Review*, 23(1), 18–28.

Baxter, P. and Jack, S. 2008. Qualitative case study methodology: Study design and implementation for novice researchers. *The Qualitative Report*, 13(4), 554–559.

Bhaduri, S. 2016. Frugal innovation by 'the small and the marginal': An alternative discourse on innovation and development. Inaugural lecture, Erasmus University, Rotterdam.

Bhaduri, S., Sinha, K. M. and Knorringa, P. 2018. Frugality and cross-sectoral policy-making for food security. *NJAS – Wageningen Journal of Life Sciences*, 84, 72–79.

Bogale, H. 2018. Challenges faced during the development of Addis Ababa Light Railway Project – with limited budget, land and time constraint in the city of Addis Ababa, Ethiopia. Ethiopian Railways Corporation. https://www.glob aldeliveryinitiative.org/sites/default/files/_gdi_day_2_delivery_lab_1_henok _bogale_presentation.pdf.

Bressers, H. 2004. Implementing sustainable development: How to know what works, where, when and how. In W. M. Lafferty (ed.), *Governance for Sustainable Development: The Challenge of Adapting Form to Function*. Cheltenham, UK and Northampton, MA, USA: Edward Elgar Publishing, 284–318.

Bressers, H. 2009. From public administration to policy networks: Contextual inter-action analysis. In S. Narath and F. Varone (eds.), *Rediscovering Public Law and Public Administration in Comparative Policy Analysis: A Tribute to Peter Knoepfel*. Berne: Haupt Verlag, 123–142.

Bressers, H., Bressers, N., Kuks, S. and Larrue, C. (eds.). 2016. *Governance for Drought Resilience: The Governance Assessment Tool and Its Use*. Cham: Springer.

Bressers, H. and Klok, P. 1988. Fundamentals for a theory of policy instruments. *International Journal of Social Economics*, 15(3–4), 22–41.

Bressers, H. and Lulofs, K. (eds.). 2010. *Governance and Complexity in Water Management: Creating Cooperation through Boundary Spanning Strategies*. Cheltenham, UK and Northampton, MA, USA: Edward Elgar Publishing.

Cheng, Y. and Huang, T. 2013. High speed rail passengers' mobile ticketing adoption. *Transportation Research Part C: Emerging Technologies*, 30, 143–160.

Cohen, W. and Lavinthal, D. 1990. Absorptive capacity: A new perspective on learning and innovation. *Administrative Science Quarterly*, 35, 128–152.

Costa, K. and Pimentel, C. 2009. Contract management for international EPC projects. Project report, Worcester Polytechnic Institute.

Drejer, A. 2002. Situations for innovation management: Towards a contingency model. *European Journal of Innovation Management*, 5(1), 4–17.

Edelenbos, J., Bressers, N. and Scholten, P. (eds.). 2013. *Water Governance as Connective Capacity*. Farnham: Ashgate Publishing.

Ernst, D. and Kim, L. 2002. Global production networks, knowledge diffusion, and local capability formation. *Research Policy*, 31(8), 1417–1429.

Fadeeva, Z. 2005. Promise of sustainability collaboration: Potential fulfilled? *Journal of Cleaner Production*, 13(2), 165–174.

Ferlie, E., Gabbay, J., Fitzgerald, L., Locock, L. and Dopson, S. 2001. Evidence-based medicine and organisational change: An overview of some recent qualitative research. In L. Ashburner (ed.), *Organisational Behaviour and Organisational Studies in Health Care: Reflections on the Future*. Basingstoke: Palgrave Macmillan, 18–42.

Fischer, F. and Gottweis, H. (eds.). 2012. *The Argumentative Turn Revisited: Public Policy as Communicative Practice*. Durham, NC: Duke University Press.

Fu, X., Pietrobelli, C. and Soete, L. 2011. The role of foreign technology and indigenous innovation in the emerging economies: Technological change and catching-up. *World Development*, 39(7), 1204–1212.

Gatersleben, B. and Vlek, C. 1998. Household consumption quality of life and environmental impacts: A psychological perspective and empirical study. In. K. J. Noorman and T. S. Uiterkamp (eds.), *Green Households? Domestic Consumers, Environment and Sustainability*. London: Earthscan, 141–183.

Kim, L. 1998. Crisis construction and organizational learning: Dynamics of capability building in catching-up at Hyundai Motor. *Organization Science*, 9(4), 506–521.

Klok, P. 1995. A classification of instruments for environmental policy. In B. Dente (ed.), *Environmental Policy in Search of New Instruments*. Dordrecht: Kluwer Academic, 21–36.

Knoepfel, P., Larrue, C., Varone, F. and Hill, M. 2011. *Public Policy Analysis*. Bristol: Policy Press.

O'Neil, H., Pouder, P. and Buchholtz, A. 2002. Patterns in the diffusion of strategies across organisations: Insights from the innovation diffusion literature. *Academy of Management Review*, 23(1), 98–114.

Owens, K. 2008. Understanding how actors influence policy implementation: A comparative study of wetland restorations in New Jersey, Oregon, the Netherlands and Finland. PhD dissertation, University of Twente, Enschede.

Pisoni, A., Michelin, L. and Martignoni, G. 2017. Frugal approach to innovation: State of the art and future perspectives. *Journal of Cleaner Production*, 171, 107–126.

Polanyi, M. 1962. *Personal Knowledge: Towards a Post-Critical Philosophy*. Chicago: University of Chicago Press.

Sabatier, P. A. and Jenkins-Smith, H. 1999. The advocacy coalition framework: An assessment. In C. Weible and P. A. Sabatier (eds.), *Theories of the Policy Process*. Boulder: Westview Press, 117–168.

Sarkis, J., Cordeiro, J., Alfonso, D. and Brust, V. (eds.). 2010. *Facilitating Sustainable Innovation through Collaboration: A Multi-Stakeholder Perspective*. Dordrecht: Springer.

Schön, D. A. (ed.). 1983. *The Reflective Practitioner: How Professionals Think in Action*. New York: Basic Books.

Schön, D. A. and Rein, M. 1994. *Frame Reflection: Toward the Resolution of Intractable Policy Controversies*. New York: Basic Books.

van Hulst, M. and Yanow, D. 2016. From policy "frames" to "framing": Theorizing a more dynamic political approach. *The American Review of Public Administration*, 46(1), 92–112.

Yeo, K. and Ning, J. 2002. Integrating supply chain and critical chain concepts in engineering-procurement-construction (EPC) projects. *International Journal of Project Management*, 20, 253–262.

Yin, R. K. 2003. *Case Study Research: Design and Methods*. London: Sage.

Zahra, A. S. and George, G. 2002. Absorptive capacity: A review, reconceptualization and extension. *Academy of Management Review*, 27(2), 185–203.

9. Financing urban infrastructure and services in Africa

Aloysius N. Bongwa and Meine Pieter van Dijk

INTRODUCTION

Investment in high quality urban infrastructure is desperately needed. Due to shortfalls in municipal budgets, cities are increasingly looking at a wider range of financing options to bridge their infrastructure needs, particularly in partnership with the private sector. While traditional forms of municipal finance – including municipal revenues, loans, or intergovernmental transfers (grants) from either national or international governments – retain their importance, there is a wide selection of financial instruments both in the private and public sector to fit a variety of infrastructure projects. In the private sector, these options include for instance bonds, public–private partnerships (PPPs), privatization/divesture, infrastructure investment funds, private risk mitigation, and crowdfunding. In the public sector, options include, among others, municipal development funds and development financing institutions, pooled financing, viability gap funding, public risk mitigation, and tax exemptions (Lindfield and Teipelke, 2014).

There is no uniform or uncontested definition of urban infrastructure. Some definitions focus on the 'hard' utilities and the material networks that underpin their provision (Leipziger et al., 2003). Other definitions include the people, practices, discourses and imaginaries that shape urban services (Amin and Thrift, 2017). There is a shared understanding that urban infrastructure is a system through which urban services, of various kinds, are provided. Hard infrastructure (i.e. bricks and mortar) mainly refers to tangible assets and is often associated with public works for core services (e.g. urban development, transportation, water and sanitation, solid waste management and energy). Soft infrastructure refers to specific operations or processes aimed at technical assistance, institutional strengthening, and human capital building (e.g. fiscal management, cadasters, operations control centers and urban governance). While the emphasis is on hard infrastructure, soft infrastructure is key, given that regulatory mechanisms and other governance structures are critical and must be put in place to facilitate the efficient operation, functioning and sustainability of the hard infrastructure component (Bonilla and Zapparoli, 2017). A robust, efficient and well-maintained infrastructure system is critical to support and sustain the economy, improve quality of life, and strengthen global competitiveness.

The literature shows that improvements in infrastructure raise productivity, stimulate private investment (Cavallo and Daude, 2011), and facilitate domestic and international trade (Bougheas et al., 1999), thereby promoting sustainable growth (Agenor, 2010). Calderon et al. (2015) estimate that a 10% increase in infrastructure provision increases output per worker by about 1% in the long run. Infrastructure has an indispensable, positive role in development, especially urban infrastructure (Kessides, 1993; World Bank, 1994).

An important distinction is between financing and funding. Infrastructure financing is raising the high upfront costs to build the infrastructure when and where needed by leveraging future revenue streams that can repay the upfront costs. Financing is the raising of this upfront capital to expedite the process. Funding is the revenue streams in the future to repay the financing.

This chapter looks at how cities cope with providing basic infrastructure services in the face of rapid urban growth globally and especially in Africa, using a multi case study approach. We identify major urban infrastructure issues. Then the theoretical underpinning of infrastructure and service provision in the context of decentralization and the subsidiarity principle are examined. The question why financing for local infrastructure is hard to get is addressed, while a range of local infrastructure financing mechanisms is presented, with Ghana as a special case. The other cases illustrate alternative methods of infrastructure financing which local governments have explored. At the end some recommendations for local government managers who are considering the use of alternative infrastructure financing options are formulated.

URBANIZATION, DECENTRALIZATION, INSTITUTIONS AND GOVERNANCE ISSUES

Rapid urbanization in Africa over the last three decades has resulted in a very high demand for basic urban infrastructure and the need for sustained and alternative mechanisms of financing and funding. Africa currently has three cities of over 10 million inhabitants (Lagos: 21 million inhabitants, Cairo: 20.4 million inhabitants, and Kinshasa: 13.3 million inhabitants); four cities with a population between 5 and 10 million; 49 cities with a population of 1 to 5 million; 53 cities whose population is between 500,000 and 1 million inhabitants; and 85 cities with a population of 300,000 to 500,000 inhabitants. This rapid increase in the urban population has put pressure on local governments to provide a wide range of infrastructure and services (public transit, roads, water and wastewater treatment, solid waste management, social services and housing) where the public sector is responsible for owning and operating the assets and where financing largely relies on grants, subsidies, taxes and other sources that are unsustainable in the long run.

Africa is suffering from a major urban infrastructure and services gap. Annual national public spending on infrastructure is exceedingly low: an average of 2% of GDP in 2009–2015, compared to 5.2% in India and 8.8% in China. Not surprisingly, African cities often succumb to fragility due to non-resilience. Sixty percent of all urbanites live in over-crowded and under-serviced slums. Around 25–45% walk to work due to lack of affordable transport. With turbo-urbanization, these appalling conditions could easily deteriorate (World Economic Forum, 2018). By every measure of infrastructure coverage, African economies lag behind their peers in other parts of the developing world.

While up to now much of the debate on infrastructure has focused on the financing challenges – how to raise finance for infrastructure projects, by using national levers and accessing international markets – the broader public governance dimension of infrastructure financing has been neglected. Governance of infrastructure refers to the processes, tools and norms of inter-action, decision-making and monitoring used by governmental organizations and their counterparts with respect to making infrastructure services available to the public and the public sector (Basedow et al., 2017; OECD, 2015). It relates to the interaction between government institutions internally, as well as their interaction with the private sector, users and citizens. It covers the entire life cycle of the asset, but the most resource intensive activities will typically be the planning and decision-making phase for most assets.

A natural starting point is to assess the challenges that arise when governance arrangements fall short (Table 9.1). Poor governance is a major reason why infrastructure projects fail to meet their timeframe, budget and service delivery objectives. Infrastructure projects with deficient governance often result in cost overruns, delays, underperformance, underutilization, acceler-ated deterioration due to poor maintenance, and, occasionally, in expensive 'white elephants' and bridges-to-nowhere. Five phases in the life cycle of an infrastructure asset project are identified; each of these relates to separate governance challenges (OECD, 2015):

- First, there is the issue of evaluating the infrastructure needs across sectors and regions.
- Second, a prioritization of these needs should take place based on plan-ning, processes and tools that allow an aggregation of the preferences of stakeholders.

Table 9.1   *Challenges in infrastructure governance*

Planning and strategic vision for infrastructure development	**Insufficient planning and lack of a strategic vision can result in suboptimal decisions and inadequate prioritization**
Involvement of interested parties	Lack of dialogue on infrastructure development with its end users, civil society, and the private sector, has a negative impact.
Coordination of stakeholders at various levels of government	The lack of coordination among the sector stakeholders and various levels of government results in unviable projects.
Technical capacities of the public sector	There can be a change in the nature of the technical capacities required for planning, implementation or evaluation, making it indispensable to acquire new capacities or skills, and maintain an institutional memory and minimum technical knowledge.
Flows and sources of financing	Whatever the source of financing (public, private or mixed), infrastructure projects require major commitments with respect to financing flows and tariff regulation.
Administrative considerations, given the substantive scopes (mandates) or geographic scopes (territorial jurisdiction) in the taking of decisions	Sector or geographic jurisdictions often do not correspond to the area of the project's socioeconomic or environmental impact, yet the decision-making process is fragmented among various institutions and is affected by the limitations of their respective mandates.
Measurement of performance in the provision of infrastructure services	The lack of reliable or relevant data and the scarce capacity for processing and analyzing available data can complicate ex ante or post facto evaluation, impeding solid decision-making.
Impact of the existing institutional or regulatory framework with their historic baggage	Past decisions (previous subsidies or investments), the prevalence of certain interest groups or the need to show results can produce important biases, resulting in suboptimal decisions for infrastructure development. Moreover, the instability or excessive complexity of the institutional framework increases vulnerability to arbitrary decisions and discourages investors.
Vulnerability to corruption	Given the amounts involved, various types of uncertainty inherent in infrastructure projects and complex processes leave the sector particularly vulnerable to the risks of corruption.
Impact of political and economic cycles	Decisions relating to infrastructure and their implementation are overly sensitive to political and economic cycles, with events such as elections or economic changes that have a direct impact.
Sharing of risk management between the public and private sectors	The distribution of risks of financing and operation of infrastructure is a complex process that requires careful consideration of the origins of risks and the responsibilities of each interested party. An inadequate allocation of risks results in disincentives for private participation and lost opportunities for infrastructure development.

Source: Adapted from OECD (2015).

- Third, in the project preparation phase, suitable procedures and skills in terms of technical design, affordability and value for money issues need to be applied.
- Fourth, in the construction phase, appropriate skills and systems should be available to ensure that project assumptions are delivered upon and changes are subject to appropriate scrutiny.
- Fifth, in the operational stage of the project, the right incentives and tools for appropriate monitoring of asset performance and maintenance should be in place as well as mechanisms for reflection on the service provided.

INFRASTRUCTURE FINANCING IN THEORY AND PRACTICE: DECENTRALIZATION AND THE SUBSIDIARITY PRINCIPLE

Governments seek to influence infrastructure investment for a number of reasons. First, governments want to ensure that infrastructure is adequate to meet demand and improve services. Private markets may not supply some goods such as street lighting so government provision may be necessary. Secondly, services may provide benefits to society over and above those that accrue to the individual. These external benefits or positive externalities are often cited to justify spending on public education. Finally, the existence of natural monopoly, that is, when the minimum efficient size of plant is so large relative to market size that the market can support only one supplier may also warrant intervention.

The outcome of this process reflects the basic, underlying rationale for fiscal decentralization generally and for the provision of urban capital projects specifically: the so-called *Subsidiarity Principle* of Oates (1972, 1993, 1999) and others, also sometimes referred to as the *Decentralization Theorem*. This principle states that government services should be provided by the lowest level of government that can do so efficiently. When tastes, incomes and needs differ across regions, local governments are or should be in the best position to determine the expenditure priorities of its citizens, and assign responsibilities to the lowest level of government. The existence of multiple local jurisdictions gives individuals the opportunity to 'vote with their feet' by moving to the jurisdiction that best meets their demands for the appropriate mix of public services and taxes, at least when mobility exists. In the same way, if local governments are assigned expenditure responsibilities, they should bear the costs of financing those expenditures because only then will they balance the benefits of public goods with the costs. A government that is 'closer to the people' will be more efficient in providing government services than a centralized government.

The Subsidiarity Principle suggests a list of fairly specific functions for urban governments. These include responsibilities for: primary and secondary education, roads and bridges, public transit, street lighting, sidewalks, water system, sewer system, garbage collection and disposal, police protection, fire suppression and prevention, primary health services, land use planning, economic development, parks and recreation, and libraries. The traditional rationale for the public provision and regulation of infrastructure is built upon the economic concepts of public goods and market failure. Infrastructure assets – which produce public goods that are not rivalrous in consumption, nonexcludable in use, or both – typically exhibit natural monopoly, and often yield positive spillovers that are hard to monetize. Due to these characteristics, private markets normally underprovide the socially desirable levels of infrastructure. This provides a rationale for public provision.

The jurisdictional responsibility for infrastructure financing and provision differs across sectors and countries in Africa. Although information and communication technology and power are usually national responsibilities, responsibility for the water supply in urban areas is widely decentralized (World Bank, 2016). In many countries, markedly the francophone African countries, operation is entrusted to utilities that remain national. Where municipal utilities do exist, municipal governments own only a few in whole or in part. Responsibility for transport infrastructure is divided between national and local jurisdictions, with boundaries varying from one country to another. The central government is typically responsible for the trunk road network, as well as railways, ports and airports. Local governments are typically responsible for local roads.

Why Financing of Local Infrastructure Is Hard to Get

Most local jurisdictions, whether urban or rural, lack the resource base to provide adequate infrastructure services to households and businesses. Many factors contribute to current challenges of infrastructure financing. On the demand side, government spending on infrastructure has not kept pace with the investment demands of population growth and urbanization. Municipal budgets are very small in relation to the cost of meeting infrastructure requirements implied by fast urban growth. On the supply side, rising capital construction costs, shrinking public infrastructure finance sources, and constrained public sector budgets due to competing priorities (rising health care and pension costs) threaten the future sustainability of local infrastructure finance.

Cities face a major investment gap in financing infrastructure projects. Local governments have two possibilities when it comes to financing infrastructure: pay-as-you-go (pay-go, or cash) and pay-as-you-use (pay-use, or debt). Pay-as-you-go capital financing refers to using cash or other current assets rather than debt issuance to fund capital projects. It is most commonly used in cases where capital project sizes are small, project sponsors have limited access to debt, local governments are closely approaching their debt limits, or there are prohibitions on use of debt. Pay-as-you-use capital financing means issuing long-term debt in the form of general obligation bonds or revenue bonds to fund capital projects. Infrastructure projects often involve large or lumpy investments and benefit both current taxpayers and future generations. The use of debt financing is justified in part by the rationale of spreading out the costs of public infrastructure investments throughout the lifespan of the asset.

Alternative and Innovative Infrastructure Financing

The sources for financing local infrastructure generally come from local general taxes, special funds such as dedicated user fees and earmarked taxes, intergovernmental grants, bond proceeds, or some combination of these sources. However, developments in regulatory frameworks and in international financial markets have opened up new opportunities not only in mobilizing more private capital for urban development but also in exploring new innovative financing and funding mechanisms for urban infrastructure. However, the opportunities need to be regulated, incentives have to be presented and relevant stakeholders should be brought on board.

Innovative or alternative infrastructure financing is an umbrella concept that supplements traditional infrastructure funding sources and financing methods, and embraces any strategy involving new funding sources, new financing mechanisms, and new financial arrangements in the provision of infrastructure. We categorize alternative infrastructure financing into three types:

- New funding sources: any new measures that generate additional revenue resources to pay for infrastructure projects. These include new taxes such as local option taxes that are earmarked for infrastructure projects, or different value-capture mechanisms such as impact fees or development exactions, which are charged to compensate the cost of constructing new infrastructure improvement projects during the development process.
- New financing mechanisms: represent new methods for borrowing money in flexible and/or potentially cost-effective ways to pay for an infrastructure project. They include new credit assistance tools (loans, loan guarantees, and lines of credit) offered by governments and alternative bond and debt financing tools (green bonds, social impact bonds).
- New financial arrangements: these involve new partners (the private sector, the nonprofit sector, or the general public) to participate in infrastructure financing and project delivery.

Table 9.2   *Infrastructure financing and funding practices*

Temporality	Type	Examples
Established, 'tried and tested'	Tax and fees	Special assessments; user fees and tolls; other taxes
	Grants	Extensive range of grant programs at multiple levels (e.g. federal national, province, state, supranational)
	Debt finance	General obligation bonds; revenue bonds; conduit bonds; national loans funds (e.g. PWLB), state bond banks, green bonds, diaspora bonds
	Tax incentives	New market/historic/housing tax credits; tax credit bonds; property tax relief; enterprise zones
	Developer fees	Impact fees, infrastructure levies
	Platforms for institutional investors	Pension and insurance infrastructure platforms; state infrastructure banks; regional infrastructure companies; real estate investment trusts; sovereign wealth funds
	Value capture mechanisms	Tax increment financing; special assessment districts; sales tax financing; infrastructure financing districts; community facilities districts; accelerated development zones
	Public–private partnerships	Private finance initiative; build–(own)–operate–(transfer); build–lease–transfer; design–build–operate–transfer
New innovative	Asset leverage and leasing mechanisms	Asset leasing; institutional lease model; local asset-backed vehicles
	Blended finance	Private equity funds
	Land-based instruments	Ad hoc contributions, sale of development rights, impact fees and development charges, public land leasing and land sales, land readjustment, betterment levies/taxes
	Financing mechanisms promoting growth	High occupancy/toll lanes; development cost charges (DCCs); parking site tax; land value taxation; stormwater utility fee credits, fuel tax transfer; tax increment financing

Source: Adapted from Strickland (2014).

Given local capital markets' lack of capacity to enable the government to adequately finance infrastructure projects, a number of nontraditional financing options have been put forward to assist governments in assembling consortiums of investors, lenders and other stakeholders to finance infrastructure projects too large for a single investor to underwrite. Table 9.2 summarizes these options.

Local governments in African countries can finance infrastructure projects in three ways: their own financial resources (e.g. intergovernmental transfers, property taxes and revenue generating facilities), borrowing, and public–private partnerships. In African countries financing systems are often built around property taxes and transfer schemes. For example, South Africa

Table 9.3   Possible mixture of finance options

Type of investment	Sub-national government income level/creditworthiness		
	Low	Medium	High
Self-financing	Mix of loans (possibly subsidized) and transfers	Mix of loans (possibly subsidized) and bonds (if feasible)	Mix of bonds and loans
Partially revenue generating	Mix of loans (likely subsidized) and transfers	Mix of loans (likely subsidized) and transfers	Mix of loans (possibly subsidized) and transfers (if justified)
Non-self financing/ social purpose	Transfers only	Mix of loans (possibly subsidized) and transfers	Mix of loans (possibly subsidized) and transfers (if justified)

Note: The mix of financing instruments would have to be based on objective criteria and the source of financing and would vary based on availability and specific criteria.
Source: Smoke (2019).

and Zambia mainly rely on local taxation and utility taxes whereas central government transfers provide a crucial share of local government finances in Ghana, Kenya and Uganda. However, in general, resources have not increased in proportion with local authorities' infrastructure investment needs. The following case studies will cover infrastructure services that perform a public role. There will be varying degrees of private participation, i.e. pure public works contracts, service concessions, full concessions, PPP arrangements. The challenge is getting the right mix of financial instruments. Some possibilities are given in Table 9.3.

EXPERIENCES OF LOCAL GOVERNMENTS IN AFRICA

This section examines first in detail the case in Ghana and then more briefly cases from Tanzania, South Africa, and Cameroon, covering a range of issues related to the governance structure or the different financing modalities.

The selected case studies cover the myriad urban infrastructure finance vehicles available to local governments today and highlight the challenges and key lessons of using them. Notwithstanding the fact that the sample is small, the diversity of urban infrastructure finance vehicles is covered. The cases are analyzed under three headings: the formula used for financing, access to capital markets, and the governance structure put in place and listed in Table 9.4.

Table 9.4   Selected case studies, short description, financing modalities and results

City, country and source	Governance of project	Financing formula	Results
Four cities in Ghana to bridge infrastructure gap, the French Development Agency (AFD) created a credit facility. More information in this chapter.	Between AFD and the Government of Ghana / municipal and metropolitan assemblies (MMAs) which make their own contribution. The objective is the development of urban infrastructure, their maintenance and capacity building, tailored to the needs of Kumasi, Tamale, Ho and Sekondi-Takoradi.	The GUMPP is a program financed by AFD for a total amount of €40.5 million. The funding is a concessionary loan to the Government of Ghana and a **capacity building grant of € 0.5** million. The Government of Ghana and the Participating Metropolitan, Municipal and District Assembles (MMDAs) are also contributing €4.0 million as counterpart funding bringing the total program package to **€44.5 million.**	– Increased income to the beneficiary MMAs. – Improvement of livening condition and livelihood. – Property valuation to enhance revenue generation. – Skills enhancement because of people working directly. – Provided residents with improved services based on municipal asset use (infrastructure, abattoirs, markets, parking, etc.). – Attracted more domestic and foreign investors. – Improved land valuation (for example, through relocation of public properties, sale and leases, and improvements in infrastructure such as better roads). – Enhanced the environment and improved quality of life (for example through public parks and greenways).

City, country and source	Governance of project	Financing formula	Results
The local government reform program (LGRP) in Tanzania to improve accountability and responsiveness of local government. Tidemand and Msami (2010), Van Dijk (2008)	LGRP aimed at transferring duties and financial resources from central to local levels, which are thought to be in a better position to identify people's needs by encouraging citizens' participation in democratic governance, and thus supply the appropriate form and level of public services. LGRP improves quality of urban service delivery by LGAs.	External finance through World Bank loan and improved funding.	– There has been substantial development in the processes of decision-making, especially through attempts to include citizens in the planning process. – The LGRP improved the access and quality of services provided by LGAs. Contributed to positive changes in provision of services, revenue enhancement, improved governance. – There are no effective instruments and procedures in place for ordinary people to use when they want to hold council officials accountable. – Corruption was perceived to be a problem for all six case councils.

City, country and source	Governance of project	Financing formula	Results
The Durban Water Recycling Project in South Africa for better treatment of municipal waste and sewerage water involving the utility and local government under a 20-year concession contract. ACBF (2016)	This R74m sewage-to-clean-water recycling plant treats 47.5 million liters of domestic and industrial wastewater to a near potable standard for sale to industrial customers. The saving of treated potable water is of great benefit to Durban. Water Recycling (DWR), a consortium led by Vivendi Water Systems (Veolia), chosen to finance, design, construct, and operate the plant.	External finance and improved funding. **Project value**: R74 million (Euro 11.3 million) Equity from **DWR shareholders**: R14 million (Euro 2.3 million). **Development Bank of Southern Africa**: R18 million (Euro 2.8 million). **Rand Merchant Bank**: R24 million (Euro 3,9 million). **French Protocol**: Euro 2.3 million.	– Promoted the use of water by others to generate revenue and comply with legal requirements. – A considerable benefit to industries is the lower tariff when compared to the normal tariff paid by industries for potable water. The two largest customers so far are the Mondi Paper Mill in Merebank and the Sapref Refinery, owned by Shell and BP. – Some of the key elements for the success of the project is eThekwini Water's (ETW's) vision in initiating the project, Vivendi's ability to provide finance and to implement innovative, tailor-made technical solutions and Mondi's endorsement of the project, by committing its entire paper production at its Merebank Mill to recycled water.

City, country and source	Governance of project	Financing formula	Results
Communauté Urbaine de Douala (CUD) means some decentralization, while the 1972 Constitution created a highly centralized system where cities are administered not by mayors but political appointees. ACBF (2016)	Douala, the financial capital of Cameroon, issued a five-year bond in 2005 through a special purpose vehicle (CUD Finance), designed to assist the municipality with raising funds for urban management and development. The regional and local authorities shall have administrative and financial autonomy in the management of regional and local interests.	This CFA 16 billion bond (approximately US$22 million) was jointly initiated by the central government and its representation in Douala in an effort to diversify the city's financial resources, but the most senior officers in municipalities shall be delegates, appointed by the President.	– A bond of CFA 16 billion (US$22 million) initiated by central government and its representation in Douala to diversify the city's financial resources, fully backed by central government in accordance with the constitution of Cameroon's unitary government. – The city's bond issuance was plagued with questions of financial and regulatory irregularities.

Financing Infrastructure through Local, National and International Funds in Ghana

The local government system in Ghana is premised on the assumptions that development must respond to people's problems and represent their objectives and priorities; and that responsibility for development is shared by central government, local governments, parastatals, non-governmental organizations (NGOs) and the people as the ultimate beneficiaries of development. The resources of Metropolitan and Municipal and District Assemblies (MMDAs) are thus essential to enable local governments to translate their powers and competences into development activities.

After some years of preparation, the Ministry of Local Government and Rural Development (MLGRD) through the Government of Ghana received in 2012 a concessionary credit facility for a total amount of €40 million with a capacity building grant component of €0.5 million from the French Government through the Agence Française de Développement (AFD). The Government of Ghana and the participating Metropolitan and Municipal Assemblies' contribution of €4 million as counterpart funding brought the total funding to €44.5 million towards the implementation of the Ghana Urban Management Pilot Program (GUMPP). This credit facility was to support the MLGRD and four participating MMAs to finance their priority infrastructure investments projects and supported by other key urban interventions such as property valuation and spatial planning and capacity building. The GUMPP is one of the largest urban management programs implemented in Africa.

This project was implemented over a seven-year period from January 2012 to December 2019. The project shows very clearly the challenges of funding municipal infrastructure under a complicated financing and governance structure: the Development and Financing Partner (AFD), the Ministry of Finance, the Ministry of Local Government and Rural Development representing the government of Ghana, a dedicated Urban Development Unit supported by a Technical Assistance Team; four Municipal and Metropolitan Assemblies; the Environmental Protection Agency (EPA) and reliable and good design and supervision consultants and contractors ready to meet their contractual arrangements. Coordination requires flexibility, responsiveness and manageable procedures. We conclude that a robust institutional arrangement matters. Table 9.5 summarizes the challenges and lessons learned.

Gaining Access to Capital Markets: Borrowing and Issuing Bonds

The conditions required to provide local governments with capital market access have been tested and developed in North America and Europe. The critical challenges, particularly in developing countries, are bringing borrowers

Table 9.5   Key challenges and lessons learned in the GUMPP project

Challenges	Lessons learned
The **Financing dimension**: Decentralized borrowing, payback, own contributions.	• Financial reporting, resettlement and compensation of displaced citizens are important. • MMAs' own contribution (through land acquisition) is a problem.
The **Expectation dimension**: Managing stakeholders' expectations is the key: making sure the key stakeholders and project beneficiaries are well informed as to what to expect.	• Need of promotion of local development and increase of local employment. • Maintenance of social network and neighborhood relations important. • Availability of amenities, economic benefits to local governments and people. • Increase participation and cooperation.
The **Synergy dimension**: Ensuring that with the multiplicity of development partners engaged in the urban sector and in financing infrastructure, GUMPP did not replicate existing projects.	• Working with a development partner makes it more challenging. • Institutional mapping was useful to find out who was financing what and where.
The **Sustainability and Management dimension**: The two key issues here are the issue of financial sustainability and the management options for the GUMPP priority assets delivered by the project. Cities have the potential to minimize their environmental footprint in GUMPP projects. Supply of relevant equipment and logistics.	• Project prioritization and selection is paramount. • The need of the specific project to transform the urban setting was key. • The GUMPP performance grant of €1,200,000 worked, using criteria like progress on implementing existing priority investment projects, resettlement and compensation payments made. • Cities can invest in infrastructure and still stay connected with the natural environment. • Sustainable development actions taken within the city level can significantly impact on the natural environment and health. • The focus should not always be only on urban infrastructure, but also the soft components: spatial planning; property valuation; revenue enhancement; street naming. • Developing and strengthening the capacity of recipient municipalities and beneficiaries is important.

and lenders together in a market relationship and managing the risks inherent in this type of financing.

However, cities also have the option of borrowing and/or the issuance of municipal bonds to finance infrastructure. The chief obstacle to municipal bond issuance for raising funds relates to the constitutional and regulatory systems in countries. Only a handful of local governments have successfully

Table 9.6   *Challenges and lessons in Douala*

Challenges	Lessons learned
Allegations of fraudulent exchanges between tranches and improper licensing of the financial arranger for the transaction were investigated and deliberated in Cameroonian courts for months. Although this did not hamper the city's ability to honor its debts, and investors received their principal and interest in full and on time, perceptions of illegality have given municipal leaders reason to doubt the likelihood of a follow-on financial transaction.	• The central government can initiate and back a change process to diversify the city's financial resources. • This approach allowed the city an opportunity to defer some of the costs of borrowing and helped to make the bond more appealing to a wider pool of investors. • This did not hamper the city's ability to honor its debts, and investors received their principal and interest in full and on time.

issued municipal bonds, almost all of them in South Africa. Direct bond issuance is likely to remain a limited option soon due to legislative constraints as well as the low borrowing capacity and lack of creditworthiness that characterizes most cities in Africa, except for Johannesburg, Lagos, Douala and Dakar. For comparison, cities in sub-Saharan Africa have raised less than 1% of the US amount since 2004.

In Douala bonds were issued, but the bond issuance was plagued with questions of financial and regulatory irregularities that ended in the dismissal and imprisonment of the government's delegate, within 18 months. Other challenges and lessons from the experience in Cameroon are listed in Table 9.6.

While the benefits are clear, the potential for and timing of capital market development are to a large extent dependent on the level of economic and structural development of a country. That is, a country's starting point heavily dictates the recipe for timing, sequencing, and even the feasibility of what can be done in terms of developing local capital markets (IFC, 2017). An essential condition for a well-functioning financial system (with both banks and capital markets) is the existence of sound macroeconomic and policy frameworks. The institutional framework is also critical, as markets depend on investor confidence and strong institutions provide the basis for investor and creditor protection.

Governance Structure Put in Place, Decentralization and PPPs: Public Pain, Private Gain?

Infrastructure governance assumes that, once central government agencies have partnered with intergovernmental counterparts, followed by financing to sub-national agencies, municipal authorities allow these entities to implement projects that respond to the differing needs of urban residents. This obscures

Table 9.7   Challenges and lessons in the Tanzanian project

Challenges	Lessons learned
LGA control over local staff is still limited, and fiscal transfers from central government are increasingly earmarked for specific purposes. The Local Government Capital Development Grant, for example, was intended to provide non-earmarked development financing, yet in practice, LGAs are often directed by central government on how to spend the grant. Other goals of local government reform, such as the transparent, formula-based fiscal allocation of resources, have also only been partially implemented and achieved.	• Restructuring: enhancing the effectiveness of local government authorities in delivering quality services in a sustainable manner. • Finance: increasing resources available to local authorities, improving the efficiency in their use. • Human resource development: improving accountability and efficiency of use of staff. • Legal: establishing an enabling legislation to support effective implementation of reforms. • Program management: supporting effective and efficient management of the reform program.

the multi-layered nature of infrastructure governance at municipal level. The Local Government Reform Program (LGRP) in Tanzania was introduced to improve the access and quality of services provided by Local Government Authorities (LGAs). It strengthened fiscal decentralization, improved accountability, and initiated intergovernmental transfers of funds. Challenges are listed in Table 9.7. One key lesson concerning the governance of the project was the need for establishing broad-based community awareness and participation, aimed at promoting principles of democracy, transparent and accountable government.

One governance structure which is often used is public–private partnerships. PPPs are promoted by many governments associated with the Organisation for Economic Co-operation and Development (OECD) and some multilateral development banks – especially the World Bank – as the solution to the financing shortfall needed to achieve development, including the Sustainable Development Goals (SDGs). Table 9.8 gives the challenges and lessons in the South African wastewater PPP project. It was shown that the current stringent legislative requirements do not seem to consider practical challenges of changing from one system to another. Hence good management and leadership are crucial, just like the ability to manage political sensitivities.

A critical issue in the design of a PPP is the sharing of risks. In general, this depends on the type of partnership. The greater the private sector's share, the greater will be its expected rate of return. In principle, the party best able to deal with each type of risk at least cost should bear that risk. PPPs take a wide range of forms (including Concessions, Build–Operate–Transfer (BOT); Build–Own–Operate (BOO), Build–Own–Operate–Transfer (BOOT)) varying in the extent of involvement of and risk taken by the private party. Normally, the risk of cost over-runs, delays, and service demand should be borne by the

Table 9.8   *Challenges and lessons in the South African wastewater PPP project*

Key challenges	Key lessons
The existing legal framework stifled creativity and innovation during the bidding negotiation process. Municipal officials were discouraged to invest time in devising solutions to long-term municipal challenges due to legislative requirements. The political climate/conditions under which some of the partnerships was undertaken increased the negotiation risks of municipalities. Visionary and long-term thinking is crucial.	• Good negotiation skills are key in ensuring such high-level partnerships. Municipal representatives must have the authority to make decisions on the spot. • International exposure can be useful when negotiating such high-profile projects. • The ability to justify risks taken is important. • The importance of pursuing a win-win result within a partnership.

private sector, whereas the risks associated with changes in regulations and legislation, including changes in local taxation and environmental standards are borne by the public sector. The objective of the negotiations should be to ensure infrastructure programs that make the right projects happen at the right scale, in a cost-efficient and affordable manner that is trusted by users and citizens and take their views into account.

DISCUSSION

Infrastructural projects in Africa face problems, frequently because these projects are complex. They require heavy, long-term investment, have strong public-good characteristics, a long life, and high sunk costs and they are overly sensitive to local political conditions. Widespread corruption in infrastructure increases project costs, lengthens delivery times, reduces output quality, and thus lowers benefits. It also undermines infrastructure maintenance and sustainability of benefits. The case studies helped identifying factors explaining the low infrastructure provision in Africa, and why infrastructure financing is hard to get right. The following factors stand out:

1. The discrepancy and mismatch between investment needs and available finance.
2. In countries without a capital market financing is dominated by banks that are risk averse and either do not have funds or are reluctant to lend long term for infrastructure projects.
3. The failure to create an enabling and a governance framework for these investments.
4. Africa's legal, regulatory, and governance frameworks are major constraints to attracting private capital to infrastructure.

5. The necessity to manage government expectations regarding what one can expect from private participation in infrastructure, with respect to the size of their contribution and the time required for processing PPP projects.
6. If laws are enacted they may lack implementation decrees or may not be implemented.
7. The absence of well-defined infrastructure programs and bankable project pipelines is also a major issue in many African countries.
8. Often the private sector is not prepared to assess, develop and prepare infrastructure projects, given the costs, risks and long time horizons.
9. In this case governments, donors and international financial institutions take action through long-term infrastructure planning based on population growth and development objectives and taking into account the economic importance of different regions.
10. Poor governance (corruption) and political economy issues can be major bottlenecks for infrastructure development.

CONCLUSIONS

To help address the challenges of infrastructure financing, local governments are taking a combination of traditional and alternative approaches to finance and fund their infrastructure investments. While infrastructure financing presents unique challenges, it also offers opportunities for both the public and private sectors. High-quality infrastructure is one of the backbones for achieving long-term inclusive development. Nevertheless, infrastructure projects can sometimes fail to meet their time frame, budget and service delivery objectives. This is often due to shortcomings in the country's governance framework for infrastructure. Good governance of infrastructure not only promotes value for money and affordability, but also helps to make the right projects happen in a manner that is trusted by users and citizens. Successful governance of infrastructure demands a clear regulatory and institutional framework, robust coordination across levels of governments and sustainable performance throughout the life cycle of the asset. It requires a comprehensive preparation phase, including overall strategic planning, open and transparent prioritization mechanisms and decision processes that are based on affordability and cost-efficiency.

Alternative infrastructure financing is not likely to replace traditional methods of infrastructure financing because it is relatively new and many local governments are well served by traditional infrastructure funding sources and municipal bonds. Nonetheless, new financing alternatives effectively complement traditional funding sources and are efficient conduits to low-cost borrowing for many local communities. These innovations can effectively stretch scarce federal and state funding sources, leverage private funds, and enable local governments to accelerate project completion with greater flexibility.

Innovations in local infrastructure financing may require changes in state and local laws and administrative arrangements. Obtaining legislative approval to authorize the use of innovative infrastructure financing is a critical first step. To win support, effective education of the public and legislators is necessary. Local government managers need to explain the feasibility and benefits of innovative infrastructure financing to legislators and be open to a frank dialogue about alternative financing options. In addition, local government managers need to patiently and persistently educate the public about the potential of innovative infrastructure finance, as well as to consider the risks.

Alternative infrastructure financing strategies often involve complex financing techniques and engage various external financial partners and stakeholders. Effective working with new partners is often required in these arrangements. Local government professionals need to strengthen their understanding of these techniques, as well as their capacity to manage these financing alternatives. They need to take actions to ensure transparency and accountability when using alternative infrastructure financing methods. For instance, local government managers may engage and inform citizens in the process of project planning, selection and funding. Managers should also provide clear explanations of new financing tools being considered.

Matching financing tools with appropriate projects is challenging but potentially rewarding for local managers. As many examples indicated, good projects with appropriate financing can enhance community wealth, safety and sustainability. The selection of the right financing tool requires matching revenues with the flow of benefits coming to the community. This may bring in private sources of funding that reduces the burden on government and achieves broader and more durable support. It is a matter of getting the right mix.

Designing a clear and coherent strategic vision is difficult due to the complex nature of infrastructure policy, as it needs to address multiple and potentially contradictory objectives such as growth, productivity, affordability, inclusive development and environmental concerns. In sum, like so many elements of local government, innovation in infrastructure financing is not for the faint of heart. However, the importance of the challenges facing our communities demands a wise and determined approach. Finance is changing, presenting new alternatives and opportunities. This approach enables cities to realize their full functional responsibilities as regards infrastructure and service financing and their developmental potential.

In the case of PPPs it is evident that an effective and efficient partnership agreement requires both parties to clearly understand the risks that each is to assume because incorrect risk assignment can lead to increased costs for the private sector and higher risk premiums than should be the case, or higher costs associated with resolving disputes for the public sector.

The challenge for urban managers is to go beyond what is available in terms of own sources (taxes, grants). Healthy urban projects, if structured properly, should be able to generate the funds necessary to repay loans, bonds or other sources of finance. An integrated and coordinated approach (including PPPs, asset leveraging – land, domestic financial institutions, multi-lateral and bi-lateral financial institutions, pension funds, insurance companies, foundations and endowments, capital markets) and new innovative mechanisms for infrastructure finance could go a long way in resolving the bottlenecks facing urban infrastructure financing thus enabling cities to realize their full functional responsibilities as regards infrastructure and service financing and their developmental potential. To summarize this chapter:

1.   There are more sources of finance than we usually think of and it may be time to think of tapping new, and in particular private, sources more often.
2.   To be able to use these sources one has to learn some 'bank speak', the language of the world of finance. To finance urban projects one has to convince financial people that it is worth putting their money into these projects. This requires identification of the possible risks and the identification of the societal costs and benefits of these projects, including the environmental and social costs as well.
3.   We can learn a lot from experiences elsewhere, gained by urban governments, NGOs, communities and other stakeholders, whose experiences are often documented in case studies.
4.   However, besides proper financing and funding options for infrastructure projects, a good governance structure is also crucial.
5.   Robust institutional arrangements matter due to the multiplicity of actors and there is a need for better project coordination mechanisms.
6.   Finally the economics of infrastructure will only work if with the infrastructure a governance structure has been put in place including some mechanism for cost recovery.

For local governments to fulfill their functions and shape the future of African cities, new and innovative revenue-raising instruments are needed or, alternatively, existing instruments must be more robustly deployed. Considering the limited extent to which transfers, cities' own-source revenue and service-provider funding are currently able to fund much-needed investments in infrastructure, land-based financing becomes an important funding option. Land-based financing refers to a broader category of financing mechanisms that include land value capture as well as contributions made by property owners or property developers, regardless of whether land values are increasing. Land-based finance is being implemented in practice (Addis Ababa, Harare, Nairobi) and discussions on the potential for wider uptake are current. We conclude that African city governments are using land-based financing, albeit in inconsistent ways.

Recommendations and the Way Forward

This chapter identified general principles that should guide policymakers' choices for financing infrastructure investment in a decentralized setting. By raising efficiency, there are substantial savings to be made from the choice of appropriate financing, given that the costs of infrastructure investment are substantial. In particular:

- The choice of financing instrument depends on the nature of the investment (size, revenue-generating capacity, potential for competition), the modality of service delivery (pure government provision, procurement, concession, PPP), the budgetary capacity of the jurisdiction (breadth and depth of own taxes, intergovernmental transfer arrangements, borrowing constraints), and the technical capacity of the jurisdiction to design and negotiate contracts with private sector providers.
- Financing options should maximize the welfare of local residents. Perception of the role of government matters and affects the willingness to pay for services. If local residents believe that provision, especially that financed locally, does not generate benefits that can be internalized by the local community, they are unlikely to be willing to pay for the services associated with the infrastructure.
- Where sub-national administrations remain important providers of infrastructure, better coordination mechanisms can help ensure that returns to scale are exploited and interjurisdictional spillovers are taken into account, including through decision-making frameworks that bring together sub-national and central governments, as well as other stakeholders.
- On the financing side, sub-national governments typically need to enhance their capacity to raise own revenue, to make the most of intergovernmental grants and transfers, and to mobilize private sector funds, including by tapping capital markets, where permitted. They also need to strengthen their technical capacity to design and implement investment projects, as well as manage increasingly complex, multi-year budgets, especially when there is private sector involvement.
- To meet the infrastructure investment challenge, making better use of user charges, while dealing with associated affordability and equity drawbacks, can help make sure existing infrastructure that can generate revenue streams is used efficiently and identify where more infrastructure

investment is needed, as well as creating more options for private sector involvement.

REFERENCES

African Capacity Building Foundation (ACBF). 2016. *Infrastructure Development and Financing in Sub-Saharan Africa: Toward a Framework for Capacity Enhancement.* Harare: ACBF.

Agenor, P.-R. 2010. A theory of infrastructure-led growth. *Journal of Economic Dynamics and Control*, 34, 932–950.

Amin, A. and Thrift, N. 2017. *Seeing Like a City.* Cambridge: Polity Press.

Basedow, J., Westrope, C. and Meaux, A. 2017. Urban stakeholder engagement and coordination: Guidance note for humanitarian practitioners. London: IIED.

Bonilla, M. and Zapparoli, I. 2017. *The Challenge of Financing Urban Infrastructure for Sustainable Cities.* Washington, DC: Inter-American Development Bank (IDB) Housing and Urban Development Division.

Bougheas, S., Panicos, O., Demetriades, P. and Morgenroth, E. L. W. 1999. Infrastructure, transport costs and trade. *Journal of International Economics*, 47, 169–189.

Calderon, C., Moral-Benito, E. and Serven, L. 2015. Is infrastructure capital productive? A dynamic heterogeneous approach. *Journal of Applied Econometrics*, 30, 177–198.

Cavallo, E. and Daude, C. 2011. Public investment in developing countries: A blessing or a curse? *Journal of Comparative Economics*, 39, 65–81.

International Finance Corporation (IFC). 2017. *Annual Report 2017.* Washington, DC: IFC.

Kessides, C. 1993. The contributions of infrastructure to economic development: A review of experience and policy implications. Discussion Paper No. 213. Washington, DC: World Bank.

Leipziger, D., Fay, M., Wodon, Q. T. and Yepes, T. 2003. Achieving the Millennium Development Goals: The role of infrastructure. Research WPS no. 3163. Washington, DC: World Bank.

Lindfield, M. and Teipelke, R. 2014. *Explainer: How to Finance Urban Infrastructure.* C40 Finance Facility. https://www.c40cff.org/knowledge-library/explainer-how-to -finance-urban-infrastructure.

Oates, W. E. 1972. *The Economic Theory of Federalism.* Englewood Cliffs, NJ: Harcourt Brace Jovanovich.

Oates, W. E. 1993. Federalism and government finance. In J. M. Quigley and E. Smolensky (eds.), *Modern Public Finance.* Cambridge, MA: Harvard University Press, 126–151.

Oates, W. E. 1999. An essay on fiscal federalism. *The Journal of Economic Literature*, 37(3), 1120–1149.

OECD. 2015. *Guidelines for Urban Infrastructure.* Paris: OECD.

Smoke, P. 2019. Improving sub-national government development finance in emerging and developing economies: Toward a strategic approach. ADBI Working Paper 921. Tokyo: Asian Development Bank Institute. https://www.adb.org/publications/ improvingsubnational-government-development-finance-emerging-developing -economies.

Strickland, T. 2014. The financialization of infrastructure funding and financing in the UK and the US. CURDS: Newcastle University.

Tidemand, P. and Msami, J. 2010. *The Impact of Local Government Reforms in Tanzania*. Dar es Salaam: REPOA.

Van Dijk, M. P. 2008. The impact of decentralization on poverty alleviation in Tanzania. In G. Crawford and C. Hartmann (eds.), *Decentralization in Africa: A Path Out of Poverty and Conflict?* Amsterdam: Amsterdam University Press, 145–169.

World Bank. 1994. *World Development Report 1994: Infrastructure for Development*. Washington, DC: World Bank.

World Bank. 2016. *The State of PPPs: Infrastructure Public–Private Partnerships in Emerging Markets and Developing Economies 1991–2015*. Washington, DC: World Bank.

World Economic Forum. 2018. *Africa Strategic Infrastructure Initiative Project Overview: Accelerating Project Infrastructure in Africa*. Geneva: World Economic Forum.

10. Collaborative capacity of public–private partnerships in housing projects: case studies from Nigeria

Daniel Adamu and Alberto Gianoli

INTRODUCTION

Developing countries and urban areas adopt different approaches, reflecting different paradigms, in order to deal with high rates of urbanization. These paradigms can be conceptualized as central planning, urban management and urban governance. These paradigms reflect phases in which developing countries intervene in cities, whereby the timing depends on among others specific institutional contexts. Nigeria mainly adopted a central planning approach between 1966 and 1999, when the military ruled Nigeria with only a single attempt at democratization. This period was characterized by acute shortages in urban infrastructure and services. The government used centralized policies like National Development Plans (1st: 1962–1970, 2nd: 1970–1974 and 3rd: 1975–1980) and the Structural Adjustment Programme 1986 in attempts to solve these problems. Transition to the urban management paradigm in Nigeria is traceable to interventions by the World Bank slum improvement projects in Bauchi in 1978, and urban infrastructure improvement projects of three cities in Ondo in 1986. However, the transition was institutionalized with a successful return to a democratic government in President Olusegun Obasanjo's government. The democratic government institutionalized a neoliberal focus in the period 1999–2007. This coincided with the time global key players (e.g. UN, World Bank, IMF, ADB) were propagating neoliberal approaches. Nigeria like most other developing countries adopted this new pathway for public service delivery.

In this chapter, we provide an account of the housing sector in Nigeria, which currently encompasses both the urban management paradigm, with its focus on market-based approaches, and the urban governance one, based on network mechanisms. Urban governance is still relatively new in Nigeria.

Between 1966 and 1999, federal and state governments under the military regime adopted central planning approaches in order to provide houses across the country via several initiatives. Housing development programmes included the Federal Housing Estates built by the Federal Housing Authority (FHA), and Shagari Housing Estates built during a short-lived democratic experiment that maintained the central planning paradigm. The state governments also weighed in by building housing estates across the local government headquarters called State Low-Cost Housing Estates. They targeted low-medium income earners, especially civil servants, and offered affordable rentals.

However, after the introduction of the neoliberal approach, publicly held housing estates were privatized through direct sales to occupants. This was accompanied with resales to speculators. The involvement of private developers meant that housing became a commercial product which was treated as an exchange commodity between investors. It offered extraordinary returns to the private developers. Due to the global economic crisis of 2008–2010, the housing market became a viable alternative for capital preservation. This fuelled a property bubble which in turn created a housing affordability crisis, as house prices increased exponentially.

The chapter examines the project processes rather than looking at the outcomes alone, an approach followed by other researchers on housing in Nigeria (Ibem, 2010, 2011; Ukoje and Kanu, 2014). In particular, the chapter aims at addressing the following question: *What is the influence of PPP models on the collaborative capacity in housing projects in Nigeria?* This is done by analysing two housing projects that were implemented by adopting different PPP models: the Talba project, implemented through an alliance model, and the Efab project, implemented through a concession model. After outlining the theoretical framework and the methodological approach, the chapter presents the empirical findings and draws relevant conclusions.

PUBLIC–PRIVATE PARTNERSHIP MODELS AND COLLABORATIVE CAPACITY

Researchers have used several approaches to classify PPPs: using semantics to explain the categorization, emphasizing organizational and functional arrangements, and looking at families of governance arrangements (Wettenhall, 2008). Classifications include the collaborative and the exchange partnerships (Weihe, 2008), concessional and alliance partnerships (Edelenbos and Teisman, 2008; Van Marrewijk et al., 2008; Willems and Van Dooren, 2011), and contractual and institutionalized partnerships (Wettenhall, 2003). This research concentrates on the concession and alliance classification of partnerships by Edelenbos and Teisman (2008) in order to benefit from the clear and unambiguous identification process that distinguishes their approach.

Concession models of PPP have distinct features, whereby the public sector controls project objectives, initiation and expected outcomes, The private partners design and implement the project(s) and in most cases finance and operate the project(s) for a defined term, after which the ownership is returned to the public partners. The relationship pattern is that the public partner is the commissioner, and the private partner a contractor (Edelenbos and Teisman, 2008). It is typically a vertical kind of relationship with minimal interdependence (Weihe, 2008). A concession model emphasizes the need for a clear contract which specifies roles and boundaries (Edelenbos and Teisman, 2008). Variants of concession PPPs include Build–Operate–Transfer (BOT) and Design–Build–Finance–Operate (DBFO).

By contrast, the alliance model engages both private and public partners in decision-making, design, and in some cases implementation. The relationship is close, highly interdependent and equal, also known as a horizontal relationship (Edelenbos and Teisman, 2008; Weihe, 2008; Willems and Van Dooren, 2011). Actors form an alliance to jointly define the problem and search for innovate solutions based on synergy and integration. This potentially leads to trustworthiness and efficiency in relationship contracts (Duffield, 2010; Willems and Van Dooren, 2011). Table 10.1 summarizes the main characteristics of the two models.

Foster-Fishman et al. (2001: 242) conceptualize collaborative capacity as:

> The conditions needed for coalitions to promote effective collaboration and build sustainable community change.

Hudson et al. (1999: 241) defined collaborative capacity as:

> The level of activity or the degree of change a collaborative relationship can sustain without any partner losing a sense of security in the relationship. This sense of security encompasses not only the tangible resources which are central to collaborative endeavours but less obvious matters such as perceived loss of autonomy and perceived change in relative strength.

Highlighting the essence of capacity in stakeholder collaborations is important because the resources that partners are able and willing to commit to, in order to realize their goal(s) are *dynamic, adjustable* and *transferrable* (Foster-Fishman et al., 2001). Foster-Fishman et al. (2001) further assert that efforts by researchers and practitioners in a collaborative capacity assessment endeavour should focus on the following four essential categories:

- The capacity of individual members of a partnership
- The relationships between partner organizations (internal and external)
- Reviewing the organizational capacity
- Assessing their programme or project capacities.

Table 10.1   Characteristics of concession and alliance models

Concession (turnkey, contractual) models	Characteristics	Alliance (collaborative, institutionalized) models
Public and private actor(s)	*Types of actors*	Public and private actor(s)
Public partner as commissioner, private partner as contractor Distant relationships Minimal attentiveness and sometimes misunderstandings Minimal interdependence	*Type of relationship*	Public and private partners relate as equals, joint decision-making, design, and implementation Close relationship Attentiveness/empathy for the partner Highly interdependent
Public partner defines problem and develop solution, private partner implements solution	*Content*	The joint effort at problem definition and collective/creative solution(s) through collaboration
Financial Efficiency Integration	*Motive*	Trust building Financial Efficiency Integration Partnership Synergy
High dependency on contract content for clarity and certainty	*Role of contract*	Higher dependence on trust-building than compliance through strict contract monitoring
High dependency on specified roles and limited to boundaries	*Project scope*	Susceptible to re-scoping base on project specifics and in a coherent manner
Strongly based on project management principles (clear objectives, schedules, supervision, and organized human resources)	*Management principles*	Anchored on the principles of process management (goal-oriented operation, development of solid cooperation process based on rules and roles and interconnecting goals)

Source: Adapted and modified from Edelenbos and Teisman (2008).

However, within the context of this research only the relational, organizational and project capacities are examined. The reason is that the projects have already ended and examining individual member capacity which requires researchers adopting a non-participatory observation method in data collection in real time during the projects' development circle is thus not possible. Table 10.2 illustrates how collaborative capacity has been operationalized in the study.

Table 10.2   Overview of collaborative capacity framework

Sub-variables	Sub-sub variables	Indicator
Relational capacity		
	Internal relational capacity	Cohesive
		Cooperative
		Trusting
		Shared vision
		Power-sharing/Values diversity
	External relational capacity	Participation of users/community
		Need assessment
		Links with other organizations
Organizational capacity		
	Resources	Ability to attract financial resources
		Availability of physical asset(s)
		Information management framework and facilities
		The reputation of the organization
		The employee experience
		The trustworthiness of the organization
		The managerial skills
	Capabilities	Ability to utilize resources
		Performance in resolving challenges
	Structures	Clarity of members' roles/responsibilities
		Availability of internal operations guidelines and procedures
		The precision of a work plan
		Availability and structure of workgroups or committees
	Autonomy	Operational transactions and social reliance on other organizations
		Statutory and fiscal limits
		Degree of exposure to political pressure
	Stimuli	Presence and perspective to threats
		Ability to identify and utilize opportunities
Project capacity		
		Project Objective
		User Need
		Cultural Sensitivity

Source: Inspired by Foster-Fishman et al. (2001); Gazley (2010); Harrison et al. (1990); Hudson et al. (1999); Lerman and Reeder (1987).

Against this background, the chapter looks at the influence of a specific PPP model on the nature and level of collaborative capacity.

Table 10.3   Cases studied

S/N	Case Name	Number of units	Location	Partnership model	Public partner	Private partner
1.	*Talba Housing Estate*	500	Minna, Niger State	Alliance	Niger State Housing Corporation	Puzzles Group of Companies
2.	*Efab Metropolis*	1500	Karsana, Abuja	Concession	Department of Mass Housing and Public Private Partnership	Blue Fountain Properties Limited

METHODOLOGY

Researchers have conducted inter-organizational studies for decades and a significant proportion of these studies utilize single or multiple case studies (Steijn et al., 2011). Case studies are used in order to be able to provide a deeper insight into how these arrangements work within local contexts. A multiple case study methodology was identified as the most suitable research method to be used because this research sought to compare two PPP models within their contexts. The advantage is that it allows for the comparison of examples to view a single phenomenon by utilizing data triangulation (Baxter and Jack, 2008; Stake, 2013). According to Yin (2011) and Baxter and Jack (2008), case studies allow for exploration of individuals or organizations, simple or complex sets of relationships, communities or programmes and they also support either the deconstruction or reconstruction of phenomena.

Case Selection

Multiple case study methodology enables researchers to select a few related cases either by their context or content (Seawright and Gerring, 2008; Stake, 2013). We selected two cases based on content. These were housing PPP projects, involving two or more primary stakeholders, identified as concession or alliance models and they both were carried out in Nigeria. One case study took place in Minna, Niger State (Talba housing estate) and another in Abuja (Efab metropolis) both in North Central Nigeria. An overview of the main characteristics of the two case studies is provided in Table 10.3.

The research applied two data collection methods. Qualitative data was collected in key informant interviews with the staff of the organizations who participated in these projects. These interviews provided in-depth information concerning the nature of the relationship in each project. Quantitative data was collected using the Organizational Capacity Assessment tool (OCA) of the US Corporation for National and Community Service (2017). OCA aims to help organizations to assess and develop their capacity for service delivery. The approach is worked out by Bateson et al. (2008). The study selected two to three core members of each organization to conduct an assessment based on the checklist of the OCA.

RESULTS

Partnership Models

The alliance partnership model utilized in the Talba project revealed a flexible sharing of responsibilities and risks throughout the project development circle. The public and private partners jointly identified and prepared projects based on proposals of private developers. The operations and management components were the prime responsibility of the public partner thus easing private investment since this reduced risks. Both parties received a return on equity on a 50 per cent basis. By contrast, the concession project which was called the Efab project had a clear division of responsibilities and risks. The public sector dominated the pre-implementation phase which was made up of the project identification, preparation and bidding arrangement, and the private sector dominated the implementation stage of the project's life cycle.

The Collaborative Capacity of the Project Partners

The relational, organizational and project capacities of partners in these two projects are discussed below.

1.   Relational capacity
In the Talba project (see case 1 in Figure 10.1), which applies an alliance PPP model, the two collaborating organizations (NSHC and PGC) had a close relationship. PGC's funding and technical input were directed at constructing the houses whereas the NSHC supplied the land and funded the infrastructure delivery. However, while this relationship was quite robust internally the two partners did not deem it fit to involve external stakeholders in the project. The project had civil servants as the priority beneficiaries, the reason being that the public representatives were civil servants too. Hence the public sector was expected to understand the needs of their colleagues.

In the concession model of the Efab project (see case 2 in Figure 10.1) internal relationships were distant and incoherent. The monitoring responsibilities suffered a significant setback due to a shortage of manpower and logistics, leaving the implementation by private partner with few fidelity checks. Consequently, the private partner (BFPL) developed three strategies to finance the project and to maximize the profit. They were able to introduce contractor developers, introduce individual developers and find funding from the First Generation Mortgage Bank (FGMB) that was a subsidiary firm in order to implement the project and provide mortgage facilities for the intending off-takers. The external relationships, unlike the internal relationships that were weak, resonated with hyperactivity. The relationships with the external organizations and individuals were cohesive and close. Sub-contractors and individual developers poured their funds into the project due to its high and promising quick returns. There was a booming property market in Abuja at the time of this project, and the city had the advantage of being the nation's capital. At the time of development, the housing prices escalated, such that despite increasing housing stock in the city, accessibility and affordability became monstrous challenges.

In conclusion, the alliance partnership model provided opportunities for the partners' joint influences in the decision-making processes and modification of strategies compared to the concession model where there was a clear partner dominance throughout the project phases thus inducing internalization of the project's benefits. The private partner prioritized profit over the importance of social variables that initially constituted the project's objectives.

2.   Organizational capacities of project partners in the two cases

This sub-section focuses on discussing the capacities of the partner organizations within two broad categories, namely *internal capabilities* which refers to a combination of resources, capabilities and competencies combined with formalized structures and procedures, and *external capabilities* which includes autonomy and stimuli.

Resources mobilization capacity
Wernerfelt (1984) conceptualizes organizations as bundles of resources, which can be tangible and intangible (Bryan, 2011; Eisinger, 2002; Honadle, 1981; Ingraham et al., 2003; Judge and Elenkov, 2005; Vinzant and Vinzant, 1996; Wernerfelt, 1984):

- Tangible resource mobilization capacity: Finance is one of the most crucial resources necessary for organizations to fulfil their objectives and the common objectives in partnerships. From the two cases it was observed that in both projects, the public partners maintained a single source of income, which was through budgetary allocations. Since their income was limited to public budgeting, their operations in the partnership at times were difficult. For example, DMHPPP in the Efab project was limited in

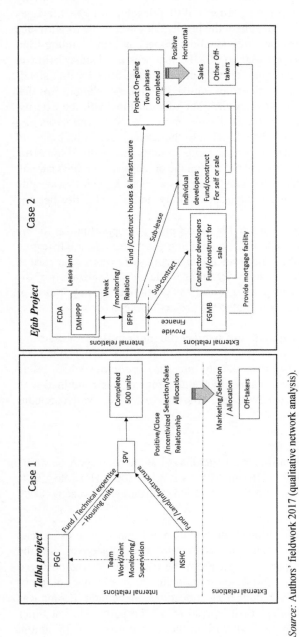

Source: Authors' fieldwork 2017 (qualitative network analysis).

Figure 10.1   Relational capacities of the two cases

financing their monitoring activities and the number of people that they were able to employ to carry out this essential role.

The NSHC also experienced challenges with such deficiency leading to the PGC (the private partner) incentivizing their supervisors to carry out their assigned supervisory tasks. This was because the fund releases from the commercial banks depended on the daily supervisory reports of the public partners. By contrast, the private partner's strategy in the Efab project to mobilize funds reinforced the prioritization of commercial considerations above social considerations.

• Intangible resources mobilization capacity: Reputation, trustworthiness and leadership were essential intangible resources in order to grow trust among partners in the two PPPs. In the Talba project, the leadership of Governor Babangida inspired the institutionalization of the alliance PPP model in Niger State thereby playing a prominent role in the ability of the project to deliver. The governor offered transformational and boundary spanning leadership, able to bring the partners of PPP together.

Capabilities

Capabilities have been measured as the availability of relevant skills and experiences necessary to execute tasks and schedules. The OCA results (see Figure 10.2) show that the public partner had moderate capacity (55 per cent) while the private partner received a slightly higher capacity rating of moderately high (70 per cent). In the Talba project, the collaboration enabled the PPP to contextualize the building designs and to resolve conflicting circumstances. However, these processes were hampered by moderate skills and knowledge, especially of the public sector. In the Efab project, weak public skills constrained the monitoring and quality control of the project.

Formalized structures and procedures

The two PPPs have many similarities. Both had defined roles and responsibilities which were provided by the terms of their contracts and agreements. Responses from interviewees were unanimous on the presence of contract documents which included clearly defined roles and responsibilities. The internal structure of each organization founded their operations. Both cases also had sets of rules which guided their operations internally and externally. These were based on the ethics and operational mandates that guided the PPP within the institutional context of their partnership activities. The policy documents (i.e. the FCT Housing Development Guideline 2011 for the Efab project, and the Niger State PPP Guideline 2011 for the Talba project) guided their operations and defined the roles of the public and private partners. These guidelines influenced the operational procedures in the projects. Both projects also used

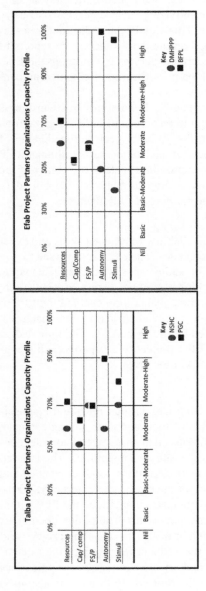

Note: Cap/Comp = capacities and competences; FS/P = formalised structures and procedures
Source: Authors' fieldwork 2017.

Figure 10.2   OCA results of organizational capacities of the two projects

intra-organizational management and technical committees and neither of the PPPs clearly defined work plans and/or met estimated target delivery dates.

There are also differences between the two PPPs. The Talba alliance model made more use of workgroups. The technical and management committees regularly met on an inter-organizational platform. While the technical committees were responsible for site daily supervisory roles, the management committee mainly met fortnightly for management decisions and monitoring purposes. In the Efab project there was a management committee that was installed but it seldom met. The private partner mentioned that they had not had any contact in three years. The nature of the concession model adopted in Efab had limited intra-organizational relations as envisaged along the project development phases. These differences are reflected in the OCA performance rating: for Talba project the two organizations scored moderate-high while in Efab the two partners assessed their performance as moderate.

Autonomy

Both DMHPPP and NSHC, the public partners of respectively Efab and Talba, were statutorily and fiscally limited by their status as public agencies. They were limited to statutory means of sourcing funds and bound by the appropriated funds for their operations. As Vinzant and Vinzant (1996) noted, organizations with multiple revenue sources like the two private partners in the two projects were more autonomous than single stream ones.

Stimuli

Dynamic or external stimulus indicates how organizations respond to threats and opportunities in their environment (Judge and Elenkov, 2005; Vinzant and Vinzant, 1996). The actors of the Talba alliance project were stimulated to address the acute housing deficit in the city of Minna and the growing agglomeration of public and private agencies and offices along the Minna-Bida road. The opportunity arose for people to work and live close to shopping facilities, as this is an important factor in a housing acquisition decision. The essence was to minimize the travel distance and reduce transport costs. The alliance also had to deal with threats. For instance, initially there were local tensions and pilfering of project materials. In response, the alliance decided to restrict low skilled and unskilled labour recruitment to those around the project community. This strategy helped to ensure public buy-in and protection for the project.

The public partner of the Efab concession project had poor capacity to cope with opportunities and threats. The private partner made use of the opportunities that arose due to weak monitoring and supervision by using the project for financial gains. It could be regarded as a case of regulatory capture because DMHPPP was the project partner and regulator of the mass housing

Table 10.4   Organizational capacities in the two cases

Alliance partnership	Organization capacity	Concession partnership
Talba		*Efab*
Joint (public–private) resource mobilization	*Resources*	Private resource mobilization, land supplied by public
Joint (public–private) skills and experiences	*Capabilities*	Private outsourced skills
Formalized	*Structures*	Formalized
Dependent public/independent private	*Autonomy*	Dependent public/independent private
Reactive partners	*Stimuli*	Hypersensitive private and placid public

programme. The knowledge that a large sum of public resources has been committed to a project with minimal monitoring by the public partner can be a recipe for failure.

Table 10.4 summarizes the organizational capacities of the two projects based on the previous analysis.

3.   Project capacity

The indicators that this research utilized to analyse project capacity included:

- The clarity and extent to which collaborative efforts were deployed to drive project objectives
- Cultural sensitivity
- The extent to which goals and objectives were fashioned to meet *user needs.*

The Talba alliance project adopted a dynamic approach, whereby the partners focused on meeting the overall objective of delivering affordable housing that the target beneficiaries could access. This project was able to deliver the social component (cultural sensitivity) as the private partner's architectural design was reviewed to suit the people's culture and local climate of the project area. This illustrates that it is possible to achieve cultural sensitivity/affordability if the public partner is able to moderate both economic spending and building design from the private partners in PPPs. With these actions, the users' needs were sufficiently prioritized in the project.

Unlike the Talba case, the Efab concession project did not achieve its core objective (reduce house prices in the city of Abuja). This was partially due to the public partners' inefficiency in monitoring the project, partly due to the choice of leasehold as the delivery model and partly due to unregulated building design which did not reflect the interest of lower-medium income earners. Based on the conditions contained in the leasehold, the private partner (BFPL) opened up the project to attract other investors negating the users' need. The high land value in Abuja combined with the private partners' motives jeopardized meeting the user needs. In summary, the two projects had clear differences on the dimension of meeting the user needs.

Influence of Partnership Models on the Collaborative Capacity of Partners

The partnership model describes the nature of the relationships, sharing of roles, risks, and benefits, who brings what resources and who makes decisions. The study analyses the impact of the partnership model on the collaborative capacity by looking at the two cases of Talba and Efab.

The alliance model represented in the Talba project revealed horizontal relationships between partners with complementary actions. Joint decision-making, joint monitoring teams and interdependence between partners reduced competition and furthered cooperation. In content development, partners in the alliance model participate in either the design or assessment and critique of the design. By doing this it is possible to create joint problem definitions and solutions which can be derived through broader perspectives. If this is achieved, then the partners are more willing to harness their joint resources into realizing predetermined objectives like in the Talba project.

Unlike the alliance model, the concession model represented by the Efab project had a vertical relationship which was characterized by command and control mechanisms whereby the public partner was the grantor and possessed the enforcement authority. The concession model project is characterized by stricter, more role-specific responsibilities and the public partners set the goals and objectives. The contract therefore becomes the central code of conduct in any concessions and actions by either partner and they are restricted to the terms and conditions of the contract. However, in alliance models, though contract terms and conditions are predefined and specific roles and responsibilities are outlined, there is more room for intuitive and discretional approaches. It makes adherence to the contract terms more flexible as long as everyone agrees with the changes. For example, while it was the private partner's responsibility to provide infrastructure in the Talba project, the public partner took over the responsibility about 30 per cent into the implementation by the private partner. This was taken into account and there were compensations for the 30 per cent investment made by the private partner in the infrastructure component which was duly altered. Unlike the alliance model, in the concession model, the developer deployed sub-contracting for crowdsourcing finance.

The results from the Talba project, which used an alliance partnership model, showed that the project was able to deliver housing to their target groups, hence meeting its objectives. Joint pricing was a critical component and the way and manner in which it organized funding acquisitions for the target groups were instrumental in attaining their objectives. Since the partners communicated with each other in developing the project content, relational capacities and internal capacities of organizations were enhanced through resource sharing, and joint tasks undertaken by these partners. Both organizational and relational capacities were enhanced as a result. In the Efab project, which utilized the concession model, the private partners pursued personal interests, and this was detrimental to the overall project objectives and the building up of capacities.

The concession model had lapses in the monitoring roles, especially by the public partner. It was observed that commercial considerations preoccupied the private partner's priority list. Thus, chances to deliver the need-oriented and affordable housing were short-changed for profit. The alliance model PPP potentially presented an alternative to the concession model PPP. The cases analysed show that there are opportunities to revise how partnership models are deployed in public service delivery, especially in urban housing projects, in order to achieve broader objectives than purely financial ones.

CONCLUSIONS

This chapter has examined the relationship between PPP models and the collaborative capacity of partnership projects for two projects in Nigeria. Evidence from the two cases analysed showed that the alliance model PPPs influence positive internal relational capacities between partners, hence, by extension boosting project capacity, as expected based on theory (Edelenbos and Teisman, 2008; Susilawati and Armitage, 2004; Williams and Van Dooren, 2011). Positive internal relational capacities often drive projects towards prioritizing overall project objectives, thereby satisfying user needs and promoting community ownership of projects. Since the alliance model supports co-sharing, less emphasis is placed on the individual organization capacities. By contrast, concession PPP models necessitate stronger organizational capacities for partner organizations. A concession partnership depends largely on the individual capacity of organizations because it promotes independence, and it is susceptible to promote the individual interest of an organization where other partners are not active participants. In essence, concession projects have the tendency of having less regard for public buy-in. The choice of a partnership model for projects should therefore consider project goals and priorities as these are influenced by the relational capacities that the partners deploy.

We recommend further research to test these research findings.

The findings in this research connect with other comparable studies. We also recommend more research on the specific roles of partners in different PPP models. By way of illustration, in a study of PPP's influence in facilitating affordable housing in Queensland, Australia, it was observed that public, private and community organizations exert different influences in projects. This study has shown that private partners were most effective in bearing construction risks, whereas public partners were most effective in asset management and performance measurement and the community associations were most effective in managing tenancy for affordable housing (Susilawati and Armitage, 2004). In another study of PPPs regarding housing affordability in China it was found that when increased synergy has been achieved, the risks and responsibilities are better handled by the private partner, thus creating opportunities for innovation and improved quality of service (Qin et al., 2017). This calls for cities in developing countries that are experiencing rapid urbanization, housing affordability issues and sharp inequalities to prioritize the assessment of internal and external relational capacities, organizational and project capacities of partner organizations to be involved in PPPs for service delivery. In this way the wider societal goal may be achieved.

REFERENCES

Bateson, D. S., Lalonde, A. B., Perron, L. and Senikas, V. 2008. Methodology for assessment and development of organizational capacity. *Journal of Obstetrics and Gynaecology Canada/Journal d'Obstetrique et Gynecologie du Canada*, 30(10), 888–895.

Baxter, P. and Jack, S. 2008. Qualitative case study methodology: Study design and implementation for novice researchers. *The Qualitative Report*, 13(4), 544–559.

Bryan, T. K. 2011. Exploring the dimensions of organizational capacity for local social service delivery organizations using a multi-method approach. DPhil dissertation, Virginia Polytechnic Institute and State University, Virginia.

Corporation for National and Community Service. 2017. *Organizational Capacity Assessment Tool*. Washington, DC: Corporation for National Community Service.

Duffield, C. F. 2010. Different delivery models, In G. A. Hodge, C. Greve and A. E. Boardman (eds.), *International Handbook on Public–Private Partnerships*. Cheltenham, UK and Northampton, MA, USA: Edward Elgar Publishing, 187–215.

Edelenbos, J. and Teisman, G. R. 2008. Public–private partnership: On the edge of project and process management. Insights from Dutch practice: The Sijtwende spatial development project. *Environment and Planning C: Government and Policy*, 26(3), 614–626.

Eisinger, P. 2002. Organizational capacity and organizational effectiveness among street-level food assistance programs. *Nonprofit and Voluntary Sector Quarterly*, 31(1), 115–130.

Foster-Fishman, P. G., Berkowitz, S. L., Lounsbury, D. W., Jacobson, S. and Allen, N. A. 2001. Building collaborative capacity in community coalitions: A review and integrative framework. *American Journal of Community Psychology*, 29(2), 241–261.

Gazley, B. 2010. Linking collaborative capacity to performance measurement in government non-profit partnerships. *Nonprofit and Voluntary Sector Quarterly*, 39(4), 653–673.

Harrison, P. J., Lynch, E. W., Rosander, K. and Borton, W. 1990. Determining success in interagency collaboration: An evaluation of processes and behaviors. *Infants & Young Children*, 3(1), 69–78.

Honadle, B. W. 1981. A capacity-building framework: A search for concept and purpose. *Public Administration Review*, 41(5), 575–580.

Hudson, B., Hardy, B., Henwood, M. and Wistow, G. 1999. In pursuit of inter-agency collaboration in the public sector: What is the contribution of theory and research? *Public Management: An International Journal of Research and Theory*, 1(2), 235–260.

Ibem, E. O. 2010. An assessment of the role of government agencies in public-private partnerships in housing delivery in Nigeria. *Journal of Construction in Developing Countries*, 15(2), 23–48.

Ibem, E. O. 2011. Public-private partnership (PPP) in housing provision in Lagos megacity region, Nigeria. *International Journal of Housing Policy*, 11(2), 133–154.

Ingraham, P., Joyce, P. and Donahue, A. 2003. *Governance Performance: Why Management Matters*. Baltimore, MD: Johns Hopkins University Press.

Judge, W. Q. and Elenkov, D. 2005. Organizational capacity for change and environmental performance: An empirical assessment of Bulgarian firms. *Journal of Business Research*, 58(7), 893–901.

Lerman, D. L. and Reeder, W. J. 1987. The affordability of adequate housing. *Real Estate Economics*, 15(4), 389–404.

Qin, W., Soliño, A. S. and de Albornoz, V. A. C. 2017. Introducing public-private partnerships for affordable housing in China. *Open House International*, 42(2), 75–81.

Seawright, J. and Gerring, J. 2008. Case selection techniques in case study research: A menu of qualitative and quantitative options. *Political Research Quarterly*, 61(2), 294–308.

Stake, R. E. 2013. *Multiple Case Study Analysis*. New York: Guilford Press.

Steijn, B., Klijn, E. and Edelenbos, J. 2011. Public private partnerships: Added value by organizational form or management? *Public Administration*, 89(4), 1235–1252.

Susilawati, C. and Armitage, L. 2004. Do public–private partnerships facilitate affordable housing outcomes in Queensland? *Australian Property Journal*, 38(3), 184–187.

Ukoje, J. and Kanu, K. 2014. Implementation and the challenges of the mass housing scheme in Abuja, Nigeria. *American International Journal of Contemporary Research*, 4(4), 209–218.

Van Marrewijk, A., Clegg, S. R., Pitsis, T. S. and Veenswijk, M. 2008. Managing public-private megaprojects: Paradoxes, complexity, and project design. *International Journal of Project Management*, 26(6), 591–600.

Vinzant, D. H. and Vinzant, J. C. 1996. Strategy and organizational capacity: Finding a fit. *Public Productivity & Management Review*, 13(1), 139–157.

Weihe, G. 2008. Public-private partnerships and public-private value trade-offs. *Public Money and Management*, 28(3), 153–158.

Wernerfelt, B. 1984. A resource-based view of the firm. *Strategic Management Journal*, 5(2), 171–180.

Wettenhall, R. 2003. The rhetoric and reality of public-private partnerships. *Public Organization Review*, 3(1), 77–107.

Wettenhall, R. 2008. Public-private mixes and partnerships: A search for understanding. *Asia Pacific Journal of Public Administration*, 30(2), 119–138.

Willems, T. and Van Dooren, W. 2011. Lost in diffusion? How collaborative arrange-ments lead to accountability paradox. *International Review of Administrative Sciences*, 77(3), 505–530.

Yin, R. K. 2011. *Applications of Case Study Research*, 3rd edition. Los Angeles: Sage.

11. Planning for all? Guiding principles for selecting multi-stakeholder tools in urban planning processes

Els Keunen and Saskia Ruijsink

INTRODUCTION

Strategic urban or spatial planning is a popular approach to address contemporary (urban) challenges and opportunities jointly (Albrechts, 2013, 2015; Davoudi, 2015; Healey, 1998; Innes and Booher, 2010; Van den Broeck, 2004). In strategic planning, integrating disciplines and using a spatial perspective is a central element and the role of the planner shifts to bringing stakeholders together, encouraging exchange of information, viewpoints and ideas between the stakeholders, and guiding them towards joint agreements: the planner as a strategist, facilitator and mediator (Tan, 2012). This contrasts with the statutory approach where the planner is concerned with efficiently organizing physical space and securing the legal basis for using space (Mäntysalo et al., 2015): as an expert and administrator (Fox-Rogers and Murphy, 2016). Engaging in strategic planning therefore requires a distinct skill-set from the skills expected in the expert driven statutory planning.

Strategic planning is more recently also conceptualized as a co-creation process, going beyond stakeholder participation, by acknowledging that any stakeholder can initiate, deliberately influence and intervene in an urban development process (Watson, 2014). Hence the role of urban planner can be taken up beyond the (formal) urban planner, by any 'city maker'. The co-productive 'turn' in strategic planning promotes an "equal and reciprocal relationship" (Albrechts, 2015: 514) between stakeholders and invites all of them to co-create and co-produce. It takes place in "a setting ... where actors can articulate their identities, their traditions, and their values" (Albrechts and Balducci, 2013: 22), also recognizing interdependence of actors in order to bring together the necessary resources for realizing urban transformations (Klijn and Koppenjan, 2012). However, as these actors or stakeholders do not always have an urban planning background, they might struggle with it. This was the case in 2018, when we (the authors in their role as integrated urban development and urban planning trainers at IHS) were approached by a Lebanese NGO, NAHNOO. NAHNOO is an organization of urban activists, consisting mostly of volunteers with various educational backgrounds (e.g. architecture, urbanism, environmental studies, health studies, management, psychology). Among others, they campaign for more and better quality public space as many public space challenges have developed under the government's top-down manner of urban planning and management. NAHNOO wanted to build its capacity in strategic urban planning, focusing on mobilizing stakeholders to come up with alternative solutions for public space in Lebanese cities.

A common way to facilitate stakeholder engagement in urban planning is by using 'tools'. Various stand-alone tools and toolkits have been designed and their number is expanding constantly. Thus, IHS, represented by the authors, together with NAHNOO, lecturers from the Notre Dame University – Louaize (NDU) in Lebanon and the Veldacademie (Rotterdam, the Netherlands) – later on referred to as 'the team' – co-designed and implemented a training course for NAHNOO staff and volunteers, in which the use of tools for guiding stakeholders through a strategic urban planning process took a central position. Yet, the selection of tools posed a challenge: how to identify those that would contribute to strategic urban planning processes, would be suitable to the local context, would be possible to facilitate by someone without a formal background in urban planning, and in a context of limited resources? More generally, how to select appropriate tools for multi-stakeholder processes in strategic urban planning in any context?

We believe that urban development processes are too complex and too contextual to be captured in a sort of 'ultimate' toolkit, as it would always (at best) reflect a specific spatio-temporal context. A more feasible and flexible approach is identifying certain guiding principles that go beyond a specific context and could assist in selecting tools. Van Dijk (2006) illustrates that the selection of tools depends on the nature of the issue identified. In this chapter the focus is on multi-stakeholder urban development processes. This chapter builds on our experiences with NAHNOO as well as literature in order to come up with guiding principles for identifying useful tools for strategic urban planning within different contexts.

These guiding principles came about using an Action Design Research methodology (Sein et al., 2011) composed of four stages. In this chapter, we first explain this methodology, then present the main findings of each stage, leading to the presentation of guiding principles in the fourth stage. We close the chapter with a reflection and conclusion.

AN ACTION DESIGN RESEARCH METHODOLOGY

Design can be understood as "a process in which something is created" (Fallman, 2007: 194). Within the act of design, a process of knowledge production occurs (Roggema, 2016). Design thinking has long been present in the practice of architecture, urban design and planning since it acknowledges that finding and exploring solutions (design options) is part of understanding the problem (Çalışkan, 2012), that there are many feedback loops and that there is not one starting point in a process.

The logic of the design approach has also found its way into doing research. Insights put forward in this chapter result from such a design research process. The research method used is framed as the Action Design Research (ADR) by Sein et al. (2011). This method starts with a problem formulation that can be framed as a more generic knowledge problem as well as a specific contextual one. In the ADR method both layers of this problem formulation (stage 1) then form the basis for the development and evaluation of an intervention, based on some preliminary research (stage 2). The focus in the third stage draws on the principle of guided emergence and is concerned with learning and reflection based on how the designed solution works in the specific context for which it is designed: "Conscious reflection on the problem framing, the theories chosen, and the emerging ensemble is critical to ensure that contributions to knowledge are identified" (Sein et al., 2011: 44). The fourth stage in the ADR method is concerned with formalization of learning and with generalizing outcomes (Sein et al., 2011: 44). In this chapter, the stages are organized as follows:

- **Stage 1:** The central problem identified in this chapter is the challenge of selecting and combining tools for multi-stakeholder processes in urban planning. This is connected to a more specific problem for NAHNOO: what tools and process guidance principles and structure can be used to train NAHNOO staff and volunteers in facilitating multi-stakeholder processes in strategic urban planning.
- **Stage 2.1:** Development of a prototype framework that can guide the use of tools in an urban planning process. This step was done based on urban planning theory and the team's understanding of the local context in Lebanon. Based on this framework, we made a selection of tools that seemed to fit in this framework and would be appropriate for the situation in Lebanon and developed a description of each tool.
- **Stage 2.2:** Application and evaluation of the tools in practice. During the training course, the tools were applied in a real case setting. For each tool, the team assessed its usefulness, how the tool related to other tools employed, the planning process, the Lebanese context and the capacities within NAHNOO for using it.

- **Stage 3:** The team revised the framework as well as the tools descriptions and came up with the selection of a set of characteristics that were important to gauge the tools' usefulness. This was done as the final component of the course in the form of a co-creation workshop. The joint reflection in this workshop introduced some generic principles but was primarily concerned with the use of tools by NAHNOO.
- **Stage 4:** The authors used the insights from piloting the toolkit and the co-created tool selection criteria and combined it with further review of literature. This resulted in the identification of a revised framework with guiding principles for selecting multi-stakeholder tools in strategic urban planning that can be applied beyond the specific case needs of NAHNOO.

These stages form the structure of the following section of the chapter.

PROTOTYPE FRAMEWORK: URBAN PLANNING PROCESS AND USING TOOLS

Developing a Prototype Toolkit for NAHNOO

NAHNOO works with volunteers who come and go and this challenges institutional memory. NAHNOO and IHS jointly came with the idea to develop a training and an urban planning process guide with tools (i.e. 'a toolkit') to deepen and structure the work with volunteers. The team developed a prototype version based on the review of theory and the reworking and selective use of available tools and toolkits. The starting points for the design prototype toolkit were rooted in strategic urban planning literature:

- Organizing the **strategic urban planning process in phases**
- A strong focus on including the **spatial dimension** in the planning process
- A strong focus on **stakeholder engagement**
- Combining **various tools and timeframes**.

These points will be elaborated below.

Strategic urban planning process in phases

Albrechts (2004: 747) identifies strategic urban planning as a "sociospatial ... process through which a vision, actions, and means for implementation are produced that shape and frame what a place is and may become". It is iterative and organized in non-linear phases: various processes might be going on at the same time, with 'going back and forth' between phases that are not clearly delineated but overlap. Based on Cities Alliance (2016), the prototype toolkit structured the process into four main phases following a more or less chronological order, however with overlaps and feedback loops: 1. Inventory and

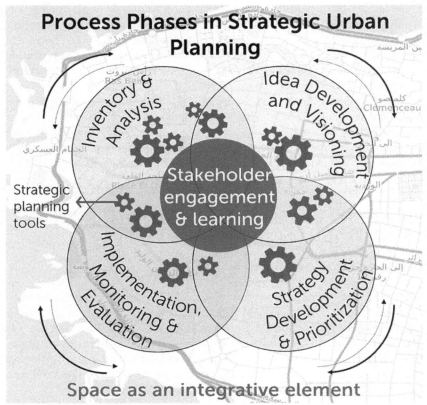

Source: Developed by the authors.

Figure 11.1　Visualization of process phases in strategic urban planning

Analysis; 2. Idea Development and Visioning; 3. Strategy Development and Prioritization; 4. Implementation, Monitoring and Evaluation (Figure 11.1). Stakeholder engagement and learning and the use of space as an integrative element are cross-cutting through all four phases. Despite its obvious importance, phase 4 was not included in the training for NAHNOO since they were primarily interested in developing alternative visions, strategies and actions used for advocacy and mobilizing stakeholders.

Spatial dimension
The spatial dimension of strategic urban planning is emphasized by many authors (Albrechts, 2004; Davoudi and Strange, 2008; Healey, 1998; Van den

Broeck, 2004). The importance of urban spatial transformation processes is also considered key for realizing sustainable development, for example in the Sustainable Development Goals, especially the 'urban' SDG11 (UNDP, n.d.). It is, however, remarkable that the toolkit for City Development Strategies (CDS) from Cities Alliance (2016) hardly covers the spatial dimension. More spatial tools, such as those developed by Gehl (n.d.), often only focus on the inventory and analytical phase. Therefore the need to include spatial tools formed a clear starting point for the prototype toolkit.

Multi-stakeholder processes in urban planning

It is widely acknowledged that addressing current urban issues and strategizing for urban transformation requires joint action and collaboration (Albrechts, 2013, 2015; Davoudi, 2015; Healey, 1998; Innes and Booher, 2010; Van den Broeck, 2004). There are several motivations to engage stakeholders in urban planning or in other forms of public policy. Fiorino (1990) identified three major categories of arguments for engaging stakeholders: (1) substantive, that is concerned with quality improvement due to a holistic approach, (2) normative, which is a democratic dimension: stakeholders have the right to be included, and (3) the instrumental argument focuses on how engaging stakeholders can facilitate implementation by their commitment and contribution with resources. In other words, multi-stakeholder processes can lead to *better, fairer and more feasible* plans and the prototype toolkit aimed at providing the equipment to do justice to all aspects. Of course one cannot be naive and expect that tools can overcome systemic (governance) issues that pose challenges and even risks to stakeholder processes including power disparities and under- and overrepresentation or clashing values systems and rationalities (see for example the work of Arnstein, 1969; Brand and Gaffikin, 2007; Cornwall, 2008; Watson, 2003; White, 1996).

Various tools and timeframes

Strategic urban planning processes are long-term, iterative processes which develop over time and that can make use of tools. In its concrete form, a tool is "a piece of equipment that you use with your hands to make or repair something"; more abstractly, it is "something that helps you to do a particular activity" (Cambridge English Dictionary, 2019). While there are many technical tools in urban planning – software programs such as GIS, visualization tools, calculation aids or programs for statistical and qualitative analysis, etc. – we primarily focused on developing a prototype toolkit with multi-stakeholder tools for collaboration in the development of urban strategies.

But tools are only a small piece of the puzzle and cannot be disconnected from the multi-stakeholder strategic urban planning process. Based on Aguirre et al. (2017), we conceptualize a 'five-level typology' (see Figure 11.2) in which tools are the smallest building block (level 1), in a strategic planning process (level 5) comprised of phases (level 4), components (level 3) and interactions between stakeholders (level 2).

Different types of tools can be employed in order to complete certain activities, and answer specific questions for each phase, and this can in turn help in creating events and it is the series of events that eventually corresponds with the strategic urban planning process.

The prototype toolkit

The prototype toolkit that was used in the training included guidance on the theoretical strategic urban planning starting points as specified above and a selection of tools as included in Table 11.1. This table is structured according to the different phases, their corresponding types of tools and an overview of tools used in the NAHNOO training.

Using the prototype toolkit with NAHNOO

NAHNOO selected a group of approximately 20 staff and volunteers for taking a training organized and implemented by the team in 2019. The first two weeks focused on using tools for carrying out an integrated urban problem analysis and developing an urban vision for a selected area in Beirut. Around three months later, a one-week training was held which focused on strategy development and making suggestions for implementation. The group composition of training participants, while overlapping, was not constant throughout the training.

Even though NAHNOO has a lot of experience, working in this manner with the tools for urban planning was new for them. In various evaluations, ranging from daily logbooks, to a survey and oral and analogue forms of evaluation, the overall assessment of working with tools was positive. They learned about the study areas in Beirut as well as about new approaches that allowed them to collaborate better. The tools offered guidance for joint work, making use of different forms of existing expertise (writing, drawing, mapping, creativity, analytical capacity, disciplinary knowledge) and combining it in new ways. However, participants shared that working with many tools was also time consuming and sometimes repetitive. It was critical that they were regularly reminded in which part of the planning process they were and what the ultimate goal was.

Outcomes of identifying guiding principles in a co-creation process

After working with the toolkit for three weeks, a small group of NAHNOO staff and volunteers, varying between four and eight persons daily, participated in a one-week co-creation workshop. This workshop focused on reviewing the toolkit, by developing a flexible roadmap with milestones that helps in

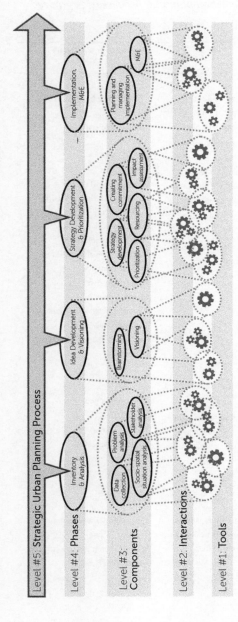

Source: Based on Aguirre et al. (2017).

Figure 11.2   Visualization of the five-level typology

Table 11.1   *Overview of types of tools used for multi-stakeholder processes in strategic urban planning processes, organized per phase*

Type of tool	Description	Tools used in NAHNOO training
Inventory and analysis		
Tools for data collection	Tools for going on the ground and collecting both quantitative and qualitative data. This can be complemented by secondary data collection.	5 Whys – Fishbone (Ishikawa) diagram
Tools for socio-spatial situation analysis	Analysis can be done by identifying layers with structuring elements, by zooming in and out of different geographical scales and by identifying clusters, connections and networks. Furthermore, there are also tools for assessing spatial qualities.	Problem tree analysis SWOT Spatial SWOT Persona Participatory Mapping Importance/Influence Matrix (Stakeholders)
Problem analysis tools	Tools designed to jointly identify and analyse specific urban problem(s).	Social network analysis Stakeholder mapping
Stakeholder analysis tools	Tools for understanding who is involved in what, their power and/or influence, resources and interrelations.	Stakeholder analysis following living labs model Street interviews Mental mapping Activity/Behavioural Mapping Transect Walk Backing up the problem statement
Idea development and visioning		
Brainstorming tools	Tools for collecting ideas from various sources of inspiration.	Collage Reference Project
Visioning tools	Visioning tools contribute to jointly developing a long-term vision, and, depending on the tool, can also include developing a mission statement and identification of core values.	Speed Date Values (Vision) Values (Manifesto) Brainstorming/ideation Storyboard Just City
Strategy development and prioritization		
Strategy development tools	Tools that help stakeholders to identify strategies for concrete action and how they can be combined to complement and strengthen each other.	Participatory Backcasting Scenario Planning SOAR (Strengths, Opportunities, Aspirations, Results)

Type of tool	Description	Tools used in NAHNOO training
(Ex ante) impact assessment tools	These tools help to identify what the potential desirable as well as undesirable impacts of proposed interventions could be. An example is cost–benefit analysis.	TOWS Analysis Trend Analysis 'HEY! Imaginable Guidelines' role-play game
Resourcing tools	Resourcing tools help to identify which actions and projects would be needed to implement the strategies. Furthermore, they also assist in identifying and analysing the financial, material and human resources as well as the time investments that are linked to these actions and projects.	Various strategic plan formats/templates (Aspirations, Results) TOWS Analysis Trend Analysis 'HEY! Imaginable Guidelines' role-play game Various strategic plan formats/templates
Prioritization tools	These tools help to prioritize which actions, strategies and/or projects should be prioritized and can assist in decision-making.	
Tools for creating commitment	These tools help in getting the buy-in from the different stakeholders with regard to the proposed strategies.	
Implementation, monitoring and evaluation		
Planning and managing implementation tools	Similar to project management tools, these tools help to coordinate the implementation of strategies, actions and projects identified in the previous phases. In this context, especially useful when (multiple) stakeholders are involved in this phase.	*Not applicable*
Monitoring and evaluation tools	Tools for joint evaluation and reflection. These can be targeted at the impacts of the actions but can also help to reflect on stakeholder interactions, level of cooperation and creation of trust.	

Source: Authors, based on Cities Alliance (2016).

organizing an urban planning process as well as in communicating to its participants 'where' they find themselves in the process. This was inspired by the project phases and related tools shown in Table 11.1, but it also included various outputs (e.g. 'a problem statement') that were helpful as milestones in the planning process. The group preferred to have a large toolkit from which they could pick and choose since the relevance of combining different tools with different characteristics to allow for diversity was deemed very important for working with a broad range of stakeholders.

Additionally, all the tool descriptions were reviewed. In several group discussions, several distinguishing characteristics of tools were identified:

- Divergence vs convergence – does the tool allow for gathering as many ideas as possible vs does it support the process of reaching consensus on an issue?
- Difficulty of using the tool – is the tool easy or difficult to use?
- Type of expertise needed of the facilitator – what kind of expertise and competences does the facilitator need?
- Type of expertise needed of the group members – what kind of expertise and competences do the group members need?
- Internal vs external – is the tool most suitable for use within NAHNOO (internal) or with stakeholders outside NAHNOO (external)?
- Spatiality of the tool – how and to what extent does the tool allow to address the spatial dimension of the urban issue/strategy?
- Time needed to use the tool – how much time is needed to use the tool?

TOWARDS GENERIC GUIDING PRINCIPLES

The starting points for the design of the toolkit, the experience and evaluation of using it (stage 2) and the reflection in the co-creation workshop (stage 3) resulted in myriad insights relevant for organizing and designing a process of strategic urban planning and for selecting tools that can be used therein. In this fourth stage of ADR, we have synthesized those findings and we have reviewed additional literature and used that to further synthesize our findings towards generic guiding principles for selecting tools in strategic urban planning that we have identified as essential principles, followed by the compounding principles as is explained further below. We then conclude with an overview table with key questions for each of the guiding principles.

Essential Principles

The prototype toolkit was based on starting points rooted in strategic urban planning theory where we explicitly go beyond seeing it as a participatory form of urban planning, but rather as a co-productive approach. Additionally it is critical to realize that strategic urban planning needs more than a focus on process. Albrechts and Balducci (2013) identify key characteristics of strategic urban planning and also recognize the importance of content, the relational nature and the institutional implications in addition to the process. All those aspects are closely interrelated and cannot be seen in separation from each other (for a similar argument, see Fainstein, 2010, 2014). So ideally the aspects are addressed in their intertwined nature when selecting and using tools. Since planning is concerned with creating 'better cities', it is unavoidably a highly normative field (Fainstein and Campbell, 2011), as it is also concerned with making explicit what a better city is or could be. We agree with Fainstein and Campbell (2011) that these values should be made explicit. We think that each and every tool that is used in the urban strategic planning process should (allow to) be used in such a manner that it is **promoting urban sustainability and urban justice**. We explicitly include promoting these two values as characteristics of strategic planning. Indeed, sustainability, understood in its broad form including environmental, social, spatial and economic considerations (Boelens, 2011), is at the core for many authors on strategic planning (e.g. Boelens, 2011; Healey, 2012; Hillier, 2008, 2011; Van den Broeck, 2013). While urban justice has been much less prominent within strategic planning literature, the work by Fainstein (2010, 2014) on the just city and by Soja (2013) on spatial justice, as well as by other authors, has brought the topic to attention within general planning theory. Urban justice strives to reduce existing inequalities in resource distribution as well as power inequalities in decision-making (Dikeç, 2001) and is concerned with democracy, diversity and equity (Fainstein, 2014). Striving for urban sustainability and urban justice is part of strategic urban planning and needs to be done in conjunction.

A second essential guiding principle is that each tool should allow for **plurality and multidisciplinarity**: when working with various stakeholders, invariably opinions, visions, perspectives, disciplines and agendas will show a variety. It is important to understand and acknowledge these different viewpoints, which often might be diverging. While there is no 'right' or 'wrong' in these different perspectives, some convergence and level of consensus will be necessary in order to come to joint and fair decision-making (Albrechts, 2015). Allowing for plurality also means paying attention to power imbalances which might exist between stakeholders and trying to address these (Brand and Gaffikin, 2007). Additionally this plurality materializes in multidisciplinarity as strategic planning is an integrated form of planning, combining understandings of different disciplines related to spatial, economic, social and environmental challenges, opportunities and possibilities into visions, plans, strategies, projects and concrete actions (Albrechts, 2004). While emphasizing working across perspectives and disciplines and hence holistically, it is key to make selective (strategic) choices since resources are limited.

Encouraging **innovation, creativity and learning** is the third essential principle. In order to come up with innovative solutions, which can deal with the complexity and uncertainty of planning and urban development, creativity is essential (Healey, 1998). Innovative approaches can unfold best when creativity and a constant curiosity and willingness to learn are combined. Tools should facilitate processes that go beyond individual learning and lead to social learning. Social learning is understood as a process of learning that can occur *between* rather than merely *within* individuals (Muro and Jeffrey, 2008; Reed et al., 2010; Rodela, 2011, 2013; Webler et al., 1995). Social learning includes both cognitive enhancement and moral development (Webler et al., 1995) and this is essential when engaging in urban strategy development, due to its highly normative nature. Social learning occurs when stakeholders are open for dialogue when dealing with complex issues (Reed et al., 2010; Rodela, 2013) or wicked problems (Muro and Jeffrey, 2008), in situations where the subject at hand is unpredictable and dynamic and requires a creative approach.

In order to allow for a plurality of views, it is important that stakeholders feel welcome to participate and are able to do so. Thus a fourth essential principle is that tools should be **inviting and captivating**. It relates to making sure that there are no barriers to participation, but also that the level of engagement expected is fitting the stakeholders involved (Sorensen and Sagaris, 2010) no matter whether planning happens within or outside the institutional realm of urban planning. Furthermore, strategic urban planning processes tend to be long-term processes. Creating and sustaining stakeholder interest throughout the entire process is key to successful stakeholder engagement. Specific attention should furthermore be paid to whose attention is captured (and whose is not) and whether there are imbalances between different groups of stakeholders (Cornwall, 2008). Furthermore, while using the tools, it has become very clear that tools should be simple enough, not only to keep people on board, but also to allow stakeholders to concentrate on the complexity of the urban issues rather than the complexity of the tool.

Finally a critical essential principle of a tool for urban planning is that it is **contextual and fitting within available resources**. Differences in legal, political, governance and socio-cultural contexts in general, but also specific conditions at a particular moment in time can greatly influence how stakeholders behave and interact with each other (Brand and Gaffikin, 2007). Any tool should allow for such diversity and leave space and encouragement for contextualization. In line with that, it should match with the type of resources that are locally available such as time, human, financial, technical and knowledge resources. There should be a balance between the input of resources and the desired outputs of the strategic planning process. Resource efficiency takes into account resource investments by those organizing the stakeholder engagement as well as by the other participants in the process (Cornwall, 2008).

Compounding Principles: Preconditions for Strategic Urban Planning

The compounding principles anchor the essence of strategic urban planning. While they might not be represented in each tool individually, the combination of tools should be such that all compounding principles are considered in the process. For example, a participatory mapping tool can be useful to demonstrate the spatial dimension and show the diversity of views, while a back-casting tool is not in itself spatial but very helpful in promoting visionary and long-term thinking and supporting dealing with uncertainty.

First, a number of tools used should explicitly allow for **dealing with uncertainty and complexity**. The notion of embracing uncertainty and addressing complexity in urban planning has reached solid ground in urban literature in the last decade, e.g. in urban planning for resilience (e.g. Jabareen, 2013), complexity in urban planning (e.g. Byrne, 2001; De Roo et al., 2016; De Roo and Silva, 2010; Portugali, 2008), contingency planning (Healey, 2012), a multiplanar theory of planning (Hillier, 2008, 2017), urban living labs (e.g. Bulkeley et al., 2016), adaptive planning (Rauws, 2017) and a focus on 'the experimental city' (Evans et al., 2016). Complexity driven planning deliberately addresses the need for imagining possible futures (Byrne, 2003). The plural here stems from the understanding that the world is developmentally open (Gerrits, 2012; Prigogine and Stengers, 1997) and that there is no such thing as one future. It is essential that in an urban strategic planning process at least some tools explicitly focus on dealing with uncertainty and complexity by allowing for experimentation, using the logic of testing rough conjectures as in design thinking and by advising rather than mandating (Balducci et al., 2011) and by addressing the dynamic nature of (urban) development. However, more static and linear tools can be complementary and relevant as well. Therefore this principle is compounding.

Secondly, being **visionary** is important for directing a focus on long-term development in a flexible manner (Byrne, 2001). While visions are a fundamental part of strategic planning, it is important to stress that they are not conjuring up an image of an end-state of the city, a final product. Urban development, and therefore also strategic planning, is a dynamic, continuous process of 'becoming'. This is understood here as "the ability to cope with action, movement, emergence, relationship, and creative experimentation" (Albrechts and Balducci, 2013: 21).

Being visionary is critical in urban strategic planning, but not enough; it needs to be complemented with a third compounding principle of being **action oriented**. Action orientation is important for dealing with urgent issues, gaining and maintaining public support and simply getting things done and seeing results (Albrechts and Balducci, 2013). This is often contrasted with the blueprint type of planning, in which the land use of the entire physical space is determined, but without considering financial resources or human capacities (Albrechts, 2004; Faludi, 2000; Mäntysalo et al., 2015).

Eventually **acknowledging spatiality** is a critical compounding principle for selecting tools, since spatiality is essential in strategic urban planning. However, a spatial approach needs to be complemented with approaches making use of narratives, images and figures. While these latter are captured in many tools that are more generic such as multi-stakeholder tools and strategic business planning tools, the spatiality deserves more attention in strategic urban planning as an integrative framework for social, economic and environmental urban development. *What* happens *where*, impacts how much and what kind of resources we use; it affects our access to employment or education and it influences how we experience and live our daily lives. Many people are only implicitly aware of the spatial dimension and will hardly consider it if it is not explicitly brought up. Spatiality is also linked to working at different **geographical scales**, from the local to the urban, regional and beyond. Localized actions take place within a certain broader context, while broad-reaching actions can have differentiated effects at local level, therefore zooming in and out to envision the impacts at different spatial scale levels is necessary. It also implies the need to include actors at various levels of governance (Albrechts and Balducci, 2013).

Key Questions for Guiding the Selection of Tools

In Table 11.2, we present the principles and their key questions for guiding the selection of tools. As can be observed, these are not yes/no questions but require a qualitative assessment of each principle.

REFLECTION AND CONCLUSION

Strategic planning aims to influence socio-spatial transformation processes (Low and Iveson, 2016). However, if we see the city as a complex system (De Roo et al., 2016) we should acknowledge that the impact of strategic planning will always be 'just one of the processes' that are going on in a city. Tools are only the smallest component within a strategic urban planning process (see Figure 11.2), which is only one component in a larger governance structure. An urban transition process requires a multitude of transition oriented management approaches including strategic urban planning processes. Even so, the quality and suitability of tools in a particular context matters, as the following quote by Lynam et al. (2007) shows:

> Any form of participation, whether in the context of research or natural resource management practice, involves far more than the mechanical application of participatory tools for capturing local stakeholder perspectives and knowledge. Nevertheless, tool selection matters: success is not guaranteed by selecting the right tool, but it is excluded by selecting the wrong one. (Lynam et al., 2007)

While various toolkits exist and can be useful, we argue that because of the dynamics, complexity and contextuality of urban planning (issues) the ulti-

Table 11.2   Guiding principles with key questions

Guiding principles	Key questions
Essential	
Promoting urban justice and sustainability	How does the tool address sustainability in strategic urban planning? How does the tool address justice in strategic urban planning?
Allowing for plurality and multidisciplinarity	How does the tool support addressing the diversity of stakeholder perspectives? How does the tool address potential power imbalances and ensure attention to more vulnerable groups? How does the tool support in integrating the diversity of (disciplinary) knowledge? How does it help to converge various ideas and reach consensus?
Encouraging innovation, creativity and learning	How does the tool encourage creativity and innovative ways of thinking, planning and/or implementing urban strategic planning processes and related actions? How does the tool facilitate continuous learning in and for urban strategic planning?
Inviting and captivating	How clear are the tools' instructions? What is the level of facilitation needed? What is the difficulty level of input requested from stakeholders? To which stakeholders is the tool attractive? What is the number of stakeholders interested in/involved in the tool? How long does the tool manage to capture the attention of stakeholders?
Contextual and fitting within available resources	In which way is the tool able to adapt to changing contexts and situations, changing times, changing levels of resource availability and other dynamics? What are the resource investments needed by the organizers and other stakeholders for using the tool? How does that compare to the results of using the tool?
Compounding: preconditions for strategic urban planning	
Dealing with uncertainty	How does the tool allow for dealing with uncertainty in strategic urban planning?
Visionary	How does the tool support developing the visionary, value-based and long-term aspect of urban strategic planning?
Action oriented	How does the tool support being action oriented and developing short-term interventions for urban strategic planning?
Acknowledging spatiality	How does the tool support in creating understanding of the spatial dimension of urban strategic planning? How does the tool enable zooming in and out across different scale levels?

Source: Authors.

mate toolkit does not exist and instead propose guiding principles for selecting tools for multi-stakeholder strategic urban planning processes. Nine guiding principles have been identified: promoting urban justice and sustainability; allowing for plurality and multidisciplinarity; encouraging innovation, creativity and learning; inviting and captivating; and contextual and fitting within available resources as five essential principles. The preconditions for strategic urban planning resulted in the following compounding principles: dealing with uncertainty; visionary; action oriented; and acknowledging spatiality.

These principles cannot be used as yes/no criteria and we proposed key questions for each principle that reflect the qualitative rather than quantitative character of the guiding principles: they invite reflection on the characteristics of a tool to qualitatively assess their suitability in a specific context. Apart from using these principles to assess existing tools, they can also be used to adapt tools to become more suitable for strategic urban planning, or as design principles for developing new tools. Many tools, especially those frequently used (e.g. participatory mapping, SWOT analysis, scenario planning, etc.), have been described and their instructions worked out in multiple ways by different actors, with slight variations between their descriptions. In our experience (since we have used many tools in lecturing and training also beyond our work with NAHNOO), we would choose a certain description of a tool as a basis and make adaptations. One example of this is that we often find tools that do not consider the spatial dimension, whereas on many occasions (e.g. tools for strategy development) it is very useful and possible to include them. A planning process, but also a tool in itself is therefore not static but dynamic, always in development, to be experimented with, adjusted and improved over time and in different contexts – and allowing for different variations of the same tool.

It should be clear that, as Lynam et al. (2007) argue, merely using the 'right' tools will not lead to a qualitative strategic urban planning process and outcome and improved stakeholder interaction; more is needed than that. Moreover, strategic urban planning tools can facilitate and enable learning, but learning is a process that needs more enabling factors than simply using tools and also involves less tangible things such as co-productive stakeholder attitudes, quality process facilitation, a safe environment, positive group dynamics, etc. In fact, in the case of Lebanon, there was a strong demand for more than guiding principles as they also worked with us on developing a process guide, helping to structure what kind of tool can be used in a specific phase and how to move from one phase to another. This shows that there is a need for flexibility as well as for structure and guidance. This is also not surprising since in practice multi-stakeholder processes are chaotic: people come and go; most stakeholders do not participate in every step of the process, thus there is a need for constant going back and forth. This complexity can be facilitated by flexible guidance and leadership of a core group of stakeholders who oversee and guide the process as a whole.

The development of guiding principles has been collaborative and explorative and we aim to keep on refining and adjusting them with further use, possibly complementing them by more guidance on how to move between the various phases of planning. We invite researchers and practitioners to provide their reflection and proposals for improvement of the principles. Furthermore, we intend to use these principles to assess different tools and make these assessments publicly available for comments and perusal. We further invite others using the guiding principles to share their findings with us. Additionally we see a possible intersection with design research that is concerned with studying how different learning environments influence learning and also on how design education is best facilitated (for example: Collins et al., 2004) and further exploring this intersection could be relevant to future research.

REFERENCES

Aguirre, M., Agudelo, N. and Romm, J. (2017). Design facilitation as emerging practice: Analyzing how designers support multi-stakeholder co-creation. *She Ji: The Journal of Design, Economics, and Innovation*, 3(3), 198–209.

Albrechts, L. (2004). Strategic (spatial) planning reexamined. *Environment and Planning B: Planning and Design*, 31(5), 743–758.

Albrechts, L. (2013). Reframing strategic spatial planning by using a coproduction perspective. *Planning Theory*, 12(1), 46–63.

Albrechts, L. (2015). Ingredients for a more radical strategic spatial planning. *Environment and Planning B: Planning and Design*, 42(3), 510–525.

Albrechts, L. and Balducci, A. (2013). Practicing strategic planning: In search of critical features to explain the strategic character of plans. *DisP – The Planning Review*, 49(3), 16–27.

Arnstein, S. R. (1969). A ladder of citizen participation. *Journal of the American Institute of Planners*, 35(4), 216–224.

Balducci, A., Boelens, L., Hillier, J., Nyseth, T. and Wilkinson, C. (2011). Introduction: Strategic spatial planning in uncertainty: Theory and exploratory practice. *Town Planning Review*, 82(5), 481–501.

Boelens, L. (2011). Going beyond planners' dependencies: An actor-relational approach to Mainport Rotterdam. *The Town Planning Review*, 82(5), 547–572.

Brand, R. and Gaffikin, F. (2007). Collaborative planning in an uncollaborative world. *Planning Theory*, 6(3), 282–313.

Bulkeley, H., Coenen, L., Frantzeskaki, N., Hartmann, C., Kronsell, A., Mai, L., Marvin, S., McCormick, K., van Steenbergen, F. and Palgan, Y. V. (2016). Urban living labs: Governing urban sustainability transitions. *Current Opinion in Environmental Sustainability*, 22, 13–17.

Byrne, D. (2001). What is complexity science? Thinking as a realist about measurement and cities and arguing for natural history. *Emergence: A Journal of Complexity Issues in Organizations and Management*, 3(1), 61–76.

Byrne, D. (2003). Complexity theory and planning theory: A necessary encounter. *Planning Theory*, 2(3), 171–178.

Çalışkan, O. (2012). Design thinking in urbanism: Learning from the designers. *Urban Design International*, 17(4), 272–296.

Cambridge English Dictionary (2019). Tool. https://dictionary.cambridge.org/dictionary/english/tool.

Cities Alliance (2016). *What is a City Development Strategy (CDS)?* City Development Strategy Toolkit. http://city-development.org/intro/.

Collins, A., Joseph, D. and Bielaczyc, K. (2004). Design research: Theoretical and methodological issues. *Journal of the Learning Sciences*, 13(1), 15–42.

Cornwall, A. (2008). Unpacking 'participation': Models, meanings and practices. *Community Development Journal*, 43(3), 269–283.

Davoudi, S. (2015). Planning as practice of knowing. *Planning Theory*, 14(3), 316–331.

Davoudi, S. and Strange, I. (eds.) (2008). *Conceptions of Space and Place in Strategic Spatial Planning*. London: Routledge.

De Roo, G., Hillier, J. and Van Wezemael (eds.) (2016). *Complexity and Planning: Systems, Assemblages and Simulations*. Aningdon: Routledge.

De Roo, G. and Silva, E. A. (eds.) (2010). *A Planner's Encounter with Complexity*. Aldershot: Ashgate.

Dikeç, M. (2001). Justice and the spatial imagination. *Environment and Planning A: Economy and Space*, 33(10), 1785–1805.

Evans, J., Karvonen, A. and Raven, R. (eds.) (2016). *The Experimental City*. London: Routledge.

Fainstein, S. S. (2010). *The Just City*. Ithaca, NY: Cornell University Press.

Fainstein, S. S. (2014). The just city. *International Journal of Urban Sciences*, 18(1), 1–18.

Fainstein, S. and Campbell, S. (2011). Introduction: Theories of urban development and their implications for policy and planning. In S. Fainstein and S. Campbell (eds.), *Readings in Urban Theory*, 3rd edition. Chichester: Wiley-Blackwell, 1–17.

Fallman, D. (2007). Why research-oriented design isn't design-oriented research: On the tensions between design and research in an implicit design discipline. *Knowledge, Technology & Policy*, 20(3), 193–200.

Faludi, A. (2000). The performance of spatial planning. *Planning Practice and Research*, 15(4), 299–318.

Fiorino, D. J. (1990). Citizen participation and environmental risk: A survey of institutional mechanisms. *Science, Technology, & Human Values*, 15(2), 226–243.

Fox-Rogers, L. and Murphy, E. (2016). Self-perceptions of the role of the planner. *Environment and Planning B: Planning and Design*, 43(1), 74–92.

Gehl (n.d.). *Tools Archive*. Gehl Institute. https://gehlpeople.com/tools/.

Gerrits, L. (2012). *Punching Clouds: An Introduction to the Complexity of Public Decision-Making*. Litchfield Park, AZ: Emergent Publications.

Healey, P. (1998). Collaborative planning in a stakeholder society. *Town Planning Review*, 69(1), 1–21.

Healey, P. (2012). The universal and the contingent: Some reflections on the transnational flow of planning ideas and practices. *Planning Theory*, 11(2), 188–207.

Hillier, J. (2008). Plan(e) speaking: A multiplanar theory of spatial planning. *Planning Theory*, 7(1), 24–50.

Hillier, J. (2011). Strategic projects: From sustainability to resilience? In S. Oosterlynck, J. Van den Broeck, L. Albrechts, F. Moulaert and A. Verhetsel (eds.), *Strategic Spatial Projects: Catalysts for Change*. London: Routledge, 212–222.

Hillier, J. (2017). *Stretching beyond the Horizon: A Multiplanar Theory of Spatial Planning and Governance*. London: Routledge.

Innes, J. E. and Booher, D. E. (2010). *Planning with Complexity: An Introduction to Collaborative Rationality for Public Policy*. London: Routledge.

Jabareen, Y. (2013). Planning the resilient city: Concepts and strategies for coping with climate change and environmental risk. *Cities*, 31, 220–229.

Klijn, E.-H. and Koppenjan, J. (2012). Governance network theory: Past, present and future. *Policy & Politics*, 40(4), 587–606.

Low, S. and Iveson, K. (2016). Propositions for more just urban public spaces. *City*, 20(1), 10–31.

Lynam, T., de Jong, W., Sheil, D., Kusumanto, T. and Evans, K. (2007). A review of tools for incorporating community knowledge, preferences, and values into decision making in natural resources management. *Ecology and Society*, 12(1). https://www .jstor.org/stable/26267832.

Mäntysalo, R., Kangasoja, J. K. and Kanninen, V. (2015). The paradox of strategic spatial planning: A theoretical outline with a view on Finland. *Planning Theory & Practice*, 16(2), 169–183.

Muro, M. and Jeffrey, P. (2008). A critical review of the theory and application of social learning in participatory natural resource management processes. *Journal of Environmental Planning and Management*, 51(3), 325–344.

Portugali, J. (2008). Learning from paradoxes about prediction and planning in self-organizing cities. *Planning Theory*, 7(3), 248–262.

Prigogine, I. and Stengers, I. (1997). *The End of Certainty*. New York: Simon & Schuster.

Rauws, W. (2017). Embracing *Uncertainty Without Abandoning Planning. DisP – The Planning Review*, 53(1), 32–45.

Reed, M. S., Evely, A. C., Cundill, G., Fazey, I., Glass, J., Laing, A., Newig, J., Parrish, B., Prell, C., Raymond, C. and Stringer, L. C. (2010). What is social learning? *Ecology and Society*, 15(4). https://doi.org/10.5751/ES-03564-1504r01.

Rodela, R. (2011). Social learning and natural resource management: The emergence of three research perspectives. *Ecology and Society*, 16(4). https://doi.org/10.5751/ ES-04554-160430.

Rodela, R. (2013). The social learning discourse: Trends, themes and interdisciplinary influences in current research. *Environmental Science & Policy*, 25, 157–166.

Roggema, R. (2016). Research by design: Proposition for a methodological approach. *Urban Science*, 1, 2. https://doi.org/10.3390/urbansci1010002.

Sein, M. K., Henfridsson, O., Purao, S., Rossi, M. and Lindgren, R. (2011). Action design research. *MIS Quarterly*, 35(1), 37–56.

Soja, E. W. (2013). *Seeking Spatial Justice*. Minneapolis: University of Minnesota Press.

Sorensen, A. and Sagaris, L. (2010). From participation to the right to the city: Democratic place management at the neighbourhood scale in comparative perspective. *Planning Practice & Research*, 25(3), 297–316.

Tan, L. (2012). Understanding the different roles of the designer in design for social good: A study of design methodology in the DOTT 07 (Designs of the Time 2007) projects. Doctoral thesis, Northumbria University. http://nrl.northumbria.ac.uk/ 8454/.

UNDP (n.d.). Goal 11: Sustainable cities and communities. Sustainable Development Goals. https://www.undp.org/content/undp/en/home/sustainable-development -goals/goal-11-sustainable-cities-and-communities.html.

Van den Broeck, J. (2004). Strategic structure planning. In A. Loeckx, K. Shannon, R. Tuts and H. Verschure (eds.), *Urban Trialogues: Visions, Projects, Co-Productions. Localising Agenda 21*. Leuven: UN Habitat, 168–184.

Van den Broeck, J. (2013). Balancing strategic and institutional planning: The search for a pro-active planning instrument. *DisP – The Planning Review*, 49(3), 43–47.

Van Dijk, M. P. (2006). *Managing Cities in Developing Countries*. Cheltenham, UK and Northampton, MA, USA: Edward Elgar Publishing.

Watson, V. (2003). Conflicting rationalities: Implications for planning theory and ethics. *Planning Theory & Practice*, 4(4), 395–407.

Watson, V. (2014). Co-production and collaboration in planning: The difference. *Planning Theory & Practice*, 15(1), 62–76.

Webler, T., Kastenholz, H. and Renn, O. (1995). Public participation in impact assessment: A social learning perspective. *Environmental Impact Assessment Review*, 15(5), 443–463.

White, S. C. (1996). Depoliticising development: The uses and abuses of participation. *Development in Practice*, 6(1), 6–15.

12. Conclusions: new insights in urban planning, management and governance in emerging economies

Jan Fransen

Chapter 1 of this book identifies centralized planning, urban management and urban governance as three contrasting paradigms that describe interventions in cities. The way in which we intervene in cities and what we aim to achieve has changed over time, in part because urban challenges have been reframed. The chapters of the book offer a rich combination of sectoral analysis and case studies, which allow us to identify new insights related to the reframing of challenges and how we intervene in cities. This concluding chapter analyses the chapters of this book based on five questions:

1. What urban challenges are addressed and how are these (re)framed?
2. What are new insights in urban planning?
3. What are new insights in urban management?
4. What are new insights in urban governance?
5. What main challenges do cities face in implementing these new insights?

REFRAMING URBAN CHALLENGES

The decision on what to include in a problem frame significantly influences the solutions put forward (Van Dijk et al., 2011). Chapter 1 describes how the perception of urban challenges has shifted over time from a massive shortage of basic infrastructure and services during the industrial revolution and after the Second World War, to the localization of urban challenges in order to address diverse needs in cities, to the recent reframing of urban challenges as wicked. A wicked problem relates a problem to broader urban issues within its context, whereby the effort to solve one aspect of a wicked problem may reveal or create other problems (Tonkinwise, 2015). Wicked problems have incomplete, contradictory and changing requirements. Actors are likely to adopt different perspectives, offering partial and incomplete solutions (Rittel and Webber, 1973).

The chapters of this book show that (1) old problems are reframed as wicked, (2) new wicked problems emerge, (3) wicked problems are not just related to other local issues but also to global issues because cities are open systems and (4) problems are reframed as flows. I will now discuss the contributions of the chapters.

Reframing Old Challenges

Various chapters describe how old problems are reframed as wicked problems and may become urgent once again. The old problems that are described include flooding, poor water and transport infrastructure and poorly maintained and unsafe public space. Other persisting problems such as poverty, inequality, exclusion and unemployment, have also been reframed over time, although they are not discussed in the book.

Van Dijk states in Chapter 6 that flooding in cities is reframed and attains new urgency because of urbanization, economic development and climate change. Climate change results in more volatility and unpredictability in rainfall, due to which cities are facing both flooding and drought (Van Dijk and Blokland, 2016). Water retention also affects related challenges such as heat waves. With ever higher densities, space for water storage is scarce. This reframing of flooding as a broader issue, interdependent with other issues, has resulted in new integrated approaches such as the smart eco city, green city and sustainable city.

In Chapter 7, Toto et al. reframe the challenge of unsafe and poorly maintained public spaces found in many cities in emerging economies. The variety of property rights arrangements and social networks complicate their design and maintenance. Local governments often fail in proper policing, maintenance, and in relating to the community, leading to the dehumanization of open space (Ondrejicka et al., 2017). The authors argue that such reframing shows the necessity of new forms of urban governance, with varying levels of community involvement.

In Chapter 9, Bongwa and Van Dijk state that Africa still suffers from a major urban infrastructure and services gap. The scholars perceive infrastructure provision as a public good with high sunk costs, which requires heavy, long-term investment and is overly sensitive to local political conditions. Widespread corruption in infrastructure increases project costs, lengthens delivery times and reduces output quality. It undermines infrastructure maintenance and sustainability of benefits. Africa's legal, institutional and governance frameworks are major constraints to attracting private capital to infrastructure. Infrastructure and service delivery is thus reframed as an issue of governance and political economy.

New Wicked Problems

The chapters refer to four new wicked problems that have emerged and have a major impact on urban development in emerging economies: climate change, sustainability, resilience and new technologies. The section above already exemplifies how climate change reframes the challenge of flooding. Barrett (2013: 1819), as noted in Chapter 3 by McCauley, argues that climate change leads to a "double inequality", where the distribution of risk and responsibility are inversed. The Global North is responsible for the large part of the negative consequences associated with climate change but remains the least affected. Conversely, the Global South is less responsible for such consequences, but is set to experience the major consequences through impacts upon livelihoods, assets and security. McCauley furthermore argues that recent crises such as climate change and the COVID-19 pandemic illustrate that cities around the world must be able to deal with uncertainty related to acute or latent shocks and wicked problems. Becoming resilient and sustainable is more than just coping with a crisis, as it requires systemic change. The persistent status quo in the way in which we govern, manage and plan cities, is therefore part of the problem. This proposition radically reframes the challenge into system failure. As systemic change results in winners and losers, McCauley recommends 'just transitions'.

In Chapter 5, Lim describes new technologies as a blessing in disguise. New technologies may be used to address urban challenges but lead to other challenges such as the digital divide. She focuses on the role of ICT as applied in smart cities. On the one hand, ICT can enable networks in order to generate greater and more sustainable economic development and an improved quality of life for urban citizens. It may also contribute to tackling corruption because open public information creates a transparent environment (Afzalan et al., 2017). On the other hand, smart cities may lead to a digital divide, privacy concerns and an increasingly skewed influence of ICT firms in urban development (Datta, 2015). It may lead to a techno-surveillance state.

Cities as Open Evolving Systems

Wicked problems such as climate change cannot be addressed at the urban level alone because cities are open systems. In Chapter 4, Van Oort et al. reframe the challenge of urban competitiveness. They argue that urban competitiveness requires well-functioning labour markets. Regions able to attract and retain a knowledge-intensive and diverse labour pool have an evolutionary advantage as they are more likely to diversify to industries and services requiring related skills and they are likely to be more innovative (Neffke et al., 2011). However, labour markets hardly ever operate at an urban level, but at the level of the mega-region (Florida et al., 2008). Attracting and retaining a diverse labour force furthermore requires attractive regions. A homogeneous skill set and technology level and low labour mobility may lead to a lock-in, while diverse skill sets, technologies, migration and FDI may open new growth pathways (Eriksson, 2011; Fransen, 2020). Van Oort et al. subsequent reframe the competitiveness challenge in emerging economies as a regional institutional challenge: according to the scholars, informal work, lack of basic infrastructure, poor quality education and weak legislation may hamper the development of knowledge-intensive and diverse labour markets.

In Chapter 8, Alade and Gianoli look at the openness of cities in emerging economies as an opportunity to catch up by absorbing advanced technologies from outside the city. Instead of being passive receivers of technologies, the scholars propose an active role, by adjusting, appropriating and integrating foreign technologies into local ways of working (Fu et al., 2011). This reframes the challenge, because cities need considerable capacity to absorb foreign technologies (Zahra and George, 2002).

Challenges Reframed as Flows

The above sections have shown that urban problems are increasingly perceived to be wicked, because they are interrelated, evolve over time in open systems and are nonlinear and indeterministic. When one problem is addressed, another problem is likely to pop up. Van Dijk therefore argues in Chapter 2 that the emphasis shifts from managing assets to governing processes based on ever-larger flows of information. The governance of flows is, however, an even bigger challenge for cities in emerging economies than managing bricks and asphalt (Van Dijk, 2018). Before discussing these challenges, I will discuss how the reframing of challenges has led to new insights in urban planning, urban management and urban governance.

NEW INSIGHTS IN URBAN PLANNING

Chapter 1 introduces traditional public administration as a centralized and standardized planning process, which was especially popular during industrialization and after the Second World War (Nederhand et al., 2019). Planners produced master plans, delivered infrastructure and services and subsequently checked building permits and minimum building standards. Local authorities comprised departments devolved from national ministries. Highly detailed urban planning models, such as the garden city or Le Corbusier's Ville Radieuse, were implemented on a massive scale irrespective of the local context (Bettencourt, 2013). In many countries, urban planning was decentralized when urban management became more popular, although some countries such as Ethiopia still depend on capacitated centralized planning departments.

Regional and urban planning remain as important as ever and scholars still develop overarching urban planning models such as innovation districts (Katz and Wagner, 2014). The World Bank (2000) states that urban development also requires strategic urban or regional planning in order to attract investments and physically locate employment, houses, amenities and transport infrastructure. Within this context, the chapters in this book note new insights in urban planning.

Strategic Planning at Times of Uncertainty

In Chapter 11, Keunen and Ruijsink link strategic planning to complexity theory. Albrechts (2004: 747) identifies strategic urban planning as a "sociospatial ... process through which a vision, actions, and means for implementation are produced that shape and frame what a place is and may become". Planning is seen as a nonlinear process, with overlapping phases 'going back and forth', while simultaneously multiple planning processes are ongoing. Scholars argue that planning is a process taking place in complex urban systems (Byrne, 2001; Portugali, 2008). Complexity-driven planning deliberately addresses the need to imagine possible futures (Byrne, 2003). The plural here stems from the understanding that the world is developmentally open (Gerrits, 2012). Urban development, and therefore also strategic planning, is a dynamic, continuous process of 'becoming'. This is understood here as "the ability to cope with action, movement, emergence, relationship, and creative experimentation" (Albrechts and Balducci, 2013: 21). This leads to the conclusion that urban planning processes are increasingly governed and that governance principles and tools have become relevant for urban planners.

Co-Creation

Keunen and Ruijsink argue that strategic planning is more recently conceptualized as a co-creation process, whereby any stakeholder can initiate and intervene in an urban development process (Watson, 2014). Hence the role of urban planner can be taken up beyond the (formal) urban planner, by any 'city maker'. The co-productive 'turn' in strategic planning promotes an equal and reciprocal relationship (Albrechts, 2015: 514). Co-creation may for instance take place in urban living labs (e.g. Bulkeley et al., 2016) or the experimental city (Evans et al., 2016).

Changing Roles of Planners

In Chapter 7, Toto et al. describe the changing roles of urban planners in designing, managing and maintaining public space. This used to be a regular, local government task, but community groups are increasingly seen as key actors. Involving communities allows for place making processes which go beyond 'cold' and 'rational' urban planning. These processes enable dialogue and networking. Polycentric governance emerges if community groups and local governments across multiple public spaces interact (McGinnis, 2011; Ostrom 1999). In such collective action, the urban planner becomes a facilitator. Public space can, however, have a variety of governance arrangements and the urban planner should adapt to varying local contexts. Unfortunately, however, Chapter 7 shows that local governments often fail to appreciate these initiatives as they 'disturb' regular management routines. Changing the roles of urban planners is more easily said than done.

Keunen and Ruijsink also argue in Chapter 11 that the role of a planner shifts from designing master plans from behind a desk, to bringing stakeholders together, encouraging exchange of information, viewpoints and ideas between the stakeholders, and guiding them towards joint agreements. The modern planner is a strategist, facilitator and mediator (Tan, 2012). Engaging in strategic planning therefore requires network and communication attitudes, skills and tools in order to come to a common understanding and agreement among multidisciplinary and diverse stakeholders. The chapter argues that the available toolset is insufficient for planners to involve other stakeholders in spatial discussions and offers recommendations.

NEW INSIGHTS IN URBAN MANAGEMENT

In the 1980s urban management emerged as a decentralized and market-driven alternative to centralized public administration. It aims to improve the efficiency and effectiveness of public service delivery, by initiating processes of privatization, result orientation, public–private partnerships and specialization. It introduces business instruments from the private sector into the public sector (Hood, 1991; Nederhand et al., 2019). At the same time, decentralization and participation aim to target infrastructure and services to citizens seen as 'customers' (Bryson et al., 2014).

Over time, scholars and practitioners have realized that urban management, with its linear and deterministic result orientation, is unable to deal with the uncertainty of wicked problems (Healey, 1995). Problems cannot easily be solved from a rationalistic urban management perspective with more information, because information is contested and urban development is nonlinear and indeterministic. The chapters in this book reflect an ongoing but slow evolution towards urban governance in emerging countries: impact instead of results and local and international networks instead of only linear service delivery.

Impact Orientation

Van Dijk (2006: 56) redefines urban management as "the effort to coordinate and integrate public as well as private actions to tackle the major problems the inhabitants of cities are facing and to make a more competitive, equitable and sustainable city". Instead of a result orientation, this definition aims for broader, long-term and more equivocal impacts. And instead of focusing on efficiency it focuses on coordination and integration. These major alterations in the definition indicate a conceptual evolution towards urban governance. The question is whether the business instruments, as taken from the private sector, remain valid when the paradigm is redefined.

Networking Within Cities

The linkages between wicked problems require government departments and non-governmental actors to network. Urban management networks are typically decentralized, efficiency-driven and output-oriented. Their linear approach has great difficulty in dealing with wicked problems, which are non-linear, hard to frame, interrelated and dynamic. As a result, urban governance networks have emerged, which are polycentric and impact-driven, whereby different actors discuss different perceptions of problems and objectives. Koppenjan and Klijn (2004: 69–70) define governance networks as "more or less stable patterns of social relations between mutual dependent actors, which form around policy program and/or cluster of means and which are formed, maintained and changed through series of games". Governance networks thus adapt to urban dynamics and differences in and evolutions of perceptions of urban challenges and solutions.

In Chapter 10, Adamu and Gianoli discuss the reframing of public–private partnerships (PPPs). PPPs are defined as inter-organizational relationships where roles, risk and benefits are shared by partners in order to attain a common goal (Steijn et al., 2011). Adamu and Gianoli compare a concession and alliance partnership in Nigeria, a country where urban governance is still relatively new and unexplored. In a concession, the public partner is the commissioner and the private partner a contractor (Edelenbos and Teisman, 2013). It is typically a vertical kind of relationship with minimal interdependence. By contrast, in an alliance model both private and public partners jointly engage in decision-making, design, and in some cases implementation. The public and private partners engage in an interdependent, horizontal relationship. A concession thus incorporates elements of urban management networks and an alliance model of urban governance networks. The chapter shows that the alliance PPP is better able to deal with the multiple challenges and shocks that arise during the design and implementation phase of housing projects. The study concludes that an alliance model offers more collaborative capacity, that is: the collaboration is more effective in dealing with uncertainty and is therefore better able to result in sustainable change.

In Chapter 6, Van Dijk notices a proliferation of management and governance models in the water sector in cities in emerging economies: water is supplied by municipal corporations, public utilities, private providers, PPPs, informal private kiosks and community-managed water supply systems. It is not useful to impose one model, as each may work within its local context. Van Dijk argues that improving water supply systems within a city requires polycentric governance networks, which bring stakeholders together without enforcing one model over the others (Boamah, 2018). The state adopts a new role of a network manager: it facilitates, regulates and enables private and community initiatives in water provision (Koppenjan and Klijn, 2004).

Networking Beyond the City Boundary

As cities are open systems, urban professionals increasingly network with stakeholders outside the city boundary as well. These processes are highly visible in the economy, as globalization has increased interdependencies. The COVID-19 pandemic has shown the level of dependency on global value chains, defined as the full range of activities required to bring a product or service from its conception to the final customers and disposal after use (Kaplinsky and Morris, 2000). However, the relationship within a global value chain, and as a result the sharing of profit, is highly skewed. Many industries in emerging economies depend on the orders, designs and brands of the headquarters of multinationals. While multinationals enable local producers to deepen their skills, they have a vested interest in keeping branding, design and markets to themselves. Upgrading within global value chains is therefore rare, which impedes the evolution towards knowledge-driven and sustainable urban economies in emerging countries (Fransen and Knorringa, 2019). Many decisions influencing the urban economy are outside the influence of urban managers. However, urban managers can enable firms to improve capacities and opportunities to enable firms to learn (Fransen and Helmsing, 2017).

An important aspect of such an enabling economic environment is a well-functioning regional labour market, as discussed by Van Oort et al. in Chapter 4. They quote Oosterwaal et al. (2017: 9) saying that "Regional governments take part in new collaborative arrangements, make agreements and conclude covenants with incidental or representative representatives of the business community and the knowledge world. These new partnerships each follow their own boundaries and do not adhere to the traditional boundaries of local authorities or to divisions such as labour market regions." While labour markets are largely self-organized, local governments have a lot to gain from place-based policies. However, because the responsibility for participation and matching on the labour market for jobseekers has been assigned to each municipality, competition between municipalities is more likely than cooperation (Broersma et al., 2016).

Chapter 9 discusses networks for infrastructure finance and delivery. As infrastructure has multiple objectives, Bongwa and Van Dijk recommend governance networks in order to decide on infrastructure projects. Such decisions are ultimately political, as rational decision-making processes are likely to lead to multiple options. A combination of management and governance networks subsequently enables local governments to attract infrastructure finance from multiple sources. Infrastructure delivery and maintenance subsequently require robust networks across levels of governments and other actors. Governance models allow for more flexibility, as discussed, and should be set within a clear institutional framework in order to reduce opportunistic behaviour (such as corruption) and poor quality. In summary: professionals in urban infrastructure, often engineers, increasingly engage in political, financial and implementation networks. They are likely to engage in other networks as well, because infrastructure is an element in addressing all other wicked problems, whether these are climate change or poverty. The engineer becomes a network manager. The chapter offers a sobering conclusion: most African cities lack the required networks, institutions and capacities, which are major causes for a failure to deliver adequate infrastructure. Networks, capacities and institutions are unevenly distributed in space. Ironically, cities with the best infrastructure also tend to have the best networks, capacities and institutions and vice versa. As long ago as 1956, Myrdal referred to this as circular cumulative causation: problems persist due to circular feedback mechanisms leading to a lock-in.

New Technologies

Technology offers new opportunities for urban managers, often portrayed as urgent and not-to-be-missed (Datta, 2015). Lim discusses the role of technologies within the smart city discourse in Chapter 5. What makes a city smart depends on how we define 'smartness' (Cocchia, 2014). Taking South Korea as an example, Lim categorizes smart into first- and second-wave smart cities. The first wave focuses on implementing ICT infrastructure (Hollands, 2008), such as South Korea's use of transportation and security surveillance. For instance: sensors at critical points (in bridges, traffic lights and parks) digitally inform transport planners about congested traffic, air pollution or noise pollution, enabling real-time traffic management and feeding into transport policies. The second wave still emphasizes ICT, but also offers smart services in public administration, health and welfare, culture and tourism, and real-time facility management. These advanced smart cities expand to 'soft' infrastructures such as policies and community initiatives (Neirotti et al., 2014). The chapter shows that the second wave South Korean smart cities perform better than first wave or non-smart cities. They enable innovation and networking in the decision-making process, while smart clusters and living labs also facilitate innovation and networking for a better urban environment and quality of life (Kraus et al., 2015).

The governance of new technologies brings together private firms, educational organizations, research institutes, government agencies and civil society (Snow et al., 2016). The South Korean experience shows how regulation and supervision can restrict opportunistic behaviour of private corporates. Top-down urban management approaches enhance efficiency in project implementation but reduce the variety of urban solutions and treat residents as consumers. It injects smartness as an exogenous stimulus. By contrast, endogenous smart cities enable bottom-up innovations of urban communities and firms, sparked by the vitality of urban networks and agency. Polycentric governance can enable smart urban vitality. However, endogenous smart city development is not (yet) found in South Korea and is only emerging in a handful of cities such as Amsterdam, Barcelona and Copenhagen.

NEW INSIGHTS IN URBAN GOVERNANCE

Healey (1995: 18) states that urban governance departs from the control perspective, because urban managers and planners cannot know all information held by the immense number of heterogeneous agents in cities and cannot predict the dynamics of cities as complex systems. In urban governance, many developmental choices are therefore left open and/or are discussed in networks of interdependent actors (Bettencourt, 2013; Edelenbos and Teisman, 2013). The above sections show that urban planning and management practices in emerging economies increasingly incorporate elements of urban governance, but also that some countries such as Nigeria have only just started doing so. This section discusses the changing role of local government, learning regions, polycentric governance and transition management. The next section discusses the challenges to incorporate these elements of urban governance within cities in emerging economies.

Role of the Local Government

At the core of the debate on urban governance is the role of local government. The role differs across time and space from being a devolved implementer of national government in centralized public administration, to an enabler of private service delivery in urban management, to a strategist and network manager in urban governance. Various chapters discuss and critically assess the role of local governments: in Chapter 4 Van Oort et al. note that labour markets are mainly self-organized, but that local governments have a lot to gain in enabling regional labour markets to work well; Chapter 10 recommends a more collaborative role of governments in PPPs instead of that of a commissioner; and various chapters recommend a role of a strategist, facilitator and mediator (see also Tan, 2012). Local governments have also attained a new role: that of a network manager. Network managers set the rules of the game and manage the process by facilitating interactions in order to meet objectives.

The debate on the role of local government is often highly politicized. Public institutions may be perceived as bureaucratic, interfering and self-serving, which reduces their potential role. Chapter 1 introduces the governance frontier, arguing that local governments may combine centralized public administration, urban management and urban governance perspectives. The challenge is empirical and grounded: to identify the most appropriate role of the city government considering urban experiences and challenges. We therefore recommend contextualized, grounded and empirical debates on the role of local governments, after which local politicians and other stakeholders can take informed decisions.

Learning and Catching Up

Learning is an evolutionary and incremental process taking place at the level of a person, organization, network and region. The concept of learning regions became popular in the 1990s, connoting that regional dynamics – the process of becoming – and innovations require constant changes of institutions, capacities, networks and attitudes (Florida, 1995). As Keunen and Ruijsink note in Chapter 11, learning takes place in schools but also in self-organized urban processes, in processes of co-creation (Watson, 2014), urban living labs (Bulkeley et al., 2016) and the experimental city (Evans et al., 2016). Urban governance has an "evolutionary advantage", as networking enables innovation and learning in a constantly changing environment (Jessop, 1998: 32–33).

However, learning and catching up may be easier than inventing new technologies, but it is a dynamic and complex multi-actor interaction process which requires robust connective and absorptive capacities (Edelenbos et al., 2013; Fransen and Helmsing, 2016). Alade and Gianoli discuss how Ethiopian actors learn and catch up by transferring knowledge and technologies on light-rail transport from China to Ethiopia. The Chinese and Ethiopian actors have developed a detailed but flexible knowledge transfer plan. The plan sets targets, whereby a ratio is given to the knowledge to be transferred every year. Various mechanisms of knowledge transfer are used: Ethiopian staff receive long-term training based on explicit job description, Chinese and Ethiopian staff are paired, responsibilities are decentralized in order to allow for adaptive decision-making processes and conflict resolution. Various Ethiopian actors are involved in order to mediate knowledge transfer, including the railway company, local and central government, universities and local contractors. Costs are controlled in time management, financial management and human resource management. The scholars thereby show that processes of learning and catching up require the management of complex governance networks as well as related capacities.

Polycentric Governance

I have already mentioned polycentric governance as an insight into urban planning and management based on Chapters 5, 6, 9 and 11. Polycentric governance is a rather complex form of governance with multiple and relatively autonomous centres of decision-making (Ostrom, 1999). The chapters perceive it to be an opportunity to humanize public space, coordinate multiple coexisting water supply systems, enable smart and vital urban communities and manage the multiple facets of urban infrastructure.

In line with Ostrom's theory of collective action, Toto et al. study public space in Eastern Europe. They define urban communing as community-led network governance. However, they found that local governments do not consider the interests of users of public squares. Considering the history of Eastern European countries, collective action has a negative connotation and the subsequent step towards polycentric governance is therefore farfetched.

Based on the chapters of this book, including its considerable literature review, we conclude that polycentric governance is often wished for but rarely a reality in emerging economies. Many city governments work as bureaucracies (with emphasis on clear responsibilities, accountabilities, rules, procedures, etc.) which undermine adaptive behaviour and polycentric modes of governance. Other constraining factors are limited networking and learning skills and limited trust among partners.

Transition Management

Transition management has emerged in response to climate change and pollution (Loorbach, 2007). Despite its reference to management, it adheres to principles of urban governance, to which it adds a vision as is common in urban planning and management. Transition management is associated with participatory, reflexive and adaptable forms of networked governance (Van Welie and Romijn, 2018).

In Chapter 3, McCauley defines just transitions as a "fair and equitable process of moving towards a post-carbon society". The vision is broadly described because it is unknown what a post-carbon society looks like. Scholars indicate that urban systems or regimes, such as the transport system or labour markets are path dependent and hard to change (Fransen, 2020). The objective of transition management is therefore to destabilize current thinking within regimes through the proactive governance of change. In many cities in emerging economies, regimes are institutionalized and therefore resistant to change, but systems which are not yet institutionalized are easier to deconstruct. Transition management is about empowering the macro-level cultural, political, institutional and market trends and micro-level niche innovations.

McCauley argues that at the macro level, a growing awareness among consumers of the need to move away from fossil fuels is the most critical influential element of a transition. At a micro or niche level, governmental and non-governmental actors experiment with new technologies and ways of working (Bulkeley et al., 2014). Experiments try out alternatives, which are – if successful – mainstreamed (Sareen and Haarstad, 2018). In contrast to traditional perceptions of urban planning, management and governance, moments of disruption are to be embraced. As for transitions towards (polycentric) governance, existing bureaucratic regime structures need to change. McCauley argues that networks of non-elite actors may also encourage, enable and enact cultural shifts among urban communities. Political activities may include deliberation, advocacy or alternative political action. Non-elite community based organizations may exemplify non-compliance and thereby directly and/ or indirectly challenge the regime (Gofen, 2015). Advocacy, pressure and niche innovations may then lead to change.

CHALLENGES AHEAD

The new challenges and insights related to urban planning, management and governance in emerging economies result in more exciting, integrated, multi-disciplinary and demanding job descriptions of urban managers. The chapters have presented best practices, such as an alliance PPP in Nigeria, knowledge transfer from China to Ethiopia, smart cities in South Korea, and criteria to select new tools for planners in dealing with uncertainty. These best practices offer hope and inspiration.

However, the chapters also report on persistent barriers to deal with wicked urban problems. Many cities are at best slowly evolving towards urban governance, face major resource constraints and sometimes follow a modernization approach at the expense of other pressing problems. At the same time the COVID-19 pandemic eats away scarce resources. Cities in emerging economies face a double inequality due to climate change, where the distribution of risk and responsibility are inversed (Barrett, 2013: 1819). Ironically, cities which are most in need of improved planning, management and governance are those with the least capacity to learn, innovate and improve (referred to as circular cumulative causation by Myrdal, 1956). And while local governments face more challenges than ever, their role and contribution to urban development is questioned. Of course there are major differences between cities in emerging economies, with some doing very well. Besides differences between countries, differences in size matter. Especially smaller cities, far away from career and growth opportunities in the capital city, face capacity constraints.

I will now briefly discuss the main challenges.

Limited Ability to Deal with Wicked Problems

The transition towards urban governance, and thereby the ability to deal with wicked problems, varies but appears to be slow on average. Local governments struggle with their new roles of strategist, facilitator, mediator and manager of networks (Tan, 2012). Especially more complex governance arrangements such as polycentricity and transition management appear to be beyond the institutional and human capacity of many cities (see for instance Chapters 4 and 6). That is not surprising: traditionally educated engineers, planners and architects are not easily turned into networkers with a sensitivity towards different agendas and perspectives. Institutions set for hierarchical management are also not easily transformed into regulations and organizational cultures enabling governance. Mistrust of governments, partially caused by decades of corruption as discussed in Chapter 9, is not a solid ground for governance networks either.

In Chapter 6, Van Dijk argues that cities claim to use integrated approaches such as sustainable city, green city and smart eco city approaches in order to govern water issues. However, cities often focus on one or two elements of the approach without integrating all its elements. Some cities which claimed to be eco cities in the 1990s are now branded as sponge cities (Zhuanghe), or smart cities (Shenzhen and Beijing). They jump from one to another bandwagon. In China and India, among others, the reason is that cities qualify for government support if they use these brands. In other countries cities want to brand themselves, without necessarily using the brand to instigate change.

Toto et al. note that local governments in Eastern Europe sometimes impose barriers for urban commoning of public squares. Weak government–community networks, weak policing and poor maintenance lead to the dehumanization of open space (Ondrejicka et al., 2017). While it is promising to see community actors as stakeholders, the transition from hierarchical management to horizontal governance has not yet taken place. The scholars recommend starting this transition in public spaces in neighbourhoods, where there is more bonding among community members and therefore more potential for commoning.

Resource Constraints

All chapters refer to limited financial, human and institutional resources in order to deal with interrelated wicked problems. Chapter 9 details financial constraints for infrastructure delivery and recommends solutions (jointly with the above-mentioned governance challenges). Human capacities are related to the number of urban professionals, the immensity of the urban challenges and the new roles, skills and attitudes of urban managers. Urban planners, managers and governors are expected to be complexity-driven network managers, able to co-create, experiment with new approaches, set up alliances, manage polycentric networks, source finance, and to enable and appreciate disruptive niche innovations and macro-level developments. These skills and attitudes are supplementary to the traditional skills of an engineer, manager, planner, sociologist, etc. The urban manager has become a sheep with five legs. At the same time, the job descriptions and curricula of (professional) universities are not always adjusted to new realities in emerging economies.

Institutional constraints are especially mentioned in relation to labour markets (Chapter 4) and infrastructure delivery (Chapter 9). Chapter 4 shows that labour markets in emerging countries are institutionally constrained by their position in global value chains, informality, poor education, weak legislation and a poor state of basic infrastructure. Chapter 9 adds corruption and misuse of public resources to the list of institutional challenges.

Modernistic Approaches

Parsons developed the modernization theory in the 1930s by building on the work of Weber. It is a highly controversial theory, which claims that external assistance can support a traditional society to become modern. Chapter 7, for instance, argues that local governments with modernist approaches, which aim for modern street views and operation and maintenance schemes, underestimate the importance of 'traditional' social networks in commoning or custodianship (Radywyl and Biggs, 2013).

The modernist approach is possibly best reflected in the smart city debate, whereby ICT technology in infrastructure and services is perceived to be an urgent necessity (Datta, 2015). It argues that modern is better than traditional and that the emerging countries follow the development trajectory of the Global North, instead of setting out their own development trajectory. More recent smart city literature partially deals with these criticisms by arguing that technological, human, social and institutional capital are intertwined in complex development processes (Batty et al., 2012; Hollands, 2008). Nevertheless, smart cities are still projected as a nirvana: increased economic productivity, reduced administrative costs of public services and a more pleasant and sustainable living environment (Caragliu et al., 2011; Neirotti et al., 2014). The positive results are emphasized in the literature (Lim et al., 2019); however, smart city development can also divert policy priority from urgent urban problems such as poverty, a housing shortage and unemployment (Afzalan et al., 2017; Datta, 2015). Cities have limited financial, human, and institutional resources and smart cities can be another burden to the city. To critics, smart cities are a marketing scheme of international ICT vendors (Hollands, 2008).

FINAL WORDS

The chapters of this book offer rich narratives of the challenges and interventions in cities in emerging economies. This chapter has bundled the new challenges and insights in urban planning, management and governance. While we are aware that the book does not and cannot cover the full variety of challenges and interventions in emerging economies, we hope to inspire readers to reframe urban problems and identify innovative ways and opportunities to intervene in cities. Based on the challenges ahead, we recommend more attention to urban governance, capacity building of people, institutions, networks and financial mechanisms, and confidence and pride in locally driven development processes based on existing resources, networks and opportunities.

We realize that it is impossible to draw conclusions which are valid for all cities in emerging economies, and therefore recommend more research. Lines for future research topics which emerge out of this book include:

* Urban governance is not a luxury, but a must in order to address wicked problems such as climate change, inequality and vulnerability to shocks. The problem lies in the fact that many cities in emerging economies face institutional challenges, resulting in great difficulty in regular service delivery. There are limited capacity and resources to introduce governance approaches. Especially the application of complex governance approaches such as multi-levelness, polycentricity and transition management requires major changes in organizational cultures, knowledge, skills and networks. This raises the following research question: How do cities with limited resources and weak institutions transform towards urban governance?

- Urban planning is a quickly changing field of practice and study, increasingly applying concepts related to uncertainty and complexity. Urban practices around the world apply both the 'old' centralized approaches and 'new' forms of complexity planning. This warrants comparative studies with the following research questions: Which perspectives, skills and tools enable planners to deal with wicked problems and uncertainty? How and under what conditions do roles of urban planners in emerging economies change towards complexity planning?
- The level of technological and social change accelerates, including change in the framing of urban problems and governance approaches. Urban professionals should both adapt to and initiate change in order to address urban wicked problems. However, change leads to new winners and losers and may thereby be unjust to part of the society. Change guided by visions of modernization and competitiveness may lead to more inequality and exclusion. That raises the following research question: How just, inclusive and environmentally friendly are urban transformations?
- The book has discussed and illustrated that the concept of urban management has changed over time. However, private business tools are still widely used in order to improve efficiency of services. That raises the question: (How) do urban managers apply private business tools in combination with governance approaches?
- The roles of actors, institutions, networks and capacities are formed in local evolutionary processes, leading to an endless and ever-changing variety of urban experiences. We recommend local, grounded and empirical research that feeds discussions on the most appropriate way of planning, managing and governing. The research question is: What are the (recommended) ways to plan, manage and govern within a local context? At the same time, the variety of perspectives and practices enables learning. We recommend urban researchers and practitioners to learn from experiences and new technologies and knowledge, adjusting those to local contexts. However, knowledge exchange is far from automatic. This leads to a last research question: How well is urban knowledge shared, contextualized and applied?

REFERENCES

Afzalan, N., Sanchez, T. W. and Evans-Cowley, J. (2017). Creating smarter cities: Considerations for selecting online participatory tools. *Cities*, 67, 21–30.

Albrechts, L. (2004). Strategic (spatial) planning reexamined. *Environment and Planning B: Planning and Design*, 31(5), 743–758.

Albrechts, L. (2015). Ingredients for a more radical strategic spatial planning. *Environment and Planning B: Planning and Design*, 42(3), 510–525.

Albrechts, L. and Balducci, A. (2013). Practicing strategic planning: In search of critical features to explain the strategic character of plans. *DisP – The Planning Review*, 49(3), 16–27.

Barrett, S. (2013). Local level climate justice? Adaptation finance and vulnerability reduction. *Global Environmental Change*, 23, 1819–1829.

Batty, M., Axhausen, K. W., Giannotti, F., Pozdnoukhov, A., Bazzani, A., Wachowicz, M., Ouzounis, G. and Portugali, Y. (2012). Smart cities of the future. *European Physical Journal Special Topics*, 214, 481–518.

Bettencourt, L. M. (2013). The origins of scaling in cities. *Science*, 340(6139), 1438–1441.

Boamah, E. F. (2018). Polycentricity of urban watershed governance: Towards a methodological approach. *Urban Studies*, 55, 3525–3544.

Broersma, L., Edzes, A. and van Dijk, J. (2016). Human capital externalities: Effects for low-educated workers and low-skilled jobs. *Regional Studies*, 50, 1675–1687.

Bryson, J. M., Crosby, B. C. and Bloomberg, L. (2014). Public value governance: Moving beyond traditional public administration and the new public management. *Public Administration Review*, 74(4), 445–456.

Bulkeley, H., Coenen, L., Frantzeskaki, N., Hartmann, C., Kronsell, A., Mai, L., Marvin, S., McCormick, K., van Steenbergen, F. and Palgan, Y. V. (2016). Urban living labs: Governing urban sustainability transitions. *Current Opinion in Environmental Sustainability*, 22, 13–17.

Bulkeley, H., Edwards, G. A. S. and Fuller, S. (2014). Contesting climate justice in the city: Examining politics and practice in urban climate change experiments. *Global Environmental Change*, 25, 31–40.

Byrne, D. (2001). What is complexity science? Thinking as a realist about measurement and cities and arguing for natural history. *Emergence: A Journal of Complexity Issues in Organizations and Management*, 3(1), 61–76.

Byrne, D. (2003). Complexity theory and planning theory: A necessary encounter. *Planning Theory*, 2(3), 171–178.

Caragliu, A., Del Bo, C. and Nijkamp, P. (2011). Smart cities in Europe. *Journal of Urban Technology*, 18, 65–82.

Cocchia, A. (2014). Smart and digital city: A systematic literature review. In R. P. Dameri and C. Rosenthal-Sabroux (eds.), *Smart City*. Cham: Springer, 13–43.

Datta, A. (2015). A 100 smart cities, a 100 utopias. *Dialogues in Human Geography*, 5, 49–53.

Edelenbos, J., Bressers, N. and Scholten, P. (eds.) (2013). *Water Governance as Connective Capacity*. Farnham: Ashgate Publishing.

Edelenbos, J. and Teisman, G. (2013). Water governance capacity: The art of dealing with a multiplicity of levels, sectors and domains. *International Journal of Water Governance*, 1(1–2), 89–108.

Eriksson, R. (2011). Localized spillovers and knowledge flows: How does proximity influence the performance of plants? *Economic Geography*, 87, 127–154.

Evans, J., Karvonen, A. and Raven, R. (eds.) (2016). *The Experimental City*. London: Routledge.

Florida, R. (1995). Toward the learning region. *Futures*, 27(5), 527–536.

Florida, R., Gulden, T. and Mellander, C. (2008). The rise of the mega-region. *Cambridge Journal of Regions, Economy and Society*, 1, 459–476.

Fransen, J. (2020). Lock-in and new path development of China commodity city: The role of policies. *Forum for Social Economics*, August, 1–16.

Fransen, J. and Helmsing, A. H. J. (2016). Breaching the barriers: The segmented business and innovation system of handicraft exports in Cape Town. *Development Southern Africa*, 33(4), 486–501.

Fransen, J. and Helmsing, A. H. J. (2017). Absorptive capacity as a mediator: Innovation of handicraft exporters in Yogyakarta, Indonesia. *Tijdschrift voor economische en sociale geografie*, 108(6), 737–752.

Fransen, J. and Knorringa, P. (2019). Learning and upgrading of craft exporters at the interface of global value chains and innovation systems. *The European Journal of Development Research*, 31(3), 530–557.

Fu, X., Pietrobelli, C. and Soete, L. (2011). The role of foreign technology and indigenous innovation in the emerging economies: Technological change and catching-up. *World Development*, 39, 1204–1212.

Gerrits, L. (2012). *Punching Clouds: An Introduction to the Complexity of Public Decision-Making*. Litchfield Park, AZ: Emergent Publications.

Gofen, A. (2015). Citizens' entrepreneurial role in public service provision. *Public Management Review*, 17(3), 404–424.

Healey, P. (1995). *Managing Cities: The New Urban Context*. New York: John Wiley & Sons.

Hollands, R. G. (2008). Will the real smart city please stand up? Intelligent, progressive or entrepreneurial? *City*, 12, 303–320.

Hood, C. (1991). A public management for all seasons. *Public Administration*, 69(1): 3–19.

Jessop, B. (1998). The rise of governance and the risks of failure: The case of economic development. *International Social Science Journal*, 50(155), 29–45.

Kaplinsky, R. and Morris, M. (2000). *A Handbook for Value Chain Research*. Brighton: University of Sussex, Institute of Development Studies.

Katz, B. and Wagner, J. (2014). *The Rise of Innovation Districts: A New Geography of Innovation in America*. Washington, DC: Brookings Institution.

Koppenjan, J. F. M. and Klijn, E. H. (2004). *Managing Uncertainties in Networks: A Network Approach to Problem Solving and Decision Making*. London: Routledge.

Kraus, S., Richter, C., Papagiannidis, S. and Durst, S. (2015). Innovating and exploiting entrepreneurial opportunities in smart cities: Evidence from Germany. *Creativity and Innovation Management*, 24, 601–616.

Lim, Y., Edelenbos, J. and Gianoli, A. (2019). Identifying the results of smart city development: Findings from systematic literature review. *Cities*, 95, 102397. https://doi.org/10.1016/j.cities.2019.102397.

Loorbach, D. (2007). *Transition Management: New Mode of Governance for Sustainable Development*. Utrecht: International Books.

McGinnis, M. D. (2011). Networks of adjacent action situations in polycentric governance. *The Policy Studies Journal*, 39(1), 51–78.

Myrdal, G. (1956). *An International Economy: Problems and Prospects*. New York: Harper & Row.

Nederhand, J., Van Der Steen, M. and Van Twist, M. (2019). Boundary-spanning strategies for aligning institutional logics: A typology. *Local Government Studies*, 45(2), 219–240.

Neffke, F., Henning, M. and Boschma, R. (2011). How do regions diversify over time? Industry relatedness and the development of new growth paths in regions. *Economic Geography*, 87, 237–265.

Neirotti, P., De Marco, A., Cagliano, A. C., Mangano, G. and Scorrano, F. (2014). Current trends in smart city initiatives: Some stylised facts. *Cities*, 38, 25–36.

Ondrejicka, V., Finka, M., Husar, M. and Jemecny, L. (2017). Urban space as the commons: New modes for urban space management. IOP Conference Series: Earth and Environmental Science 95, 052004.

Oosterwaal, L., Stam, E. and van der Toren, J. P. (2017). *Openbaar bestuur in regionale ecosystemen van ondernemerschap.* The Hague: Ministerie van Binnenlandse Zaken.

Ostrom, E. (1999). Design principles and threats to sustainable organizations that manage commons. Workshop in Political Theory and Policy Analysis. Bloomington: Indiana University.

Portugali, J. (2008). Learning from paradoxes about prediction and planning in self-organizing cities. *Planning Theory,* 7(3), 248–262.

Radywyl, N. and Biggs, C. (2013). Reclaiming the commons for urban transformation. *Journal of Cleaner Production,* 50, 159–170.

Rittel, H. W. J. and Webber, M. M. (1973). Dilemmas in a general theory of planning. *Policy Sciences,* 4(2), 155–169.

Sareen, S. and Haarstad, H. (2018). Bridging socio-technical and justice aspects of sustainable energy transitions. *Applied Energy,* 228, 624–632.

Snow, C. C., Hakonsson, D. D. and Obel, B. (2016). A smart city is a collaborative community: Lessons from smart Aarhus. *California Management Review,* 59, 92–108.

Steijn, B., Klijn, E. and Edelenbos, J. (2011). Public private partnerships: Added value by organizational form or management? *Public Administration,* 89(4), 1235–1252.

Tan, L. (2012). Understanding the different roles of the designer in design for social good: A study of design methodology in the DOTT 07 (Designs of the Time 2007) projects. Doctoral thesis, Northumbria University. http://nrl.northumbria.ac.uk/8454/.

Tonkinwise, C. (2015). Design for transitions: From and to what? *Design Philosophy Papers,* 13(1), 85–92.

Van Dijk, M. P. (2006). *Managing Cities in Developing Countries.* Cheltenham, UK and Northampton, MA, USA: Edward Elgar Publishing.

Van Dijk, M. P. (2018). Smart eco cities are managing information flows in an integrated way: The example of water, electricity and solid waste. In M. Dastbaz, W. Naude and J. Manoochehri (eds.), *Smart Futures: Challenges of Urbanization and Social Sustainability.* Berlin: Springer, 149–169.

Van Dijk, M. P. and Blokland, M. W. (2016). Introduction and reflection on benchmarking for the delivery of water and sanitation services to the urban poor. In M. P. Van Dijk and M. W. Blokland (eds.), Special issue: Benchmarking for the delivery of water and sanitation services to the urban poor, *International Journal of Water,* 10, 109–121.

Van Dijk, T., Aarts, N. and De Wit, A. (2011). Frames to the planning game. *International Journal of Urban and Regional Research,* 35(5), 969–987.

Van Welie, M. J. and Romijn, H. A. (2018). NGOs fostering transitions towards sustainable urban sanitation in low-income countries: Insights from transition management and development studies. *Environmental Science and Policy,* 84, 250–260.

Watson, V. (2014). Co-production and collaboration in planning: The difference. *Planning Theory & Practice,* 15(1), 62–76.

World Bank (2000). *Attacking Poverty.* World Bank Development Report. New York: Oxford University Press.

Zahra, A. S. and George, G. (2002). Absorptive capacity: A review, reconceptualization and extension. *Academy of Management Review,* 27(2), 185–203.

Index